MANAGING THE NURSING SHORTAGE

Contributors

TERENCE F. MOORE, *Editor*
EARL A. SIMENDINGER, PHD, *Editor*

David P. Berry, Esq.
Fay L. Bower, RN, DNSc, FAAN
Kathryn L. Bray, RN, MBA
Gregory L. Crow, RN, MS
Catherine DeVet, RN, EdD
Ellen Thomas Eggland, RN, MN
Pamela S. Erb, RN, MPA, CNAA
Patricia K. Findling, MHA
Carolyn E. Fraser, RN
Cecelia K. Golightly, RN, MPH
Laurin Paul Hafner, PhD candidate
Abby M. Heydman, RN, PhD
Bernard S. Hodes
R. Edward Howell, MHA
Janet Y. Jackson, RN, MSN
Marlene Kramer, RN, PhD, FAAN

Jean C. Lyon, RN, MS, MSN, PhD candidate
Pamela A. MacFalda, RN, MS
Kathleen A. McManus, RN
Nancy Madsen, RN, MS
Doris M. Modly, RN, PhD
J. Mark Montobbio, Esq.
Terence F. Moore, MHA, MBA
Joanne Olsen, RN, MSN
Philip L. Ross, Esq.
Claudia Schmalenberg, RN, MS
Barbara L. Shockey, RN, BS
Joseph M. Smith
Terry Stukalin, RN, MA
John F. Turck III
Kathleen M. Weiss, RN, MSN
Donna D. Young, RN, MAM

MANAGING THE NURSING SHORTAGE

A Guide to Recruitment and Retention

Terence F. Moore

President
Mid-Michigan Healthcare Systems, Inc.
Midland, Michigan

Earl A. Simendinger, PhD

Professor and Chairman
Department of Health Education and Health Science
Central Michigan University
Mt. Pleasant, Michigan

AN ASPEN PUBLICATION®
Aspen Publishers, Inc.

1989

Rockville, Maryland
Royal Tunbridge Wells

Library of Congress Cataloging-in-Publication Data

Managing the nursing shortage: a guide to recruitment and
retention/[edited by] Terence F. Moore, Earl A. Simendinger
p. cm.
"An Aspen publication."
Includes bibliographies and index.
ISBN: 0-8342-0046-5
1. Nurses--United States--Recruiting. 2. Nurses--United States--Supply and demand.
I. Moore, Terence F. II. Simendinger, Earl A.
[DNLM: 1. Nursing--manpower--United States. 2. Personnel Management--methods.
WY 30 M266] RT86.73.M35 1989 362.1'73'0683--dc19
DNLM/DLC
for Library of Congress
88-38665
CIP

Editorial Services: Ruth Bloom

Library of Congress Catalog Card Number: 88-38665
ISBN: 0-8342-0046-5

Printed in the United States of America

1 2 3 4 5

To
Carleen K. Moore, RN,
and every nurse in the United States

Table of Contents

Preface

If nursing recruitment and retention are not the primary issues in many health care institutions in the United States, they are at least two of the major issues.

Health care institutions—both large and small, all across the United States—are closing entire units because they cannot recruit and retain enough nurses to staff them. The competition for well-qualified nursing personnel is at its highest level ever. It is not uncommon to see five or six full pages of advertising for nurses in newspapers of large metropolitan areas in some parts of our country. This unfortunate situation is projected to worsen in the immediate future. The population of college-age students has decreased since 1975 and is projected to continue to decrease until the year 2000. Enrollments in nursing programs have decreased 13 percent since 1983, with an estimated loss of 50,000 students as reported by the National League of Nursing.

Health care executives are challenged as never before to find innovative ways of attracting and retaining nurses. To do so, these same executives must understand the causes of the problem before they can employ techniques to alleviate it. It is our hope that health care executives will use the information contained herein as a basis for understanding the factors that cause problems in nurse recruitment and retention. Moreover, health care executives can benefit from the observations of these authors, who have outlined methods that can reduce the rate of turnover in nursing and assist organizations in recruiting quality nursing personnel. If the situation is to be alleviated it will be because we, the health care providers, demonstrate the leadership necessary to change it. This book provides knowledge that is necessary if such leadership is to be exercised.

Terence F. Moore
Earl A. Simendinger, PhD

Acknowledgments

We wish to extend our deep appreciation to the authors of the various chapters who made this book possible. Each made a significant commitment in time and effort to make the necessary deadlines and develop their respective chapters in spite of their hectic schedules. Peggy Oliver provided invaluable assistance in the coordination of the project. The staff of Aspen Publishers, particularly Steve Mautner, Mary Taylor, Ruth Bloom, Betty Bruner, and all those who reviewed and revised the various drafts of the manuscript, deserve special credit. We are grateful for the excellence they each brought to this project.

Introduction

A review of the literature shows that numerous journal articles have been published—especially during the past four years—about the nursing shortage, but most of these have covered only one aspect of the problem. The purpose of this book is to provide a comprehensive resource for top-level management and all those involved in nursing recruitment to assist in better addressing both the recruitment and retention of nurses.

The first few chapters provide a basis for better understanding the magnitude and causes of the nursing shortage: Why do nurses drop out? What are the causes of job satisfaction? What are the nursing manpower projections?

Chapters 5 and 6 describe effective marketing and advertising techniques for nurse recruitment and retention. Other factors, such as incentive programs and the influence of the medical staff on nurse recruitment and retention, are also explored in subsequent chapters.

In later chapters, nurse recruitment and retention are described from an educator's perspective and a recruiter's perspective, and an overview is provided of the special problems of recruiting to rural hospitals and urban hospitals.

Last, nursing's changing roles, the use of supplemental nurses, the use of alternative care providers, and the recruitment of foreign nurses are discussed in separate chapters.

These chapters are written by some of the foremost practitioners in the field of nurse recruitment and retention.

Chapter 1

Status of the Nursing Shortage and Projections

Janet Y. Jackson, Pamela A. MacFalda, and Kathleen A. McManus

There is no security; there is only opportunity.

—*General Douglas MacArthur*

It used to be that *R and R* meant rest and recuperation from the stress and rigors of battle, a stratagem to assure that the battalion numbers would be sufficient and the abilities and motivation of the personnel would be adequate to meet the task at hand. Today that same *R and R* might stand for *recruitment and retention* of personnel in a different kind of battle, that of health care. In this scenario the personnel are not soldiers but nurses. The discrepancy between the numbers needed for the battle and the numbers available forms one of the most widely discussed topics in health care. H. Robert Cathcart, president of University of Pennsylvania Hospital in Philadelphia, speaking as a member of *Modern Healthcare's* editorial board, discussed the diminished interest of talented young people in medicine and nursing. The board further defined the shortage of nurses as one of the primary challenges for the health care industry in 1988 and beyond.[1] Carol McCarthy, American Hospital Association president, writes about the situation more narrowly as a "severe shortage of hospital nurses."[2]

Webster defines *shortage* as a lack or deficit. A nursing shortage now means insufficient numbers of qualified nurses to provide patient care on the days and at the times and places that patients require them.[3] Questions about the extent of, reasons for, and solutions to the "shortage" as well as whether that shortage is real appear with increasing regularity in many publications, even those of other disciplines. Indeed, these are appropriate questions. So, too, is the question of what is likely to be the situation of health care in the future with respect to the adequacy of the supply of nurses. These questions are the bases for the material presented in this chapter.

HISTORICAL PERSPECTIVE

Nursing shortages are not novel phenomena; they assumed a cyclic pattern even before World War II. During World War I, young women were recruited from colleges, trained rather quickly, and sent to the front in Europe to care for American soldiers. During World War II, in order to respond to a similar unmet need, nurses were graduated quickly from nursing schools—often before the completion of their final year—and sent overseas.

After the war, the medical technology developed in battle was beginning to be used for civilians. Expectations about health care expanded markedly, and the possibilities of new treatments for disease and the need to care for wounded service personnel increased the demand for hospital beds. In response to this demand, Congress enacted the Hill-Burton Act of 1946, which authorized and supported the addition of large numbers of hospital beds. However, little thought was given to the numbers of personnel, especially nurses, needed to provide care to the increasing numbers of patients treated in hospitals. The shortage of nurses, when it occurred, was met by training and licensing a new level of nursing personnel, the licensed practical nurse (LPN). Nurses aides were utilized, too, for the first time in patient care roles.

Shortages occurred again in the 1960s, the 1970s, and now twice in the 1980s. Each time, the causes and proposed cures were discussed in the professional literature and the lay press. In fact, the verbiage written about shortages of past decades could be applied to each succeeding shortage cycle. The media response is no different today, although many believe that this shortage is different. Spencer Johnson, president of the Michigan Hospital Association, wrote:

> In the past, we weathered the shortages, looking ahead to better days. But the shortage isn't like the others. . . . Not only are we short nurses right now, we are faced with dramatic declines in nursing school enrollment. . . . Couple this shrinking pool of nurses with the increasing demands on nursing by our changing health care system and it spells crisis.''[4]

Johnson's use of the word *crisis* is worth noting. The feeling evoked by the word is one of insecurity and suspense; a crisis is usually perceived as a time of difficulty. This is certainly descriptive of the experiences of hospital and nursing administrators as well as staff nurses and patients as they seek to cope with partially filled work schedules that prevent full use of licensed patient beds and lead to increased workloads and fragmented services. *Crisis* may also mean a turning point or a state in which a decisive change for better or worse is imminent. The nursing profession, as well as the health care industry, as it confronts this shortage, is at a point where a decisive change may be imminent. The opportunity exists to make that decisive change for the better.

THE CURRENT SHORTAGE IN NURSING

In order to understand the complex nature of the nursing shortage, it is pertinent to explore the current status of the nurse supply and the demand for nursing services.

The need for nurses has never been greater. Although there are more licensed professional nurses than ever before (1.8 million) and although 80 percent of registered nurses (RNs) currently licensed are working (68 percent in hospitals), the hospital demands for nursing services are not being met.[5]

The proportion of RNs employed by institutions has increased markedly over the past 15 years. In 1975, for example, hospitals employed 50 RNs per 100 patients; by 1986 that ratio had risen to 91 per 100, an 82 percent increase—this is in spite of the fact that the number of hospital beds has decreased since 1976. Twenty years ago RNs accounted for 33 percent of hospitals' total nursing service personnel; at present RNs account for 58 percent.[6] While some of this increase is attributable to the response to an increased severity of illness, some has resulted from qualitative improvements.

Vacant positions for RNs in hospitals have doubled since 1985, according to a study conducted by the American Hospital Association in December 1986.[7] While vacancies varied by region, hospital size, and nursing specialty, it was clear that all across the nation the short supply of nurses was a concern. Fifty-four percent of hospitals indicated that they had a moderate or severe nursing shortage.[8] An unusual aspect of this survey is that many respondents indicated that they did not have a nursing shortage only six months before. While most respondents indicated that they had openings for medical-surgical nurses, the more difficult task was in filling openings for positions in intensive or coronary care.

Just as positions are remaining open for longer periods, more opportunities are available for nurses as hospitals expand into other markets such as home care or satellite clinics or create other roles that demand the versatile knowledge and experience of the registered nurse. Even non-nurses are being replaced by nurses; therefore, even though 68 percent of nurses may be employed in hospitals, they may not necessarily be employed in direct acute patient care.

Those nurses employed in patient care, however, are more likely to be RNs, as their efficiency and universal utility are recognized as being more economical in caring for the very ill patient. Specialization in nursing has increased as technology has grown, creating a more narrowly versatile work force. Indeed, in many parts of the country it is the intensive care area where the shortage of RNs is greatest.[9] Hospitals across the country have indicated that filling these vacancies is difficult or very difficult. At the same time, hospitals have also indicated that they do not have openings for LPNs or licensed vocational nurses (LVNs).

The changing health care delivery system requires a better-educated nurse, one who provides autonomous care in the community and hospital, makes on-the-spot decisions, supervises other nurses, represents nursing to the hospital administration, and participates in research.

While nursing continues to be practiced primarily by women (97 percent), the changing role of women in this society has created more opportunities in less traditional roles. More and more women are choosing careers in medicine, engineering, and law. For the first time, in 1987, more freshman women who were surveyed indicated they intended to pursue a career in medicine rather than nursing.[10]

Furthermore, an assessment of the scholastic aptitude test scores of freshmen entering college revealed that students who selected nursing achieved lower scores than most of their classmates who selected other professional programs. This finding has been characterized as reflecting a shrinking talent pool for nursing, an ominous circumstance when the increased demand for numbers and sophistication is contemplated.

The shift away from nursing as a career choice occurs at a time when the size of the 18-year-old cohort is smaller than in previous years. These factors account for the decline in the numbers of admissions to all types of nursing schools. In 1986 enrollments dropped to slightly more than 200,000 students, which represents a decline of more than 50,000 students in a three-year period.[11]

Although much of what has been discussed has been directed toward the acute care setting, long-term care is facing a dilemma of equal magnitude. The National Foundation for Long-Term Health Care held an invitational conference to address the current problems of nurse recruitment and retention in long-term care. Participants discussed the impact of education on the industry and identified key issues causing the problems. The viewpoint expressed by the participants was that there was widespread avoidance of long-term care facilities by nursing educators and that the image of the nursing home was often depressing and demoralizing for students and faculty.

Another issue addressed at the conference was the financial competition for nurses. Salary and benefit packages at long-term care facilities often are not competitive with those of acute care facilities. This hampers attracting not only the numbers of nurses required but also those with advanced preparation. Currently there are few RNs practicing within long-term care facilities, causing a feeling of professional isolation within their work environment. The reality of this isolation makes it difficult to recruit nurses but even more greatly hampers the ability to retain nurses.[12]

The authors believe that, with the move of more acutely ill patients into nursing homes, the shortage of RNs in long-term care will become increasingly more critical. The lack of available RNs in long-term care facilities is currently hindering the ability of acute care institutions to transfer patients who are ill, as they might have done in past years. This resulting lengthened stay puts financial burdens on acute care hospitals without hope of reimbursement.

As the levels of acuity within long-term facilities begin to climb to the current levels within hospitals, the health care system will experience greater difficulty in placing elderly patients and those requiring extended care within the appropriate facility. The increased need for professional nurses to care for long-term patients will also further drain an already scarce pool of RNs from acute care.

The unsettling numbers related to nursing come at a time when there are in this country great expectations about the quality of health care and its outcomes. It is certain that the public will be involved in decisions affecting them, and that access to health care will be perceived as a right as important as almost any other.

CAUSES OF THE SHORTAGE

The causes postulated for the shortage of nurses in this country are many. They are "predictably complex."[13] One of the most interesting theories is extrapolated from the change in student values and life goals as demonstrated by data from the annual American Council on Education-University of California at Los Angeles (ACE-UCLA) Freshman Survey Program. Kenneth Green, associate director of the Higher Education Research Institute at the University of California in Los Angeles, presented these data before the 1988 conference of the American Organization of Nurse Executives. In his address, Green reported that there have been dramatic shifts in the values and life goals expressed by students entering college. Specifically, there has been a dramatic decline in values related to altruistic activities and social concerns such as the environment, participation in community action programs, and keeping up with political affairs. Equally dramatic was the precipitous decline of the importance of developing a meaningful philosophy of life: both male and female students expressed a decline in commitment to that value. Conversely, the value whose endorsement increased dramatically was being very well off financially. In fact, most of the values items on the Freshman Survey that showed large increases were concerned with money, power, and status. Being well off financially, being in authority, having administrative responsibility for others, and obtaining recognition showed the greatest increases.[14] Many of the teens of today have set their career paths toward wealth, time off, and upward mobility in their professions. Clearly, nursing does not fulfill the values of these students.

Part of this change in attitude may be attributable to the fact that incoming freshmen are children of an economic upheaval—a time when a college education does not guarantee security or a job. The popular wisdom is that a nurse is always employable. However, during the early 1980s there were much-publicized layoffs of nurses as the prospective payment system encouraged the rapid discharge of patients from hospitals and shorter patient stays, resulting in lower incomes for many institutions. As the patient census dropped, the need for the patient care staff also dropped, and so nurses were laid off in many communities. This instability and lack of job security, coupled with values concerned with money and power, make nursing a less attractive occupational option.

The women's movement at its height encouraged women to seek validation in the formerly all-male corridors of commerce, politics, and industry. In so doing, women have created a trap for themselves that has forced them to move out of "feminine" pursuits, among them nursing, social work, and education. Despite the changes in the role of women in this country, the role of men has changed far less, and most men continue to perceive nursing as women's work; very few men choose to enter the profession.[15]

The nursing profession's image continues to be hampered by a negative public perception. It is not considered to be a prestigious profession. In fact, in a survey conducted by *Working Woman* magazine, nursing was named as one of the ten least desirable professions for women.

The image of nurses as portrayed in the literature, movies, and television soap operas—as handmaidens of physicians, as powerless to take any autonomous action, as sex objects, and as puppets of others—makes nursing a less than attractive career for the intelligent, autonomous, upwardly mobile young person of today. High school counselors who, in ignorance of the demands of the profession, continue to offer nursing as a career choice for the girl they describe as "nice," who babysits, and for whom they think nursing would be good preparation for marriage and motherhood are somewhat responsible for the lack of entry into the nursing profession.

The level of salary, in contrast to the level of responsibility of the nurse, is listed frequently as a cause of the nursing shortage. In fact, most nurses in their first jobs earn about what other young professionals earn. However, their salaries peak after five or six years in practice, while the professional in another field has a potential for much greater growth. Whereas starting salaries of nurses are now comparable with those of other college graduates, the average maximum salary for nurses is only $7,000 higher than the average starting salary.[16] It is well known that in most hospitals nurses with five years' experience in the profession are in fact at the same rate of pay as an individual with 35 years of continuous nursing service. The constrained financial reimbursement that hospitals face does not promise much possibility of more than modest increases in salary for nurses overall.

Furthermore, many hospitals do not distinguish, to any great degree, among levels of education when considering salary. This may make the work and financial sacrifice of returning to school a source of dissatisfaction for nurses. In contrast, advanced education in other fields may provide more lucrative options, and these are enhanced further by the fact that most of the jobs less frequently require night and weekend work.

Nurses, by virtue of breadth of education and work experience, may be the most versatile of health care employees. This versatility is one factor that makes nurses employable in many non-hospital or non-direct care roles. They have expanded their spheres to include home care, education, marketing, corporate quality assurance, fitness, law, insurance, and operational administration.

The employment of nurses in other than direct patient care roles in hospitals, coupled with a growing need to provide the more concentrated care required by sicker patients, increases the pressure on the supply.

The heightened demand for nursing care also may be caused by an increase in the number of physicians in practice. It has been demonstrated that the work of nursing and other health care workers increases as the numbers of physicians increase. As technology has expanded and the number of physicians has grown, the elements of care ordered for a patient population that is increasingly more ill have also escalated. This creates additional demands for intervention by nurses and other health care workers.[17]

Stress in today's environment is frequently cited as a reason for the lack of nurses. Not only are the needs of patients greater, their illnesses are more severe, they require more concentrated care as patients in general, and they are discharged earlier. The pace is faster, and the physical and emotional demands are greater. The pressure is constant, with little relief in the course of the average work day. The rapid turnover of patients reduces the ability to create satisfying relationships and to see the outcome of the care given. Expanding technology has created dilemmas about whether the kinds of health care that are possible should be pursued. These ethical dilemmas create moral distress for the nurse. The context in which most nurses work, which limits their freedom to implement moral decisions, can be cited as one reason nurses leave the profession. It may also be responsible for a potential decrease in productivity. It is well known that stress reduces the ability to be productive, and surely this is no different in nursing.

No matter how good a nurse is, or how skilled, he or she cannot be stretched so thin that demands for his or her skills are impossible to meet.[18] The inability to do a good job creates exceptional stress for nurses, leading in some cases to professional burnout.

PROJECTIONS FOR THE FUTURE

It has been projected that by the year 2010 the proportion of the over-65 population to the under-65 population will be 23 percent; by 2020, 33 percent; by 2055, the figure could be more than 50 percent, and that is without a significant change in the life expectancy or retirement age of the population. In the longer term, the implications for health care are profound.

It is well known that individuals over age 65 use the majority of health care services in this country. While better health care may create healthier segments of society, advances in science may sustain life in other segments with chronic disease. If the population of persons over 65 is greater than 50 percent, the incidence of chronic illness is likely to be staggering. Furthermore, as the population ages, the percentage of females will increase and the female component of the population will account for a greater percentage of personal health care use.[19] These elders after the year 2000, products of the baby boom, will be more affluent, educated, and knowledgeable about health care practice than probably any previous generation of elders.

Health maintenance and the care of chronic illness are expected to comprise 75 percent of tomorrow's health care market. Health supervision and teaching, two of the specialties of the professional nurse, will be more and more important as this young elderly group requires health care. Infectious diseases such as Acquired

Immune Deficiency Syndrome (AIDS) and the potential recurrence of preventable epidemic disease will become major health problems. Societal illness—social isolation, substance abuse, and mental illness—will also be critical problems.

The hospital, however, in the first quarter of the twenty-first century will have a population that is incredibly frail and very costly to treat, with acuity levels that are higher probably than those of today's intensive care units.

The balance of patient care will move toward services provided outside of hospital settings. In the future it is anticipated that hospitals will become exclusively critical care centers. Services such as surgery and birthing will be performed at free-standing centers, and patients will be discharged immediately to home care.

As a result of this change in health care, the need for highly technical, highly specialized, autonomous nurses in most hospitals will be much greater than in current institutions. Where the nurse to patient ratio might have been two patients to one nurse, very likely it may come to be two nurses to one patient. The need for very well prepared nurses in this setting will be critical. Indeed, nursing may require more specialists than ever before—those who are skilled in dealing with a labile population with complex needs in the intensive care unit of the future and those prepared in a broader sense to care for nonacute patients in other settings where the relationship between the nurse and other health care providers is different. These nurses will be required to have much greater autonomy than the nurses we are accustomed to finding in today's environment.

Using statistics provided by the U.S. Department of Health and Human Services, which has considered the changes in delivery of service, the National League for Nursing (NLN) has made the following projections for future needs in nursing: The demand for RNs is expected to reach 2.3 million by 2000 with a projected supply of 1.7 million. The NLN further states that shortages of baccalaureate-prepared nurses will be particularly critical, with a demand of 1 million compared with a supply of 510,000.[20] These statistics support the belief that the major deficit will occur in the category of nurses with advanced degrees. The picture for LPNs/LVNs is differently bleak in that projections depict declining opportunities for employment. These two circumstances will strain the resources allocated for nursing education either by institutions or the government.

What will be the impact of these changes in nurse supply and demand? While speculative at best, a number of possibilities are seen by the writers. One possibility is an increased number of what we term nomadic nurses. Already there are traveling nurses who fly from one part of the country to another to work for a few months in hospitals to fill in and to enjoy at least in some limited fashion the benefits of a particular geographic area. If the shortage continues it could be expected that the more adventuresome nurses who do not wish to become involved in their profession may become more and more nomadic. These nurses may go from place to place until they decide to settle in one area, find another role, or perhaps leave nursing altogether.

Nurse involvement is a critical component in most advancements in the delivery of patient care in today's hospitals. If nurses do not continue to fulfill this responsibility for qualitative improvement in patient care as part of their roles, the redistribution of an increased workload over fewer nurses will result in a further decline in health care. We would expect that more and more hospital units will close if the shortage continues or that attempts will be made to have elements of care provided by individuals who are rapidly and marginally trained to take over specific aspects of patient care. The fragmentation that this type of system implies will further decrease the gratification of nurses as well as erode the public's rapport with nursing and its satisfaction with the delivery system.

Salaries may increase. This has been one way of dealing with nursing shortages in the past. There are pronouncements of goals to increase the staff nurse salary to $50,000 annually in some hospitals. Others are providing higher-than-average salary increases to RNs while freezing those of other hospital employees. Whether these strategies will be successful in retaining nurses or whether they will result in the movement of nurses from one institution to another to take advantage of better wages remains to be seen. Whether the implementation of these strategies in the face of increased fiscal constraints and declining reimbursement can be maintained is also at issue.

The short-term impact of this deficit in nurse manpower can be expected to result in higher cost, more fragmented care, a more mobile nurse population with perhaps less commitment to individual institutions, a potential escalation in the vacancy rate and an increase in hospital unit closure, and perhaps a downward spiral of health care availability to the patient population. "The quality of hospital care depends upon the quality of hospital nursing. And where hospital nursing is involved, quality is exceptionally hard to maintain without quantity."[21]

In the near term, a continuing nursing shortage will surely diminish the quality and quantity of health care services to patients. In the longer term, this lack may also warp the fabric of our society, creating inequities of access to care and, where that access is unequal, a decline in minimum levels of care for some segments of society. The consequences of that occurrence may jeopardize our status among the civilized natives in the area of health care and may intensify the competition for and the conflict surrounding the allocation of tax dollars in this nation.

SUMMARY

The shortage of nurses in this country is real. Currently it is not from a lack of licensed RNs, nor is it really from a lack of nurses who are employed; rather it is due to the increased demand and the increased opportunities for individuals with nursing education, background, and experience. The shortage is also attributed to the perception and the reality of the nurse's image, the discrepancy between salary and responsibility, the compression of pay at the top of the scale, the hours of work and their incompatibility with the good life, the decline in human reward, the insufficient respect from others, and the penchant of nurses continually to be adaptable and accommodating to the needs of others—patients and other workers.

In the most recent cycle of the early 1980s, health care institutions were fortunate enough to have studied themselves out of the shortage. In the past the answer to the shortage has always been to increase support for tuition in nursing schools; to raise the salaries of practicing nurses; to add longevity bonuses, recruitment bonuses, benefits, and differentials for shift work; and to implement quality circles, professional conference days, collaborative practice committees, professional nurse practice committees, and flexible scheduling. All of these options are certainly helpful, and they address in the immediate term the cyclic shortages of nurses that have been experienced during the last 50 years. What these solutions do not address is the continuous adaptation of nurses to the needs and wishes of all others—patients, physicians, other healthcare workers, and the public. Remarkably little progress has been made in improving the working conditions of nurses to ensure future stability for them and their institutions.

This current, more complex, shortage will have to be answered now, or other disciplines will attempt to resolve the shortage independent of nursing. This, then, is the crisis. A state of affairs does exist in which a decisive change is imminent. The essential question is this: Will the cycle of shortage and quick fix be repeated yet again or will the nursing profession use this current shortage as an opportunity to redefine itself and its mission to achieve the autonomy its members require and to set its own destiny? Only when that question is resolved can nursing and nurses set about to really examine the need for nursing services and to devise the means to meet the need in a manner that provides for cost-effective service delivery and adequate rewards for its practitioners. When that balance is achieved, the shortage of nurses will give way to the appropriate utilization of resources in nursing. This balance, we believe, will be the most appropriate response to the needs of the people of the United States for health care into the next century.

NOTES

1. David Burda, "Reimbursement, Nurse Shortage Top Panel's List of Challenges in 1988," *Modern Healthcare* (January 1, 1988): 33.

2. Carol M. McCarthy, "Nursing Crisis: A Shortage of Solutions," *AHA News* 23 (May 18, 1987): 4.

3. Marjorie Beyers and Joseph Damore, "Nursing Shortage Requires Lasting Solution, Not a Quick Fix," *Health Progress* (May 1987): 33.

4. Spencer C. Johnson, "MHA Viewpoint, the Nursing Shortage Not Just the Same Old Thing," *Michigan Hospitals* 24 (March 1988): 5.

5. Linda A. Aiken and Connie Flynt Mullinix, "The Nurse Shortage, Myth or Reality?" *New England Journal of Medicine* 317 (September 3, 1987): 642.

6. Ibid., 643.

7. Connie R. Curran, Ann Minnick, and Joan Moss, "Who Needs Nurses?" *American Journal of Nursing* 87 (April 1987): 444.

8. Ibid., 445.

9. Ibid., 446.

10. Cooperative Institutional Research Program, *The American Freshman: Twenty Year Trends* (Los Angeles: Higher Education Research Institute, University of California at Los Angeles, 1987).

11. Peri Rosenfeld, "The Nursing Supply: What Do the Data Suggest?" *Michigan Hospitals* 24 (March 1988): 11.

12. Information contained in a summary letter to participants in the National Foundation for Long Term Health Care/Ross Laboratories Invitational Conference, January 6–8, 1988.

13. McCarthy, "Nursing Crisis: A Shortage of Solutions," 4.

14. Cooperative Institutional Research Program, *The American Freshman*.

15. Clair M. Fagin, "The Visible Problems of an 'Invisible' Profession: The Crisis and Challenge for Nursing," *Inquiry* 24 (Summer 1987): 121.

16. Aiken and Mullinix, "The Nurse Shortage, Myth or Reality?" 643.

17. William A. Rushing, "The Supply of Physicians and Expenditures of Health Services with Implications for the Coming Physician Surplus," *Journal of Health and Social Behavior* 26 (December 1985): 303.

18. McCarthy, "Nursing Crisis: A Shortage of Solutions," 4.

19. Russell C. Coile, Jr., "The Health Care System in 2010: Trends for a Changing Industry," *Health Care Executive* 1 (December 1986): 15.

20. National League for Nursing, *Nursing Shortage Fact Sheet* (New York: National League for Nursing, 1987).

21. McCarthy, "Nursing Crisis: A Shortage of Solutions," 4.

Chapter 2

What Causes Job Satisfaction and Productivity of Quality Nursing Care?

Marlene Kramer, Claudia Schmalenberg, and Laurin Paul Hafner

> What are the important variables in the hospital organization and its nursing service that create a magnetism that attracts and retains professional nurses on its staff? What particular combination of variables produces models of hospital nursing practice in which nurses receive professional and personal satisfaction to the degree that recruitment and retention of qualified staff are achieved?
> —McClure, Poulin, Sovie, and Wandelt, *Magnet Hospitals: Attraction and Retention of Professional Nurses*

The original magnet hospital study[1] sought answers to the above two questions. It described variables present in specific hospitals considered to be good places to work and good places in which to practice professional nursing. While the study provided much food for thought, the questions still remain: What variables create the magnetism, which in turn cause attraction and retention, which in turn cause nurse job satisfaction and production of quality care? What combinations of variables produce or account for variation in nurse job satisfaction and quality care? Is it the quality of the leadership team? The organizational structure? Adequacy of staffing? The presence of clinical nurse specialists? Perhaps it is the emphasis on professional development through career ladders? Or is it some combination of all of these factors? The purpose of this chapter is to answer the questions posed in the title and in this opening paragraph. This will be done by utilizing the results of a follow-up study of the magnet hospitals. This multipurpose study was designed to (1) describe in detail a random sample of magnet hospitals and the nurses who worked in them; (2) assess the impact of prospective payment systems (PPS) on nurses and nursing practice in magnet hospitals; (3) compare the magnet hospitals with the excellent companies in the corporate community on the attributes of excellence; (4) assess the causative relationship between designated variables in the hospital organization and its nursing service and the outcomes of job satisfaction and production of quality nursing care; (5) describe the attributes of nurses working in different types of hospitals; and (6) ascertain the impact of congruence in work values on nurse job satisfaction and

12

productivity. This chapter focuses primarily on the fourth purpose but uses data derived from the comparison of magnet hospitals with excellent companies where appropriate. (All other purposes have been reported elsewhere in the literature.) Unique to this study was an attempt to develop causal models to explain the "throughput"; i.e., what, if anything, happens to the nurse as a result of the impact of hospital variables on him or her, and how are these "nurse" effects related to job satisfaction and the staff nurses's perception that she or he can produce quality care?

The study *Magnet Hospitals: Attraction and Retention of Professional Nurses,* [2] conducted by the American Academy of Nursing's Task Force on Nursing Practice in Hospitals, described the perceptions of staff nurses and directors of nursing about the conditions that contribute to career satisfaction for registered nurses. Following regional interviews with the chief nursing executive (CNE) and one staff nurse from each of the 41 hospitals, descriptive data on the factors that seemed to be related to magnetism, recruitment, retention, and professional satisfaction were reported. Among the elements reported were:

- opportunity to maximize professional nursing practice through primary nursing, autonomy, availability of consultation, and resource personnel
- support of nursing personnel by hospital administration
- decentralized departmental structures
- adequate staffing
- employer support for professional development and continued formal education
- attractive employment benefits such as competitive salaries and flexible scheduling
- positive overall image of nursing both within and outside the institution

With this kind of satisfying professional environment, nurses remained in their positions; presumably, job satisfaction and quality nursing care followed or coexisted. Some magnet hospitals reported a 30 percent decrease in turnover among the nursing staff during the two years prior to the study. These relationships were not and have not been tested; testing them was the purpose of the current study.

SIGNIFICANCE OF THE STUDY

The original magnet hospital study was carried out toward the end of one nursing shortage; we are now in or moving into another. The worst is yet to come. The demand-side shortage that is being felt now is due largely to the ever-expanding diversity of employment opportunities for nurses and the upgrading of hospital nursing personnel due to diagnosis-related groups (DRGs) and PPS.[3] The supply-side shortage caused by the diminishing pool of college-age students, declining enrollments in schools of nursing, and increased competition from other women-opened occupations and professions is still in the offing. These external causes of nurse shortage are magnified when they coexist with internal causes of nurse shortage such as those produced by heavy turnover, constant orientation of new nurses, large numbers of inexperienced nurses who do not work regularly together, heavy supervisory responsibilities for lesser-trained workers, improper staff mix, large numbers of agency and part-time nurses, and inadequate support departments. The magnet hospitals have demonstrated what can be done to decrease or eliminate internal nurse shortage.[4] We can also learn from them which environmental factors are, in fact, instrumental in producing staff nurse job satisfaction and quality nursing care, and hence nurse attraction and retention.

FRAMEWORK OF THE STUDY

Increasingly, attempts are being made to establish causal models for nurse turnover[5,6]; job satisfaction is often included as an intervening variable in such models. To date, no attempt to establish the cause of either job satisfaction or perceived productivity of quality care can be found in the literature. Moreover, these areas, as yet, are too unexplored for any single theory to suggest itself for testing.

The conceptual base for this study was constructed from those factors identified in the original magnet hospital study as being associated with job satisfaction and quality care, and from a thorough review of the literature in the suggested areas. From these sources, a causal model was constructed for both job satisfaction and perceived productivity of quality nursing care.

The causes and correlates of job satisfaction have been studied by using varying theoretical models and methodological approaches. Communication theory, role conflict theory, motivational theory, expectancy theory, and social and industrial psychology models have been used to determine or explain job satisfaction. For the most part, job satisfaction is used as the antecedent variable from which to look at outcome variables such as intent to leave, or turnover itself.

Job Satisfaction Variables

Job satisfaction studies have been criticized for their failure to be predictive,[7] for their lack of standardization in framework and measurement questionnaires,[8,9] and for their low explained variance.[10] However, despite the varying approaches, theories, and methodological criticisms, the studies have produced some fairly consistent results. In the area of communication, several factors correlate with increased job satisfaction. When communications with top-level executives, supervisors, and peers are perceived as open and honest, the result is increased job satisfaction.[11,12] Communication that is regular and sincere heavily influences a nurse's perception of satisfaction. Two aspects of communication had a positive effect on job performance: communication with supervisors and personal feedback. Both improve job performance.[13,14] Communication, therefore, can be viewed as having two effects: increased satisfaction and, as a result of improved job performance, increased quality care.

Related to communication is the structural component of centralization. Generally, the more centralized the structure, the greater the turnover and dissatisfaction with work.[15,16] The reverse is also true: the greater the degree of participation in decision making, the greater the expressed satisfaction.[17] Thus one could expect that the more decentralized an organization and the more participative the decision making, the greater the satisfaction and the less the turnover. Related to this finding is that increased autonomy leads to increased satisfaction.[18] Since autonomy is concerned with the freedom to exercise decision making in the job, it adds support for linking job satisfaction with increased decision making.

Related to structure and centralization is the kind of nursing philosophy, often translated into the type of nursing care delivery system—specifically primary nursing. While the findings are mixed, primary nursing has been described as increasing nurse autonomy and job satisfaction.[19–21] While the dynamics behind the increased satisfaction are unknown, it is suggested that control of one's work and being able to perform meaningful work are likely the bases.

Another fairly common finding in terms of job satisfaction is related to opportunities for growth and development: the greater the opportunity for growth, the higher the degree of satisfaction with the job.[22–24] Somewhat related is the finding that jobs that contain highly repetitive work create increased job dissatisfaction,[25] probably because highly repetitive work does not offer much opportunity for growth.

Several other factors related to job satisfaction are experience, education, and staff mix. It has been established that a collegiate nursing education (BSN) predisposes an individual to increased professional role conflict and thus increased dissatisfaction.[26–28] Increased experience, on the other hand, leads to greater overall satisfaction with work but also greater dissatisfaction with pay.[29,30] Increased numbers of registered nurses and decreased numbers of ancillary personnel lead to decreased turnover.[31] In accordance with Price and Mueller's view that job satisfaction is a variable intervening to turnover,[32] it can be concluded that increased registered nurse to ancillary staff ratios will result in increased nurse job satisfaction.

Another study suggests that the importance one attributes to job factors and the differential expectations of a job that one holds may be key to job satisfaction.[33] Basically, the premise is that if the expectations an individual brings at entry into an organization are unmet, depending upon the importance placed on these expectations by the individual, the more dissatisfied an individual will be with his or her job.

In summary, it can be expected that

- Open, honest, sincere communication with top-level executives, super- visors, and peers will lead to increased job satisfaction.
- Increased autonomy, participation in decision making, and decreased cen- tralization will increase job satisfaction.
- Increased opportunities for promotion, growth, and development will lead to increased job satisfaction.
- Increased experience will lead to generally increased job satisfaction but decreased satisfaction with pay.
- A baccalaureate education will cause increased dissatisfaction.
- Increased registered nurse to ancillary worker ratios will lead to increased satisfaction.
- Consistency between individual and organizational expectations will increase job satisfaction.

Variables Related to Production of Quality Nursing Care

Two specific factors—communication with supervisors and personal feed- back—that are related to job satisfaction have also been shown to be related to effective performance.[34] More effective performance leads to increased quality in the nursing care delivered. What other factors affect the quality of care in a hospital?

Quality care is strongly linked to the individual nurse in his or her care of patients: it is dependent on the nurse's performance. In looking at the effect of education on individual performance, there is little hard evidence to support differences in performance based on type of education. The *total number* of years of education appears to be the best indicator of job effectiveness.[35] The more education, the better the performance. Not only does formal education lead to increased effectiveness, but continuing education also produces more job effec- tiveness.[36]

The presence of clinical nurse specialists has been noted to lead to positive patient opinions about quality care[37]; also noted is that clinical nurse specialists are cost-effective and improve quality of care.[38] Since clinical nurse specialists have more education than staff nurses, their impact would appear to be twofold. The clinical nurse specialist may also effect improved quality of care through interac- tion with the staff. The literature indicates that the clinical specialist is valued by administrators for his or her consultant functions, assistance in the inservice education of the staff, support and development of the staff, and promotion and maintenance of standards.[39] The specialist may contribute to quality care, there- fore, not only through his or her own efforts but as a result of contributing to the continuing education of the staff.

The type of nursing care delivery system plays a role in the quality of care delivered. Although there is no comparative evidence as to whether or not primary nursing is more effective than team or functional nursing in increasing quality, primary nursing is said to improve individual nurse competence because of its motivational effect. With the introduction of the primary nursing delivery system, nurses have found it necessary to review disease entities and relevant clinical material.[40] Also, because in this delivery system the nurse has total responsibility for a group of patients, the quality of care a patient receives is immediately apparent, and accountability can be established. Thus unacceptable performance can be corrected, and overall quality of nursing care can be improved because incompetence is weeded out.[41] Primary nursing has also been noted to improve quality of care without particular attention to the exact mechanism.[42,43] Both nurses and physicians noted improved communication and relationships under a primary nursing system, thus improving quality of care.[44,45] Effective nurse-physician collaboration has also been linked with positive patient care outcomes, thus permitting the inference that quality nursing care intervened.[46]

Quality of nursing care is also said to be influenced by the presence of a clinical ladder program. While there are as yet no research data, clinical ladders are said to increase the opportunity for professional growth and to encourage clinical experts to remain at the bedside, thus improving quality of care and resulting in increased job satisfaction.[47,48]

In summary, the review of the literature supports the following relationships with respect to productivity of quality nursing care:

- Increased years of education lead to improved quality of care.
- The presence of clinical nurse specialists is associated with increased education of staff and thus increased quality of care.
- A primary nursing delivery system leads to increased quality care.
- Clinical ladder programs lead to increased quality of care.
- Good physician-nurse relationships lead to increased quality of care.

Nurse Attribute Variables

Isolated findings on the relationship between personal attributes of the nurse and nurse job satisfaction and productivity were noted in the literature. Individuals who have an internal locus of control have greater general satisfaction with their jobs than those who attribute causation externally.[49] A positive correlation exists between an internal locus of control and a strong self-concept.[50] Lack of self-esteem was identified as a primary dissatisfier.[51] Thus it can be expected that individuals with high self-esteem and internality will be more satisfied with their jobs than will their counterparts with low self-esteem and externality.

While not directly measured in terms of quality care, the higher an individual's self-esteem, the higher the perceived competence,[52] the more effectively he or she will function. Individuals with positive self-esteem are more secure, confident, and self-respecting; are less prone to influence by others; are less threatened by difficult tasks and situations; and relate to and work with others more comfortably and effectively.[53] Staff nurses with high levels of self-esteem therefore should be more effective, and thus improved quality care should result. A positive correlation between self-esteem and an internal locus of control has been noted.[54] This would lead one to expect to find an internal locus of control in individuals with high self-esteem.

There is considerable literature on the effects of autonomy on job satisfaction and productivity. A positive correlation between professional identity and perceived autonomy has been found.[55] Increased education leads to increased feelings of autonomy; however, a baccalaureate education leads to a perception of decreased autonomy in the work setting,[56] although it is a prerequisite to effective nurse-physician collaboration.[57] Internal control and a primary nursing delivery system increase perception of nurse autonomy.[58] Internality has also been noted to increase autonomy and job satisfaction.[59]

Both primary nursing and a participatory head nurse leadership style lead to increased professional role orientation.[60,61] Primary nursing is seen as physically linking nurse and patient, thus improving nurse-physician collaboration and quality of care.[62]

In summary, then, the following relationships between nurse attributes and job satisfaction and productivity can be hypothesized:

- Internal locus of control and high self-esteem lead to increased job satisfaction.
- High self-esteem leads to increased perceptions of competence and quality of care.
- High self-esteem and internal locus of control lead to increased quality of care.

Based on the foregoing, a causal model to explain staff nurse job satisfaction and productivity was constructed. The model consisted of five categories of variables: exogenous, i.e., preexisting or external to the model; hospital variables as perceived by staff nurses; nurse attribute variables; professional behavior variables; and outcome variables. The purely exogenous variables were education (measured as total number of years of basic nursing education plus subsequent degree education); current employment status (full- or part-time); hospital years (number of years of employment in current hospital); and internality (internal attribution of causation). Hospital variables were high specialization (the number of discrete patient services such as thoracic-surgical units, hospice, etc., offered by the hospital); the presence of clinical nurse specialists; the ability to work with clinically competent nurses; positive nurse-physician relationships; collaborative practice; the presence of a primary nursing delivery system; the presence of an operational clinical ladder system; satisfactory salary; flexible work schedules; degree of recognition of nurses; adequate support services; institutional autonomy of the nursing department (positive response to statements such as "nursing controls its own practice" and "nursing participates in making important decisions"); adequate staffing; expectation of high standards; and high-quality leadership. The nurse attribute variables were nurse self-concept and self-esteem. The professional behavior variables were autonomy, professional role behavior, bicultural role behavior, concern for patient rights, and rejection of traditional limitations of the nurse role. Outcome variables were job satisfaction values (factors judged to be important to the individual for his or her job satisfaction), job productivity values (factors perceived by the individual as important to being able to produce quality nursing care), job satisfaction (important job factors are perceived as present in the current job); and perceived productivity (factors important to producing quality nursing care are perceived as present).

The description and psychometric properties of the tools used to measure the nurse attribute and professional behavior variables can be found in an article by Kramer, Hafner, and Hoerle.[63] The nursing work index, a tool used to measure hospital and outcome variables, has been described by Kramer and Hafner.[64] Data for exogenous variables were collected from each nurse individually.

PROCEDURE FOR THE STUDY

Utilizing the same regionalization (BLS) as described in the original magnet hospital study, a one-third sample, proportionate by regions of the country, of the 41 magnet hospitals was drawn. Because in some regions where there were only two magnet hospitals a 50 percent sample had to be drawn, the final sample comprised 16 hospitals. Between November 1985 and September 1986, each of these hospitals was visited and studied for periods of two to six days. (In 1987 and 1988, brief telephone and personal contacts were made with 14 of the 16 hospitals to ascertain the current status of the nursing shortage.) Interviews, individual and group, were held with more than 800 staff nurses. In addition, group interviews were conducted with 273 (93 percent) of the total of 295 head nurses; with 225 (91 percent) of the total of 247 in the clinical expert group, which consisted of clinical nurse specialists, staff development instructors, and clinicians; and with 102 of the 108 (94 percent) assistant and associate clinical directors in the 16 participating magnet hospitals. Individual interviews were conducted with each of the 16 CNEs. Hospital units were visited and studied on all three shifts. Nursing care plans, card indexes, and computer printouts were studied. Departmental and hospital committee meetings, including staff nurse councils, peer review sessions, and union-prescribed meetings, were attended and observed.

Much of the written history and materials of the nursing department were studied and analyzed. All publications produced by the staff of the nursing department were read and analyzed. The study technique of total immersion was used as extensively as possible throughout the period of study.

In addition to the interviews and study of the printed materials of these nursing departments, quantitative data were collected on a 25 percent random sample of the entire staff nurse population employed in each of the 16 hospitals. Respondents provided demographic data on education, experience, marital status, dependents, length of time working at that hospital, and so on. Each of the 1634 participating nurses completed the Levenson locus of control scales, the Pankratz autonomy-patient advocacy/RTRL instrument, the Taylor self-concept/self-esteem tool, the role behavior scales, and the nursing work index. The nursing work index was also completed by the top nursing management team, the clinical expert group, and the head nurse group.

The CNE in each of the participating hospitals was contacted by mail, the study was explained, and research committee/human experimentation procedures were fulfilled. The investigator provided a table of random numbers, which the hospital matched with a computerized list of all staff nurses employed full- or part-time, to obtain the 25 percent random sample. An individualized letter was sent to each nurse in the random sample that explained the study and the importance of his or her participation. To promote participation and provide personal incentive, participants were promised individual interpretations of the questionnaire results mailed to their home addresses. All data were collected by one of the investigators, were held in confidence, and were anonymous unless an individual report was desired.

For about half of the participants, the data were collected during 90-minute testing sessions held in a hospital conference room. Many nurses, particularly those working evenings and nights, preferred to complete the test packets either at home or on the unit if patient care activities permitted. Cooperation and participation in the study were outstanding—both on the part of the individual participants and on the part of the various nursing administrations. Participation of the 25 percent random sample ranged from 88 percent to 100 percent, with a median of 96 percent.

RESULTS

With 31 variables, the causal model is too large to draw, but using the five categories to represent the individual variables, the model could be drawn as in Figure 2-1. The lines in Figure 2-1 represent hypothesized explanations of the causes of nurse job satisfaction and productivity (the outcome variables). (Curved as well as straight lines indicate causal paths in this model.) For example, in this model, we are saying that the nurse's type of education (baccalaureate, diploma, associate degree) not only will have a direct effect on how he or she perceives or

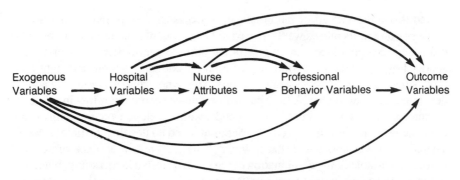

Figure 2-1 Model of Five Categories Representing Individual Variables

reacts to hospital variables such as type of nursing care delivery system, but it also will have a direct effect on the nurse's self-concept and self-esteem (nurse attributes), on professional role behavior, and on the outcome variables of job satisfaction and productivity of quality nursing care. The most direct effect hypothesized is that the exogenous variables affect the perception of the hospital variables that influence the nurses's self-concept and self-esteem, which affect how he or she enacts professional role behavior, and this determines nurse job satisfaction and perceived productivity.

The saturated model was tested, meaning that all direct and indirect paths of all variables were tested simultaneously. For each of the 26 regressions, all of the appropriate predictors were entered simultaneously (in contrast to a hierarchical or stepwise regression where the entry of variables is in a certain order). In this study, we were not trying to predict but rather to understand and explain how all of these variables go together to influence each other. It was hypothesized that they would go together in a certain way, and that hypothesis was tested.

Relevant parameters and statistics in tabular form are available from the authors. Briefly stated, the analysis indicated that there were significant coefficients in all five categories of variables. The variance explained for job satisfaction was .75; perceived productivity of quality care, = .69; job satisfaction values, = .27; and job productivity values, = .22. These seem to be, and are, large numbers but they undoubtedly are inflated because of the large numbers of predictors. Also, the coefficients, while significant, are almost all less than .10.

It must therefore be concluded that the causal model tested, while explaining some of the variation in staff nurse job satisfaction and productivity, is not sufficient and is not complete. More of the differences in the variables were explained by the actual hospitals in which the 1634 nurses were employed. In spite of the fact that all of the nurses in the sample were from magnet hospitals, there were significant differences in test scores among the nurses in the 16 participating hospitals. This hospital variable represents each hospital's unique combination of hospital variables. For example, the hospital in this study whose staff nurses scored the highest in all of the outcome variables utilized primary nursing as a delivery system, its nurses were salaried, it had self-contained nursing units, but it did not have a developed nursing information computer system. Another high-scoring hospital had a superb nursing information computer system and eight-hour total patient care delivery systems, its nurses were not salaried, but it had a well-developed clinical ladder. A hospital whose nurses scored quite low in all of the outcome variables had primary nursing and a well-developed nursing information computer system, its nurses were salaried, but it had no developed clinical ladder. Therefore, it was concluded that it was not the presence or absence of any one particular variable or the combination of variables as tested in this study, but rather the particular combination or constellation of hospital variables that made some hospitals so effective in attracting and retaining nurses and so effective in producing staff nurse job satisfaction and quality nursing care.

Another result of this study was that the causal model tested was incomplete. From observation and contact with the nurses in this sample, it was immediately evident that there were variables not mentioned earlier in the literature or in the original study that were very important, both alone and in combination, to staff nurse job satisfaction and productivity. High among these "undiscovered" variables was the salaried or exempt status of staff nurses. As frequently explained: "Nothing makes me feel less like a professional than punching a time clock or filling in a time card." A salaried status represents the difference between "working hours" and "performing a job or service." Comments such as these are evidence that staff nurses who were salaried saw themselves and their jobs differently from those who were hourly workers; there were also marked differences (increases) in the self-concept and self-esteem of staff nurses who were salaried.

While virtually all of the magnet hospitals were decentralized, with head nurses serving as department heads, the salaried status of staff nurses was frequently linked to "self-contained units," meaning that a particular unit or service was independent and fully functional unto itself. This was particularly noticeable with respect to staffing (no floating in or out of the unit), and to the cohesiveness, stability, and solidarity of relationships among staff members (all of which are factors important to decreasing internal nurse shortage).

Other previously "undiscovered" variables of considerable importance include a computerized nursing information system, salary decompression, a case manager delivery system, an opportunity to participate in nursing research, and child care facilities. To the extent that they were discovered early, data were collected on the presence or absence of these variables. In a few instances, retrospective data were collected. However, omission of these variables from the model undoubtedly created a deficit in the model's explanatory powers.

The most useful and constructive way of looking at the results of this study is to visualize that, in effect, each of these 16 hospitals had constructed its own causal model for nurse job satisfaction and productivity that led to its being able to attract and retain nurses. There were some features that were common to all of the magnet hospital models studied, such as a primary nursing delivery system or at least an eight-hour total patient care delivery system, staff nurse self-governance, self-contained units, flexible work schedules with staff nurse input, clinical career ladders, and creative nurse leadership. But each hospital's model also had unique or distinct characteristics: some of the models were more effective than others in producing nurse job satisfaction and job productivity. By tallying the variables present in those magnet hospitals whose nurses scored highest in job values, job satisfaction, and job productivity, the variables of greatest significance were salaried status, salary decompression, staff nurse involvement in decision making, self-scheduling flexibility, support for education, the presence of self-contained units, opportunity for specialized practice, high nurse self-concept and self-esteem, and high individual autonomy.

CORPORATE CULTURE OF EXCELLENCE

Additional insight into the questions raised by the title and opening paragraphs of this chapter—What causes nurse job satisfaction and productivity of quality nursing care? What are the important variables in the hospital organization and its nursing service that create a magnetism that attracts and retains professional nurses on its staff?—is provided when one examines and assesses the magnet hospitals on the attributes of "excellence" found to be characteristic of highly successful companies in the corporate community. While quantification such as that represented by the causal model tested in this study can explain some of the variation, it does not explain enough. For example, some of these hospitals had high rates of attraction and retention and high job satisfaction and productivity even though they did not have some of the features ordinarily thought to promote nurse attraction and retention, such as straight shifts rather than rotating shifts.

What was found in all of the magnet hospitals visited was evidence of a corporate culture of excellence. Modern hospitals are complex, complicated organizations that operate in an economic climate of turbulence and rapid change. Managerial success in these organizations cannot be predicted by a single factor or theory. One perspective, however, that emphasizes the importance of shared values and norms rather than the structural or rational variables stressed in traditional theories is the symbolic or cultural view.[65]

Culture is the combination of symbols, language, assumptions, and behaviors through which an organization manifests its norms and values. An understanding of these cultural concepts can help managers enhance and expand their personal management philosophy of practice, thereby increasing their probability of success.

In 1982, in *In Search of Excellence*,[66] a study was reported that identified the essential characteristics of America's "best-run" business firms. To be selected as a best-run company, one had to have the reputation of being innovative and excellent and had to meet certain criteria of financial performance. After intensive, lengthy, on-site visiting, interviewing, and study, 15 companies were selected as "exemplars." These companies were found to possess an identifiable corporate culture consisting of eight functional attributes or values. The magnet hospitals visited were studied and analyzed and were found to possess many of the same characteristics and values as a corporate culture of excellence.

Principle 1: Bias for Action. One of the attributes that characterized excellence in both the corporate community and in the magnet hospitals was an inclination to act. Permission did not need to be sought and approval obtained at multiple levels before action began. "Chaotic action was preferable to orderly inaction!"[67] This did not mean that study and thought were not given to problems, but it did mean that "paralysis through analysis" was avoided. The principle can be summarized as "ready, fire, aim" and "learn from one's tries."

Principle 2: Close to the Customer. In the excellent companies there was an almost fanatic zeal about the quality of the product, about service reliability, and about staying in touch with the customer. To achieve and maintain these virtues, companies must inculcate and reward the values of quality and service in their employees. Enactment of this principle was profoundly evident in the nursing departments of the magnet hospitals: "We give Cadillac, not Volkswagen care here." "Love and high quality workmanship." "Competent, personalized and cost effective care: those are the values here."[68]

In their pursuit of service, the excellent companies placed all resources of the company behind service to the customer. The magnet hospital corollary of this philosophy was shown by the extent and quality of support services provided to the nursing department.

> There are many built-in time savers here so nurses have time to give quality patient care. The whole hospital values quality patient care and everything here . . . is done with that purpose in mind. There is no excuse for the nurses not to deliver high quality care. The administration expects it and we expect it of ourselves.
>
> The caring, quality values here are demonstrated by everyone: nurses, mail clerks, orderlies, dietary, and the maintenance men. You either buy into these values or you get out.[69]

Other evidence of this principle, in both the best-run companies and the magnet hospitals, was intensive, active involvement on the part of senior executives; employee relations that mirrored customer relations; a remarkable people orientation; and a high degree of feedback. With respect to the latter, many nurses repeatedly commented that they expected and received answers to queries or problems expressed to management within 48 hours.

Delivery of a quality product was also ensured through a reward system that valued performance, experience, and education. Many systems—role model awards, "Care Bear" awards, "Primary Pig" awards—gave public recognition for outstanding performance. Although not necessarily distinguished by high entry pay, most of the magnet hospitals focused on decompressing salary scales. This as well as the general movement toward salaried (exempt) status rewarded experienced nurses. To provide a quality product—competent and effective nursing care—you have to have quality people. This was evidenced by the tremendous push and support for education. In the magnet hospitals studied, 51 percent of the staff were prepared with at least the baccalaureate; in some, almost 90 percent were prepared at this level. Virtually all of the magnet hospitals had both tuition reimbursement and different types of scholarship programs in place.

Principle 3: Autonomy and Entrepreneurship. This principle means creating an environment that supports experimentation from both a value perspective and a physical resource perspective. Autonomy, the freedom to act on what one knows, includes the freedom to act and succeed but also to act and fail. In the magnet hospitals visited, staff nurses were trained to feel empowered; they exuded power and confidence. The same type of intense, informal communication that supports a "bias for action" supports innovation. Internal competition and nonstandardization between subunits was not only fostered but encouraged.

> There are high expectations here that you will be creative. This is an atmosphere where creativity flourishes. When it occurs, it is recognized and rewarded.
> Great autonomy and creativity are stressed here, because this leads to quality care. You are free to function professionally. For me, this makes up for the additional salary that I could earn working somewhere else or in a different profession.[70]

Another manifestation of Principle 3 was the heavy emphasis on staff nurse involvement in both nursing department and hospital committees and policy formation. In some instances this involvement took the form of fully developed "shared governance" models; in others, it was done through well-developed and fully operational staff nurse organizations.

The magnet hospitals were also well known for their innovations and for sharing their accomplishments and ideas with the broader nursing community. The names of 13 of the 16 CNEs turned up in a computer search of the literature. In virtually all of the magnet hospitals, additional works were published by many others within the nursing departments. Several of the hospitals had or were publishing books written by teams of nurses including staff nurses.

The end result of encouraging individual autonomy, of creating a climate for risk taking to flourish, is the reduction of bureaucratic rules and structure to the absolute minimum. In such a climate, the individual develops and flourishes. "Substituting rules for judgment starts a self-defeating cycle, since judgment can only be developed by using it."[71]

Principle 4: Productivity through People. Both the excellent companies and the magnet hospitals were marked by a true respect for the individual, a people orientation. This respect takes the form of treating people with dignity and holding high performance expectations. There is reward for productivity, often associated with a great deal of "show." Peers control each other through norms established for performance. Employees of the magnet hospitals often viewed themselves as an extended family, with a prevalent use of terms such as "family feeling," "belongingness," and "caring." One of the magnet hospitals openly described itself as a "hugging organization"; this openness and warmth was genuinely felt throughout the organization.

One of the reward systems in place in many of the magnet hospitals was the clinical ladder, or credentialling process. Although many felt that the clinical ladders did not distinguish excellent nurses—"because we are all excellent here; we can't be otherwise"—they also felt that administration "cared" enough to offer this form of recognition.

Other aspects of this principle of productivity through people was the necessity for providing information to people, keeping them informed at all times, and giving feedback to peers surrounding performance. Again, as in other aspects of this corporate culture of excellence, the emphasis on informality—particularly in day-to-day information exchange—and the absence of a rigidly followed chain of command were the norms.

Principle 5: Hands-on, Value-Driven. The major role of leadership in excellent organizations, whether in the corporate community or magnet hospitals, was to create, instill, and clarify the value system. The role of management was to generate enthusiasm down to the very last worker, and leaders took this process of value shaping very seriously. Values and beliefs were not usually transmitted through formal written procedures, but rather through stories, myths, legends, and metaphors.

The top nursing executives in the magnet hospitals were highly visible and accessible; they were seen by their people as visionary, enthusiastic leaders in nursing. Many had national reputations and held national office. They set value standards for nursing locally, regionally, and nationally. Many staff nurses commented on this leadership and exclaimed that it made them feel good to know that the values promulgated in their hospital were also those that were leading the country. There was an enthusiasm and an excitement in the staff nurses when they talked about their leaders.

> _____ is the visionary with the ideas; the directors implement and carry forth the ideas. There's a oneness about the leadership here that's hard to explain.
> _____ is a leader who really cares about the nurses and the patient. She knows everyone and is always accessible. But most important, she makes you *feel* like you are someone; she makes you proud to be a nurse.

> Her vision is grandiose but it is based in reality. She's not always clear
> about the vision, but she is trusting and enthusiastic, so that carries you
> along.[72]

Consistent with the excellence study, the magnet hospitals had strong, albeit small, top nursing management teams with a common set of shared values. Genuine liking, enthusiasm, humor, and an excitement about nursing characterized this group. They were also very well educated, with most prepared at least at the master's level, and one-third who were prepared at the doctoral level.

The pervasive infusion of the values of excellence and quality existed not only in the nursing department, but was evident throughout the hospital. The support of these values by hospital administrators and physician chiefs of staff is crucial if such values are to be institutional norms, and the nursing staff was well aware of when that support was there and when it was absent. How the CNE got along with the hospital administrator was a relationship that virtually all nurses knew and could comment on.

The magnet hospitals protected their value system through selective hiring practices. Head nurses reported that they hired people who had a value system consonant with the one they were trying to promote, and that they would leave a position open rather than fill it with an inappropriate person. New graduates as well as experienced nurses had to compete for positions. Once they were successful, they perceived that they had a worthwhile job and jealously guarded the extant value system. New graduates were desired because of their enthusiasm, well-grounded book knowledge, and creativity, but their selection was balanced with the employment of experienced nurses who were dissatisfied with the practice of nursing elsewhere.

Principle 6: Sticking to the Knitting. This principle means to remain with the business that the company knows best. It was the only principle in which there was divergence between the best-run companies and the magnet hospitals. The latter had to diversify vertically in order to survive in the current healthcare market.

Principle 7: Simple Form, Lean Staff. Most large enterprises respond to bigness by designing complex systems and structures; the excellent companies were radically decentralized, had comparatively few people at the corporate level, had a minimum number of levels, and *appeared* to be reorganizing all the time.

All but two of the magnet hospitals studied had adopted very flat, lean, decentralized structures. In some there were only two levels: the CNE and the head nurse department heads. Most had one other level between the CNE and the head nurse. With stable, educated staff, the need for supervision is markedly decreased; therefore, many had eliminated some of the clinical director positions and the traditional house supervisory position.

While the enduring values of the organization pervaded all units, the move toward greater decentralization did create the small adaptive units that Peters and

Waterman talk about.[73] Considerable autonomy and nonstandardized operations and practice were permitted on these adaptive units. Individual head nurses determined their own unit-based standards and policies, provided that they followed the broad general outlines of the department and hospital. They were proud of the quick decisions and quality actions that the flexibility and control of practice at the unit level permitted. They were willing to tolerate the messiness and nonstandardization that such flexibility demanded.

Principle 8: Simultaneous Loose-Tight Properties. This principle means the coexistence of firm central direction and optimum individual employee autonomy. *Loose-tight* is about rope and about culture: give lots of rope when it comes to individual autonomy, flexible organizational structure, extensive experimentation, copious feedback, and informality; but at the same time, maintain a remarkably tight, culturally driven, and controlled set of rigidly shared values. Nothing then gets very far out of line.

This principle may seem to be a series of paradoxes, particularly with respect to individual autonomy within a rigid discipline of shared values. Such is not the case. Autonomy is a product of discipline. The discipline of a few shared values provides the framework. It gives people confidence to experiment—experimentation that stems from a stable expectation about what really counts.

Much of the evidence relative to the other attributes supports the existence of this principle within the magnet hospitals: a unifying set of values, established and guarded by the leadership of the nursing department and extant within the organization as a whole; decentralized departments that allow for autonomy at the bedside and for fast, appropriate, consumer-oriented decision making; employees who own and control their own practice, assuring competent, effective, and personalized care to each patient. Basic simple form at the top with systems for the introduction of innovation are present. The institutional culture of quality service through productive people is pervasive.

SUMMARY

This then is the whole story: Staff nurse job satisfaction and productivity of quality nursing care, staff nurse attraction, and retention in jobs cannot be adequately explained through the causal model developed and tested in this research. Individual hospital models, i.e., combinations of organizational variables, are more explanatory than a universal model applicable to all hospitals, although there is a set of common factors. Through inductive research methods, it was determined that the magnet hospitals possessed a corporate culture of excellence. Although the extent to which this culture contributes to nurse job satisfaction and productivity was not quantitatively determined, it is clear that the presence of such a corporate culture of excellence is a major determining factor—along with hospital and nurse attribute variables—in nurse job satisfaction, productivity, attraction, and retention. By infusing it with values, one converts an organization into an institution. Such a transition involves transforming men and women from neutral, technical units into participants who have a particular stamp, sensitivity, and commitment.[74] By combining this corporate culture with hospital and departmental variables shown to be important—salaried status, salary decompression, support for education, self-governance, the presence of self-contained units, self-scheduling flexibility, and opportunity for specialized practice—an environment can be created that not only eliminates internal nurse shortage but successfully attracts and retains satisfied, productive nurses.

NOTES

1. M. McClure et al., *Magnet Hospitals: Attraction and Retention of Professional Nurses* (Kansas City, Kans.: ANA Publishing Co., 1983): 2–3.

2. McClure et al., *Magnet Hospitals*.

3. M. Kramer and C. Schmalenberg, "Magnet Hospitals Talk about the Impact of DRGs on Nursing Care," *Nursing Management* 18, part I, no. 9 (September 1987): 38–42; part II, no. 10 (October 1987): 33–40.

4. M. Kramer and C. Schmalenberg, "Magnet Hospitals: Institutions of Excellence," *Journal of Nursing Administration* 18, part I, no. 1 (January 1988): 13–24; part II, no. 2 (February 1988): 12–27.

5. J.L. Price and C.W. Mueller, "A Causal Model of Turnover for Nurses," *Academy Medical Journal* 24 (1981): 543–565.

6. Ada Sue Hinshaw and Jan R. Atwood, "Nursing Staff Turnover, Stress, and Satisfaction: Models, Measures, and Management," *Annual Review of Nursing Research* 1 (1983): 133–153.

7. Dinah B. Slavitt et al., "Nurses' Satisfaction with Their Work Situation," *Nursing Research* 27, no. 2 (March–April 1978): 114–120.

8. Lyman W. Porter and Richard M. Steers, "Organization, Work, and Personal Factors in Employee Turnover and Absenteeism," *Psychological Bulletin* 80, no. 2 (1973): 151–176.

9. P. Stamps and E. Piedmonte, *Nurses and Work Satisfaction: An Index for Measurement* (Ann Arbor, Mich.: Health Administration Press Perspectives, 1986).

10. Hinshaw and Atwood, "Nursing Staff Turnover, Stress, and Satisfaction," 133–153.

11. J. David Pincus, "Communication: Key Contribution to Effectiveness—The Research," *Journal of Nursing Administration* 16, no. 9 (September 1986): 24–25.

12. Mark F. Peterson, "Co-workers and Hospital Staff's Work Attitudes: Individual Difference Moderators," *Nursing Research* 32, no. 2 (March–April 1983): 120.

13. Pincus, "Communication: Key Contribution," 24–25.

14. Peterson, "Co-workers and Hospital Staff's Work Attitudes," 120.

15. Price and Mueller, "A Causal Model of Turnover for Nurses," 543–565.

16. J.P. Curry et al., "Determinants of Turnover among Nursing Department Employees," *Research in Nursing and Health* 8 (1985): 397–411.

17. Ibid.

18. Ibid.

19. Norma Lang and Jacqueline Clinton, "Assessment of Quality of Nursing Care," *Annual Review of Nursing Research* 2 (1984): 135–155.

20. Tanna Ferrin, "One Hospital's Successful Implementation of Primary Nursing," *Nursing Administrative Quarterly* 6, no. 4 (Summer 1981): 1–12.

21. P. Giovannetti, "Evaluation of Primary Nursing," *Annual Review of Nursing Research* 4 (1986): 127–151.

22. Curry et al., "Determinants of Turnover among Nursing Department Employees," 397–411.

23. Richard O. Blaleck, "How Satisfied Are Hospital Staff Nurses with Their Jobs?" *Hospital Topics* 64, no. 3 (May–June 1986): 14–18.

24. B.P.V. Sarata, "Changes in Staff Satisfactions after Increases in Pay, Autonomy, and Participation," *American Journal of Community Psychology* 12, no. 4 (1984): 431–444.

25. Curry et al., "Determinants of Turnover among Nursing Department Employees," 397–411.

26. Frederic Decker, "Socialization and Interpersonal Environment in Nurses' Affective Reactions to Work," *Social Science Medicine* 20, no. 5 (1985): 499–509.

27. M.F. Kramer, "Some Effects of Exposure to Employing Bureaucracies on the Role Conceptions and Role Deprivation of Neophyte Collegiate Nurses." Doctoral Dissertation, School of Education, Stanford University, Palo Alto, Calif. (1966).

28. R. Corwin, "Role Conception and Career Aspirations: A Study of Identity in Nursing," *Sociological Quarterly* (April 1961): 69–86.

29. Kathleen Simpson, "Job Satisfaction or Dissatisfaction Reported by Registered Nurses," *Nursing Administrative Quarterly* 9, no. 3 (September 1985): 64–73.

30. Decker, "Socialization and Interpersonal Environment," 499–509.

31. Curry et al., "Determinants of Turnover among Nursing Department Employees," 397–411.

32. Price and Mueller, "A Causal Model of Turnover for Nurses," 543–565.

33. E. Larson et al., "Job Satisfaction: Assumptions and Complexities," *Journal of Nursing Administration* 14, no. 1 (1984): 31–38.

34. Pincus, "Communication: Key Contribution," 24–25.

35. Joanne McCloskey, "Nursing Education and Job Effectiveness," *Nursing Research* 32, no. 2 (January–February 1983): 53–58.

36. Joanne McCloskey, *Toward an Educational Model of Nursing Effectiveness* (Ann Arbor, Mich.: University of Michigan Press, 1983).

37. Lang and Clinton, "Assessment of Quality of Nursing Care," 135–155.

38. Marcus I. Walker, "How Nursing Service Administrators View Clinical Nurse Specialists," *Nursing Management* 17, no. 3 (March 1986): 52–54.

39. B.J. Tarsitano, E. Brophy, and D.J. Snyder, "A Demystification of the Clinical Nurse Specialist Role: Perceptions of Clinical Nurse Specialists and Nurse Administrator," *Journal of Nursing Education* 25, no. 1 (January 1986): 4–9.

40. Olga Church, "The Primary Nursing Care Project," *Nursing Administrative Quarterly* 1, no. 2 (Winter 1977): 16–20.

41. Marie Manthey, *The Practice of Primary Nursing* (Boston: Blackwell Scientific Publications Inc., 1980).

42. Giovannetti, "Evaluation of Primary Nursing," 127–151.

43. Lang and Clinton, "Assessment of Quality of Nursing Care," 135–155.

44. L. Weeks, M. Barrett, and C. Snead, "Primary Nursing: Teamwork Is the Answer," *Journal of Nursing Administration* 15, no. 9 (September 1985): 21–26.

45. Marilyn S. Notkin, "Collaboration and Communication," *Nursing Administrative Quarterly* 8, no. 1 (Fall 1983): 1–7.

46. Elizabeth A. Draper, "Effects of Nurse/Physician Collaboration and Nursing Standards on ICU Patients' Outcomes," *Current Concepts in Nursing* 1, no. 4 (1987): 2–9.

47. Paula M. Sigmon, "Clinical Ladders and Primary Nursing: the Wedding of the Two," *Nursing Administrative Quarterly* 5, no. 3 (Spring 1981): 63–67.

48. Betty Ann Taylor and Patricia Salome, "Mount Sinai's Four-Track Career Ladder Program," *Nursing Administrative Quarterly* 9, no. 1 (Fall 1984): 73–81.

49. Taggart Frost and Hoyt Wilson, "Effects of Locus of Control and A–B Personality Type on Job Satisfaction within the Health Care Field," *Psychological Reports* 53 (1983): 399–405.

50. William H. Fitts, *The Self Concept and Performance* (Nashville, Tenn.: Counselor Recordings and Tests, 1972).

51. Blaleck, "How Satisfied Are Hospital Staff Nurses?" 14–18.

52. Patricia Rosman and Ronald J. Burke, "Job Satisfaction, Self-Esteem, and the Fit between Perceived Self and Job on Valued Competencies," *Journal of Psychology* 105 (1980): 259–269.

53. S. Coopersmith, *The Antecedents of Self-Esteem* (San Francisco: W.H. Freeman & Co., 1967).

54. Marlene Dufault, "Changing the Locus of Control of Registered Nurse Students with a Futuristic-Oriented Course," *Journal of Nursing Education* 24, no. 8 (October 1985): 314–320.

55. Jeffrey A. Alexander, *Nursing Unit Organization: Its Effect on Staff Professionalism* (Ann Arbor, Mich.: UMI Research Press, 1982).

56. L. Pankratz and D. Pankratz, "Nursing Autonomy and Patient's Rights: Development of a Nursing Attitude Scale," *Journal of Health and Social Behavior* 15, no. 3 (September 1974): 211–216.

57. Luther Christman, "The Autonomous Nursing Staff in the Hospital," in "A Luther Christman Anthology," ed. Jerome P. Lysaught, *Nursing Digest* 6, no. 2 (Summer 1978): 71–74.

58. C. Alexander, C. Weisman, and G. Chase, "Determinants of Staff Nurses' Perceptions of Autonomy within Different Clinical Contexts," *Nursing Research* 31, no. 1 (January–February 1982): 48–52.

59. Robert Knoop, "Locus of Control As Moderator between Job Characteristics and Job Attitudes," *Psychological Reports* 48 (1981): 519–525.

60. Lang and Clinton, "Assessment of Quality of Nursing Care," 135–155.

61. Alexander, *Nursing Unit Organization.*

62. Notkin, "Collaboration and Communication," 1–7.

63. M. Kramer, L. Hafner, and B. Hoerle, "Relationship between External System of the Hospital and Staff Nurse Characteristics and Attitudes," *Research in Nursing and Health* (in press).

64. M. Kramer and L. Hafner, "Shared Values: Impact on Perceived Productivity and Job Satisfaction," *Nursing Research* (in press).

65. D. DelBueno and P. Vincent, "Organizational Culture: How Important Is It?" *Journal of Nursing Administration* 16, no. 10 (October 1986): 15–24.

66. T.J. Peters and R.N. Waterman, Jr., *In Search of Excellence* (New York: Harper & Row, 1982).

67. K.E. Weick, *The Social Psychology of Organizing,* 2nd ed. (Reading, Mass.: Addison-Wesley Publishing Co., Inc., 1969), 72.

68. All quoted material are comments by the staff nurses at magnet hospitals in interviews with the authors.

69. Ibid.

70. Ibid.

71. Peters and Waterman, *In Search of Excellence,* 278.

72. Comments by the staff nurses at magnet hospitals in interviews with the authors.

73. Peters and Waterman, *In Search of Excellence*.

74. P. Selznick, *Leadership in Administration: A Sociological Interpretation* (New York: Harper & Row, 1957): 28.

Chapter 3

Institutional Approaches to Preventing Nurse Burnout

Terry Stukalin

In the last decade numerous articles have been written about nurse burnout. Burnout occurs in work environments, as in hospitals, where responsibilities are fast-paced, emotionally demanding, and constantly changing. In our hospital settings there are multiple levels of activity, interdependence in the work world, downsizing of enterprises, acquisitions and mergers, census fluctuations, and a bottom-line focus. These are factors that I have found to be positively related to nurse burnout. Professional nurses enter a setting of this kind with personal needs and desires, looking for job satisfaction. When these needs and desires are unrecognized and/or unmet, job dissatisfaction increases. If no steps are taken to meet these needs and desires, disillusionment is often the result. For the employer, this job dissatisfaction, or burnout, manifests itself in lower productivity, higher absenteeism, increased work errors, poor judgment, defensive behavior, hostility, reduction in creativity, and job turnover. Turnover that grows out of job dissatisfaction and unrecognized and/or unmet needs seems unavoidable. Turnover is a natural consequence whenever burnout occurs; it is a waste of time, energy, and money to nurse and hospital alike.

When a professional nurse leaves the staff of a hospital, patient care is disrupted to some extent. Morale sags as the remaining staff makes another adjustment; responsibility for patient care shifts; and the process of recruitment, hiring, orientation, and training is set in motion once more. For the new nurse, changing jobs requires a period of orientation to a new work setting, where new ways of doing things and new working relationships with a new set of nursing colleagues have to be established.

Unfilled nursing positions result in the following: (1) fewer nurses than needed are available to carry the responsibility of delivering nursing care; (2) additional stress may lead to the resignations of those nurses who remain; (3) operating costs soar as management finds it necessary to utilize the services of nurse registries to provide a safe level of nursing care; and (4) hospital units with unoccupied beds that are not producing revenues are closed. These situations cause deterioration of morale among permanent personnel, and everyone becomes less productive. The economic impact on hospitals in replacing professional staff is staggering (see Exhibit 3-1). For each registered nurse (RN) who must be replaced the following steps are usually taken:

- Need advertising is initiated.
- Outside nursing registries are used to cover until a qualified replacement is found.
- Applicants are interviewed and individuals are selected.
- Relocation expenses of the selected candidate are paid.
- Physical examination of the selected candidate is performed.
- Orientation and training are given to the replacement.
- Overtime is required of other employees to take up the slack created by the turnover.

Exhibit 3-1 The Economic Impact of Turnover

Assumptions:	• Turnover of one 3–11 charge nurse for 44-bed medical-surgical service
	• No interval candidates
	• It will take 6 weeks to fill position

Process	Factor/Rate	Approximate cost
Advertising	5 insertions in local newspaper × $300/insertion	$1,500
Interviewing candidates	40 hr direct/indirect time × $15/hr	$600
Entertaining candidates	4 candidates × $25/hr	$100
Paper work generated	16 hr × $8/hr	$128
Use of supplemental staffing agency	240 hr × $24/hr	$5,760
Overtime required by other employees to take up slack	96 hr × $18/hr	$1,728
Relocation expense	(out of town only)	$2,000
Orientation and training of selected applicant	160 hr × $15/hr	$2,400
Total		$14,216

There are numerous approaches that institutions can take to prevent nurse burnout. As a nursing consultant I have made many of the recommendations to hospital managers that I identify here.

The nursing administrator and the nursing management team should perform external and internal assessments of the department of nursing annually. Surprisingly, the internal assessment is overlooked more frequently and is undertaken with greater resistance than is the external assessment. As hospital managers we seem to know more about who our competition is and what our community thinks about us than what our own employees think about us. The nursing administrator or her or his designee should review methodically these factors within the service. It is more manageable to spread the review throughout the year rather than conduct one intensive survey. A yearly calendar can pinpoint the targeted areas to review monthly.

INTERNAL ASSESSMENT

As the first step in internal assessment the following factors should be evaluated:

- nursing organization and the management team
- salary and benefit program
- utilization of supplemental staffing agencies
- employee morale
- nursing turnover statistics
- staffing and scheduling practices
- nursing policies
- absenteeism statistics
- physician-nurse collaboration
- physician climate
- staff orientation and education
- the interview process
- performance appraisal process
- promotion policies
- personnel policies
- recruitment-retention program
- physical plant and unit design
- support services provided to nursing
- state of the equipment
- patient care delivery systems
- work methods and work flow on each patient care unit

- patient acuity statistics
- assignment of staff methodology
- medication and IV administration practices
- medication errors
- the charting system
- nursing report
- patient care conferences
- rounds
- patient teaching program
- patient admitting practices
- discharge planning system
- utilization review program
- compliance with regulatory requirements
- adherence to standards of practice

In the second step in the internal assessment process, the nursing administrator or designee should interview personally and communicate with randomly selected staff members. This assessment should be performed at different hours, days, and shifts throughout the year. Ask the staff members in their department their perceptions of

- how patient care is being delivered
- leadership on each shift
- staffing and scheduling practices
- workload
- organizational changes
- staff morale
- new policies
- unit activity
- recommendations for improvement

The third stage in the assessment process by the nursing administrator is random observation of selected nursing staff members performing their assigned patient care responsibilities. Observe nursing reports, medication and IV administration, morning and evening care being delivered, meal delivery to the bedside, preparation of a patient prior to a test, preoperative and postoperative care, physician rounding, charting practices, and other patient care delivery practices.

As a diagnostician, the nursing administrator or designee will determine whether the department of nursing has created an environment that is conducive to nursing growth and development and not to nurse burnout. He or she can define problem areas before the nursing care practice, policy, or procedure becomes detrimental to the nursing department with the result of nursing turnover. A plan of action should be formulated and a time line written to enhance immediately the nursing working environment.

SYMPTOMS OF NURSE BURNOUT

To date in over 700 hospitals with which I have consulted, there are what I refer to as the symptoms of nurse burnout. These glaring deficiencies within the department of nursing make the symptoms easy to detect: inadequate nursing managers, overutilization of supplemental staffing services, unrealistic job expectations within the nurses' work world, lack of physician-nurse collaboration, and inconsistent hospitalwide policies. Although salary and benefit packages may be an issue at a hospital, nurse burnout does not occur because of it. Let us dissect some of the probable symptoms of nurse burnout.

The Nurse Manager

In the fast-paced work world the manager, whether at the unit level or the administrative level, yields power—the power to hire, fire, promote, demote, evaluate, set work schedules, set practice standards, change policy and procedures, set staffing guidelines, motivate, delegate, and develop the team. How competent are the managers to perform all of the above? Use a questionnaire to find out.

The first section of the questionnaire (Exhibit 3-2) is one that I have staff nurses fill out as questions 1–10. The second section begins with information that gives me insight into the RN's work history and feelings about quality of care and job satisfaction.

After the assessment has been performed, a preceptor should be assigned to the nurse manager. The preceptor, depending on the size and complexity of the hospital, can be the nursing administrator, assistant, nurse educator, personnel administrator, or peer who will function as a role model for the nurse manager. Identifying the manager's weakness, setting up a plan of action, and evaluating the results should be the responsibility of the nurse manager and her or his preceptor (Exhibit 3-3).

Custom-tailoring management development training for each nurse manager to his or her specific requirements is a sound approach. This process should encourage all nurse managers to become involved in the process. It is a more cost-effective approach than spending endless classroom hours on those managers whose needs are not met in a classroom or workshop setting. Encouraged that we are imparting our management expertise to others, we move to our next symptom.

Exhibit 3-2 Questionnaire Sample—Rate Your Head Nurse's Leadership Skills

Score from 1–5 (1, the lowest score)

She is/He is

    1....A seasoned professional who makes good judgment calls.
    2....Caring. Interested in staff growth and development.
    3....A role model for us.
    4....Supportive of our creative ideas.
    5....An effective communicator, both in verbal and written skills.
    6....Consistently fair.
    7....An astute financial manager.
    8....A proficient manager of our time.
    9....Able to build our confidence in ourselves, without overwhelming us.
  10....Consistently exhibiting a good attitude.

A. How long have you been a nurse? _____

B. How long have you worked on this unit? _____

C. Do you get job satisfaction from your present staff position? _____

D. Does the leadership on this unit contribute to your feeling of job satisfaction? _____

E. How would you score the quality of nursing care given on this unit? (from 1 to 10) _____

F. Does the leader on this unit strive to improve the quality of patient care? _____

G. Has she/he improved patient care? _____

H. Is the leader on this unit successful in reducing job related stress? _____

Source: Questions A through H are from *Up the Organization* by Robert Townsend. Copyright © 1970 by Robert Townsend. Reprinted by permission of Alfred A. Knopf, Inc.

Overutilization of Supplemental Staffing Agencies

It is very easy for hospital managers to rely on temporary nursing agencies. Were these issues identified when the internal audit was performed?

- lack of flexibility in the work schedule
- inconsistent salary program
- obsolete benefit package
- inadequate nursing leadership and supervision
- fragmented nursing care delivery systems
- conflict between the physician-nursing team
- deficiencies in the support services

Exhibit 3-3 Plan of Action

	Management Development		
	Manager	Jane Doe, R N	
	Preceptor	Ann Green, R N	
Action	*Who*	*Time Line*	*Accomplishment*
1. Perform needs assessment	Ann Green, RN RN staff on unit	May 14	
2. Hold conference with Jane Doe and Ms. Brown, Assoc. Dir., to discuss results of needs assessment	Jane Doe	May 21	
3. Set up weekly management training activities	Jane Doe	June 5	
4. Leadership/delegation motivation session	G. Grey	June 12	
5. Teamwork-team development	Ann Brown	June 19	
6. Time management/planning	G. Grey	June 26	
7. Communication Flexibility Evaluating staff performance	Dir. of Personnel	July 10	
8. Feedback session	*All preceptors*	July 31	

All of these issues can increase the utilization of supplemental staffing within a facility by causing nurse turnover. What can be done to decrease the utilization? Staff nurses often ask me why the hospital cannot take the money they are paying for agency nurses and share it with all of the hospital employees. They relate endless anecdotes about how those temporary nurses cannot provide the continuity of care that permanent staff members can provide; temporary nurses come into a hospital and are unfamiliar with the patients, physicians, and procedures. Many times this represents an additional workload for the permanent staff RN who must stop what he or she is doing to train the temporary; and of course the temporary tells the staff RN about how much money he or she makes, which is often close to double per hour what the permanent nurse can expect. And last, many of the temporaries are marginal nurses who "hide out" with the registries, moving from registry to registry. Let's be realistic. Supplemental agencies can be heaven-sent when we need vacation relief and maternity replacement and when the census jumps, but to utilize five to 10 shifts per day is excessive. There are some solutions.

For: Lack of flexibility in the work schedule
      Try the: It's your choice program
Choice #1   7–3 permanent shift, every other weekend off
Choice #2   3–11 Monday through Friday; weekends off with full benefits
Choice #3   work Saturday and Sunday only double shifts and receive
             40 hours' pay for 32 hours' work with full benefits
Choice #4   float pool, flexible schedule and shifts
Choice #5   6-hour shifts (6 A.M.–12 noon)
                          (6 P.M.–12 midnight)
Choice #6   10-hour day, 4-day work week
Choice #7   7/70 work week
Choice #8   9-hour shifts
Choice #9   12-hour shifts
Choice #10   Baylor plan

Ten-Hour Day, Four-Day Work Week

This type of scheduling is presently the schedule of choice for future consideration for a variety of work environments. For nursing, this approach is dependent upon an established cyclic schedule with defined days off.

There are a number of ways in which this approach can be utilized. If rotating shifts are used, numbers can be assigned to shifts and a fixed or assigned rotation can be designated for a position.

S	M	T	W	T	F	S
X	X	1	1	X	1	1
1	1	X	X	1	1	X
X	X	1	1	X	2	2
2	2	X	2	2	X	X
X	X	3	3	3	X	3
3	3	X	X	3	3	X

Code: 1 = 7:00 A.M. to 5:30 P.M.
       2 = 1:00 P.M. to 11:30 P.M.
       3 = 9:00 P.M. to 7:30 A.M.   X = DAYS OFF

If shift assignment is constant, a block schedule or continuous cycle can be established that repeats itself over time, with no individual nurse working a consecutive period of time that amounts to more than four days. Positions not covered during assigned days off are filled by part-time cycles that are alternates to the full-time positions.

Ten-Hour Day, Seven-Day Work Week

One of the more imaginative and creative approaches to nurse scheduling is the 7/70 work week. This approach utilizes a 10-hour work day seven days a week followed by seven days off consecutively. Following are some primary considerations of this scheduling approach:

- Every nurse works seven days, 10 hours daily, and is paid for 80 hours.
- Seven days of work are followed by seven days off work.
- There is no shift differential.
- Holidays are not paid since that time is covered in the 80 hours of pay per week.
- Vacation pay is also covered by paying 80 hours for 70 hours worked.
- Each nurse can be allowed a predetermined number of hours of sick leave every year.
- Shift times can be scheduled variably to meet the needs of both patients and staff.

The 7/70 approach has the following advantages:

- improved continuity of care
- better understanding of patient needs based on longer follow-through
- increased satisfaction of staff based on knowing the schedule a year in advance and prolonged rest each biweekly cycle
- decreased intershift communication problems because of overlap in shifts
- improved interdisciplinary communication as a result of continuity of care by nurse providers and planned service
- more consistent patient teaching
- more flexibility in planning daily nursing activities to meet patient needs rather than hospital regimens
- equalization of staffing between shifts and on weekends and holidays
- reduced administrative time in planning for staffing.

A variety of staffing approaches can be used according to individual situations. The staffing plan shown in Exhibit 3-4 is one that is utilized at a few hospitals and is presently meeting their variable census requirements and personnel desires. Again, it is important that any scheduling approach remain flexible and adaptable for individual institutions.

Exhibit 3-4 Sample Staffing Plan

	M–F occupancy 35
	S–S occupancy 25

2 RNs
1 LPN
1 NA*   **Day Shift 7/70**
1 UC

1 RN
1 LPN   **Evening Shift 7/70**   *Based on Census of 25*
1 NA

1 RN
1 NA   **Night Shift 7/70**
1 NA†

AND

1 PCC—Monday through Friday   40 hours/week
1 RN   **Day Shift**   40 hours/week
1 NA

1 NA   **Night Shift**   40 hours/week

Assume 35 patients:

Personnel on duty:	6:45– 7:45 A.M.	6	10
	7:45– 9:00 A.M.	4	8
	9:00–12:45 P.M.	5	9
	12:45– 5:15 P.M.	8	13
	5:15– 7:30 P.M.	4	5
	7:30– 9:15 P.M.	3	4
	9:15–11:15 P.M.	5	7

Core staff (including PCC):	9 RNs	43%
	4 LPNs	19%
	6 NAs	29%
	2 UCs	9%
	21 FTEs	

Maximum staff (including PCC):	10 RNs	38% (8 are 7/70; 2 are 8/80)
	4 LPNs	(all are 7/70)
	10 NAs	38% (8 are 7/70; 2 are 8/80)
	2 UCs	(both are 7/70)
	26 FTEs	

*Definitions: NA, nursing assistant; UC, unit coordinator; PCC, patient care coordinator; S–S, Saturday and Sunday; FTE, full-time employee.
†Two-month trial basis.

Staffing for the Night Shift

What makes the night shift undesirable, even with competitive shift differential? Some of the reasons are lack of sleep; insufficient numbers of experienced staff members for new nurses to learn from, creating low morale and difficulty in convincing new graduates to work that shift; constant pressure from spouse and family to get off nights; inability to obtain registry nurses for night shift duty; decreasing morale of long-time, dependable night nurses who watch this problem develop over time.

In order to deal effectively with this issue, another creative staffing program can be implemented—the nine-hour shift. Many hospitals have found that many night nurses already are utilizing the ninth hour to complete their work, resulting in overtime payment. This four-day work schedule also gives the night staff the benefit of additional days off for family and school activities. It also permits longer weekend time off.

Nine-Hour Program for Nights

Assumptions: It would be determined that the four-shift 11:00 P.M. to 8:00 A.M. work week would represent a 25 percent increase in salary dollars and required full-time employees, but the increased cost would be more than offset by the following factors:

First, it would be shown that incidental end-of-shift overtime for night nurses, when annualized, would reflect a dollar figure equal to half the amount of the above-mentioned 25 percent increase. The other half of the cost to convert to the four-shift work week would be offset by implementation of the proposed nine-hour program and the savings that would result from diminishing the registry fees.

Comparison: Traditional two-week pay period of eight-hour shifts, five shifts per week.

Example:

- hourly wage $13.00
- 8 hours per day × $13.00 per hour = $104
- 5 nights per week = 10 shifts per pay period
- $104 per shift × 10 shifts = $1,040

New Plan: Nine-Hour Shifts, Four Shifts per Week

Example: Same hourly wage of $13 (11:00 P.M. to 8:00 A.M.)
  1. First 8 hours (11:00 P.M.–7:00 A.M.)
     at straight time $104
  2. Ninth hour (7:00 A.M.–8:00 A.M.) paid time
     and a half $19.50

3. Half-hour bonus paid for each 9-hour shift $6.50

Earn $832 per eight shifts
Earn $156 time and a half for eight shifts
Earn $52 bonus for eight shifts

Gross dollar amount $1,040

Inconsistent Salary Programs

We must restructure nursing salaries to correct internal inequities. Adjustments should be made to compensate for different educational levels (i.e., AD diploma, BSN, or MSN). Credentials such as CCRN and RNC should be given value. Validation in skills specific to a specialty should be included. And most of all, our experienced nurses must be compensated to widen the gap between them and the new graduates. This will become the basis for a career incentive salary program.

Bonus Incentives

Another incentive to retain experienced staff is to utilize an incentive dollar bonus program. This program is in the early stages of development and is used primarily in the proprietary setting. This program rewards the managers and staff members who have met predetermined, measurable patient care and operational goals. This program can be structured.

Career Incentives

It is not uncommon to the nursing professional to remunerate an RN with 10 years of experience only $1,000 to $2,000 more annually than a new graduate. As motivation, compensation is close to the top for most RNs. But it is understood in our industry that only nurses who move into management are rewarded. We must develop a salary scale that can compensate not only for different educational levels, but for clinical skills. We must build into our salary programs long-range career incentives.

Nursing Care Delivery Systems

Nursing care delivery systems that are disorganized and fragmented are great dissatisfiers in nursing. RNs want to deliver comprehensive, coordinated, and individualized nursing care. In evaluating all of the systems that nursing uses to deliver care—functional, primary, team case management, patient-centered, and all of the variations of each model—we must decide whether each methodology meets the needs of the RNs as well as the patients in our facilities. Are we flexible? Do we utilize different models and utilize our staff more efficiently daily, or do we utilize our nursing resources haphazardly? Did our internal audit validate the following?

- Utilization of registry and per diem staff fragments the daily patient care assignments and consistency overall.
- The role definition between RN and LPN needs to be defined.
- Aides are underutilized.
- There is overall lack of continuity of assignment day to day, shift to shift.
- Staffing ratios of nurse to patient are unrealistic. They are based on numbers and fairness, not on the acuity of the patient care and the qualifications of licensed and unlicensed staff.
- Patient documentation is cumbersome and a lengthy process. The existing documentation process encourages licensed nurse overtime shift to shift.
- Patient call lights go unanswered.
- Nursing care plans do not reflect the patients' current courses of progress.
- Rounding with physicians is not an expectation.
- Report is lengthy and time-consuming.
- RNs cannot find the time to attend staff development programs inhouse— "too busy."
- Staff members never get off shift on time. Absenteeism is high and staff members are tardy.

This is not a scenario of the worst case—I find these problems identified by RNs in their work world. Many nurses will not deal with the frustrations of working within a patient care delivery system that will not meet the patients' needs effectively. They leave to join registries, pools, and other hospital settings, hoping that the organization they are joining cares about patient care.

Any care delivery system must be founded on the premise that the patient, not the task, is the major focus of nursing care. Multiple-assignment methods can be utilized weekly within the same department. This flexibility in assignments can be adapted in a number of ways to utilize available nursing personnel. Thus, the staffing methodology is specific to each hospital and each unit.

The staffing formats shown in Figure 3-1 show the relationship and responsibility of the various levels of nursing personnel in reference to acuity and census.

SUMMARY

There are no immediate knee-jerk solutions to the issue of nurse burnout and turnover. Developing a comprehensive, practical, cost-effective recruitment and retention program would be a good start. A task force should be charged with the responsibilities of identifying problems; investigating cost-effective avenues;

Figure 3-1 Staffing Methods in Patient-Centered Care

* 7 — 3 Shift
Medical Unit — 30 Pts

Example I

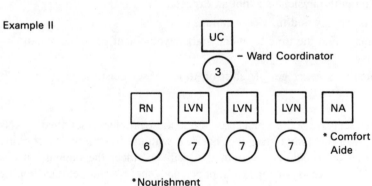

Unit Coordinator — Secretary

RN	LVN	LVN	LVN	NA
4	6	7	7	6

- Direct Care
- Unit Coordinator is responsible for the aides, patients, medications, special treatments

Example II

UC

— Ward Coordinator

3

RN	LVN	LVN	LVN	NA
6	7	7	7	

* Comfort Aide

*Nourishment
*Assists professional under direction of Unit Coordinator

Example III

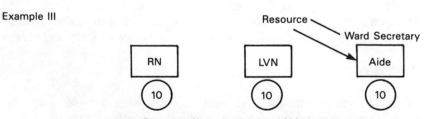

Resource
Ward Secretary

RN	LVN	Aide
10	10	10

- Resource Nurse supervises Aide.
- Performs complicated treatments and medications.

Figure 3-1 continued

Example IV

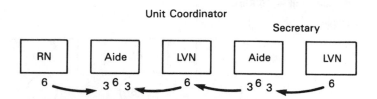

- Professional supervision of the Aides
- Professionals pass medications and complicated treatments for Aides
- Aide performs direct care for his or her module of patients

Example V

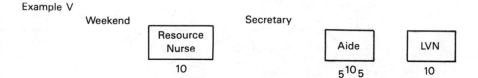

Example VI

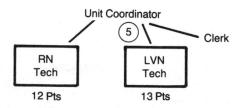

- Professional supervision of all staff
- Direct care model—mini-team concept

Figure 3-1 continued

* 3 — 11 Shift
Medical Unit — 30 Pts

Example I

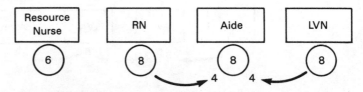

- Professional supervision of the Aides, patients
- Direct care by the Aide
- Medications and treatments for Aide's patients performed by professionals
- Resource Nurse performs direct care and functions as an advisor in the absence of the Unit Coordinator

Example II

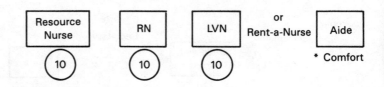

Example III

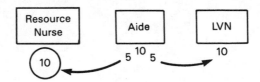

Example IV

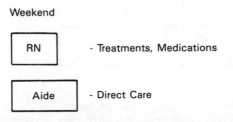

Figure 3-1 continued

Example V

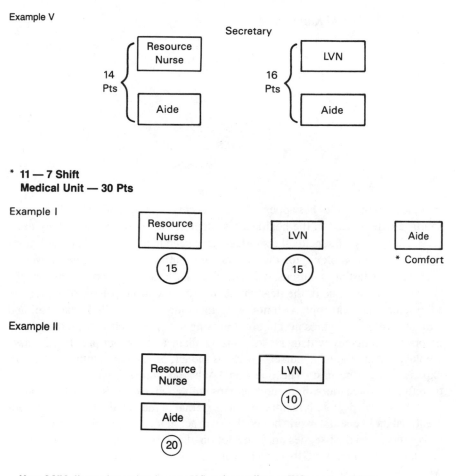

* **11 — 7 Shift**
  Medical Unit — 30 Pts

Example I

Example II

Note: LVN, licensed vocational nurse; UC, unit coordinator; WC, ward coordinator.

increasing the ability to recruit new nurses; and reinforcing the internal work climate, allowing the institution the opportunity to retain the nurses it has attracted. Then, with a strategic plan at hand, facilities can stop the drain of their natural resources—the nurses.

Chapter 4

Why Nurses Leave Nursing

Doris M. Modly and Kathleen Weiss

A plethora of articles has appeared in the recent literature discussing the nursing shortage experienced in the healthcare system in the United States. Many quite plausible factors influencing the shortage have been identified and some solutions proposed. The complexity of the factors contributing to the shortage, however, suggests that lasting solutions will not be found easily. Experts warn that the shortage will continue in the near future and that the usual pattern of a shortage followed by an oversupply will not occur this time.[1] If that will be the case, and current enrollment figures in schools of nursing indicate that it will be, the burden of practicing nurses will increase, causing them to burn out and leave active employment as practicing nurses—perhaps sooner, or in larger numbers, than was experienced in the past. The question "Why do nurses leave nursing?" will therefore be asked more often, and perhaps with good reason. Responses abound; most, however, deal with factors that are external to the nurse: the work environment, salary, benefits, work hours, lack of autonomy of practice, and lack of recognition, and the list goes on.[2] The notion of a fit between the practicing nurse and the requirements of the practice is not as often discussed as perhaps is warranted.

Data about the personality characteristics of nursing students provide insight into the nature of the fit of novice nurses in their work environment. Exploratory studies by Hafer and Ambrose of nursing students' psychographic characteristics indicate that these comprise complex combinations of personality traits that broaden the potential of the profession. However, these combinations also result in variances in professional commitment and motivational differences among nurses.[3] The heterogeneity of personalities attracted to nursing as a career warrants a closer look at the process of professional development of persons who choose to practice nursing. Nurturance of personality traits effective for the advancement of the professionals' career goals enhances the fit between the work environment and the practitioner. Marketing nursing as a career rich in opportunity and variety will attract different types of persons to nursing in the future.

50

Aggressively seeking the "best and brightest" students for nursing is a must if the nursing profession is to attain its potential.

It is proposed in this chapter that nurses do not cease to "be" nurses, that they do not "leave nursing," but that they cease to fit well into the work environment and therefore are unable to attain their full potential as practitioners of nursing and as human beings. Nurses who are not satisfied with themselves in their work environment are not as productive as they could be. This heightens the critical shortage of numbers to a shortage in "production."

Before exploring the question further, however, it might be useful to review the literature on nurse turnover. This review reveals that more nurses in the U.S. practice nursing than ever before in history. Approximately 75 to 80 percent of those educated as nurses are actively employed. Nursing is the most practiced profession among women. Nurses might leave one institution only to reapply and take another, similar position in another institution. If nurses leave their employment, their absence is most often by personal choice, and it is temporary in nature. According to the experts, 35 percent of nurses who leave active employment never really depart: they return to practice within two years.[4] The above data support the thesis of this chapter that once a person "becomes" a nurse in that personal encounter with the patient, in addition to having acquired the knowledge and skills necessary to practice nursing, that person will always "be" a nurse, even when not engaged in direct patient care.

Rather than examine the external factors contributing to the problem, in this chapter we propose to examine the "becoming" of a nurse and the ways that this becoming can be enhanced to assure that the nurse over time develops into an active, productive, mature practitioner who is able to nurture the next generation of nurses. The problem is examined from both nursing and developmental perspectives that consider the individual nurse as a developing human being. The assumption is made that once a person becomes a nurse that person cannot in fact "leave nursing," but only unsuccessfully master the next phase. The question, therefore, "Why do nurses leave nursing?" becomes a moot one. It is better to ask, What can be done so that nurses attain their full potential as nurses? What are the strengths and assets on each developmental phase of a nursing career trajectory that need to be fostered? Data to support the points made in this chapter are anecdotal notes collected by the authors during their tenures as caregivers and counselors to practicing nurses. In these roles, both authors have observed nursing careers unfold and novices become experts and then mentors in nursing. Others, challenged by their nursing careers, explored new avenues of practicing nursing as managers, lawyers, psychologists, etc. Some who could not master the challenges of their career trajectories became stuck (fixated) at different levels of development and thus were unable to develop fully at the next phase. There were nurses who appeared to have left nursing. They might have been actively employed as nurses but were not fully productive. As caregivers to nurses, the authors have learned to view each nurse as an individual who is striving in his or her own way to "become" (a nurse). It was observed that nurses often changed direction in that process but rarely ceased to be nurses. They did not regress on the trajectory but moved forward slowly or stagnated.

A parallel with Eric Erikson's conceptualization of personality development is used therefore as the framework for organizing the observations made.[5] The close similarities of the human developmental conflicts and those experienced by individuals moving along a nursing career trajectory are examined. Erikson's epigenetic principle is used to draw conclusions about consequences and to suggest interventions that support the development of the person as a nurse and consequently also as a human being.

PHASE I: CONFIDENCE (TRUST/MISTRUST)

Development of trust in one's practice is fundamental to optimal growth as a professional nurse. Similar to the earliest stages of human development, novice nurses learn to trust their own evolving abilities as practitioners of nursing during the first phase of their nursing careers. Every time a new situation is encountered, the opportunity for the development of this trust is tested. As new procedures are mastered and difficult situations resolved, novice nurses build a cognitive as well as an emotional foundation leading to confidence and satisfaction in their practice of nursing, nurturant of hope in their abilities as practitioners.

The development of trust in one's own practice is a process that reoccurs to varying degrees and with a variety of outcomes throughout one's career, although the earliest challenges, the first-time jobs, and the adaptations to new roles are probably the most critical. Indeed, the development of trust in one's practice is not necessarily related to age. Rather, internal and external factors are major variables influencing the early formation of trust. If the educational experience has been positive, effective problem-solving skills of the novice are well-developed and the scientific method is routinely applied to issues of practice; nurses then will develop confidence in their practice. Thus, the novice nurse can experience and demonstrate a positive sense of self-worth. This sense of self-worth determines the nature of interactions with patients, nurses, and other health care providers. The novice's confidence, consistency, interdependence, and continuity will be the basis for all working relationships of the practitioner—first with instructors, later with preceptors and supervisors. Recognition of individual worth, unique contributions, talents, and skills affirm the novice's sense of confidence in his or her own practice of nursing and in nursing as a practice profession.

If these early activities are not successful and novices continually redefine themselves, or are defined by others as failures in their activities, then a sense of mistrust in themselves as nurses will be inevitable. Furthermore, if novice nurses are not provided the opportunity for positive experiences to counteract their sense of incompetence or failure, feelings of estrangement from the profession and a sense of separation and abandonment are likely to occur. Managers conscious of retention, therefore, foster skill development and competence in practice by all manners of supervision, particularly through the helping relationship skills suggested by Vogt and Velthouse.[6]

If the new graduate has not been nurtured sufficiently, either cognitively or emotionally, self-doubt begins a downward spiral toward alienation and separation from the profession. In fact, any time throughout a professional career, lack of trust and confidence in oneself and in one's practice can occur. The qualities associated with this occurrence are inconsistencies: extreme doubts can lead to the overvaluation of other health professionals and an inability to recognize one's contributions as essential in the care of patients. Many nurses move through their careers with a basic lack of confidence that continues to hinder them in other phases of their career development. Unfortunately, the personality characteristics of many nurses predispose them to this lack of self-confidence.[7] Just as some persons never gain a firm sense of their own trustworthiness or trust in others, some nurses never go beyond their ambivalence about nursing as a career. This results in an inability to foster hope in others. Nursing tasks may get completed, but the patient is without the comfort of a nurse who has hope and is able to foster hope in patients that many things are possible, that suffering can be limited, that illness can be modified, and that the human spirit can overcome many handicaps.

Unfortunately, many nurses who do not trust their ability to practice nursing are employed as nurses. Dissatisfaction with their own practice prevents their progress through the developmental opportunities available to them. Not only are they not able to develop themselves but, through their lack of confidence, they often hinder others in their progress.

Nursing is rich in history, traditions, and rituals that clamor for recognition. Socialization into the profession needs to be such that all nurses become aware of the contributions made by nurses before them. Values that once attracted people into the nursing profession need to be reaffirmed and supported by today's practitioners. Opportunities should be created to advance clinical skills while supporting the level of practice already attained. The notion of precepting need not be limited to practical skills but can be expanded into areas of values clarification and personal growth as well.

As novice nurses assume their first positions, nurse educators and administrators must recognize the skills, talents, and potentials of each new nurse. Repetition, familiarity, and acceptance foster inner certainty and trust of novices in their practices. Moreover, supervisors need to praise the daily accomplishments that so often are taken for granted. The delicate balance between praise and challenge is essential for the development of confidence in one's own practice.

PHASE II: AUTONOMY OF PRACTICE/AUTONOMY/DOUBT AND SHAME

Without basic trust and confidence in the value of nursing and the nurses' contributions to patients, the novice cannot begin to develop an autonomy of

practice. Most studies that explored work satisfaction of nurses found that a perceived lack of autonomy of practice is one of the most significant factors that
contribute to the level of dissatisfaction of nurses with their work environment.
Autonomy of practice, however, is based on a sense of confidence in the profession and in one's practice skills. As these are nurtured, an optimal balance is
achieved between the need to practice nursing independently of other healthcare
providers and in interdependence with them.

There is a dual demand—one for self-control and a second for acceptance of
control from others in the environment. Reassurance from those in control assists
the development of autonomy. Freedom of self-expression, freedom to choose,
and freedom to be creative in the provision of nursing care are the qualities most
present when autonomy is experienced. Communication with others reflects the
interdependence necessary for sophisticated practice. As the novice nurse seeks
out new experiences and values the challenge of complicated procedures or
difficult interpersonal interactions, control over the environment lends itself to
mastery over self-doubt and insecurity. An autonomous nurse accepts with pride
his or her own abilities and exudes a feeling of good will and confidence in
dealings with others. A growing awareness of self as an autonomous practitioner
contributes to the differentiation of the quality of care given by others. Judgments
about quality, about appropriateness of care, and about moral and ethical dilemmas of practice are formed.

A danger at this stage of development is to exclude all nurses who do not
practice the same kind of nursing as one's own peer group. When other nurses are
viewed as "sub-nurses" or other disciplines as "sub-caregivers," then a preju-
dicial system results that diminishes the value of care and instills a sense of doubt
into the caregiver.

Nursing practices dominated by a strong sense of doubt require a multitude of
policies and procedure manuals. Nursing hierarchies become top-heavy. There are
few occasions for creative problem solving since practice is dictated by the book or
by the supervisor. Little recognition is given for individual accomplishments.
Consequently, praise, peer review, and positive feedback are kept to a minimum
while mistakes, omissions, and variances from the established norm are highly
disparaged. There is little room for professional growth, since the expectation is
that the nurse must already know the entire range of nursing practice. Not knowing
a particular procedure, protocol, or practice is equal to not being a "real" nurse.
Shame in what the nurse is not, or in what the nurse has not done, is emphasized,
rather than recognition given for what the nurse contributed or what the nurse has
accomplished.

Environments that support autonomy should allow freedom to practice professional nursing in a variety of ways. Whenever possible, decision making should be
left to those responsible for the consequences of the decision. Self-scheduling,
flextime, choice of assignments, peer selection, peer review, peer termination,
salary allocation, and retention strategies represent a few opportunities for such

decision making to occur. An autonomous nursing practice can occur in any setting, at any age. Those in control need to model openness, self-control, responsibility, and the valuation and adherence to professional nursing care. Standards of nursing practice that are attainable and reflective of quality care need to be supported and maintained. A statement of the philosophy of nursing held by an organization, congruent with the philosophy of practice adhered to by nurses, serves as a foundation for practice and fosters the elements of pride, confidence, and freedom necessary for an autonomous practice. The autonomy thus developed results in the willpower to strive forward and to bring about changes. The lack of autonomy results in automatic performance of tasks and leads to the loss of joy in nursing.

PHASE III: MASTERY AND SPECIALIZATION (INITIATIVE/GUILT AND INDUSTRY/INFERIORITY)

The next developmental phase, comparable to Erikson's stages of initiative/guilt and industry/inferiority, leads to the nurse's expanding mastery and specialization. The nurse demonstrates competencies decisively more advanced on all levels of practice. Assessments include advanced biopsychosocial data that are well-organized, based on sound theoretical principles, and relevant to the creation of a plan of care. Interventions mutually negotiated with the patient are sophisticated and reflect compassion for the patient. Evaluations of patient outcomes dictate the care given and form the bases for ongoing assessments and modifications in the plan of care. With this process fully employed in practice, the nurse is able to pursue sophisticated patient care goals. A sense of purpose and eagerness provides the energy for the nurse's professional growth. Having mastered the tasks of this developmental phase, the nurse is now free to explore a variety of settings in which to practice. The danger at this stage is that the individual's idealized vision of nursing may never be realized. Limited career opportunities may not satisfy, and the overzealous career expectations may lead to overbearing obligations and disappointments. Finally, a sense of guilt and/or inferiority for not achieving expectations eradicate all initiatives.

To enhance this stage, nursing initiatives need to be encouraged by employers. Efforts to provide competent, creative nursing care must receive financial and moral support from nursing managers. The structure of the nursing organization needs to be such that the bedside practitioner is given every resource to provide creative, complete care to the patient. Opportunities to develop, to change, to persevere, and to succeed need to exist in every practice setting.

Managers also need to be creative in providing the opportunities nurses may require to be innovative in their practice. To promote initiative, periods for "rest and relaxation" should be strategized and encouraged by nursing managers. Working retreats, off-service rotations, and teaching and learning opportunities provide a change in environment conducive to creativity. Imagination and spontaneity can be financially rewarding when patient outcomes are affected.

Nurses in general must learn to enjoy the variety of practices they can carry out, not rigidly fixate on the empty rituals and meaningless formalities of the traditional nursing practices. The challenge of this phase is to retain an excitement and enthusiasm for nursing, regardless of specialty or practice setting.

PHASE IV: PROFESSIONAL IDENTITY (IDENTITY/ROLE CONFUSION)

A sense of uniqueness and discovery of one's special fit in the profession results in identification with nursing during the fourth developmental phase. At this point the nurse has the capacity to develop and integrate his or her own skills and talents into a fitting practice arena. The nurse is then able to identify himself or herself with nursing, which has become a positive stabilizing force in life. Socialization into a community of nurses leads to acceptance by like-minded people and adaptation to the environment, whatever work is selected. Roles are readily negotiated with confidence, since competence has already been achieved. In spite of external pressures or inevitable contradictions in practice and among practitioners, the value of fidelity develops toward one's own career choice. A clarity of mission and a definition of professional practice are attained during this phase. If nurses are not able to define themselves clearly in terms of being a nurse, identity confusion results. A manifestation of this is a negative identity, which is then projected onto other nurses. Devaluing, discrediting, and doubting one's role in the profession and in society at large are characteristic of this stage.

If nurses as a professional group support experimentation with new roles and nurse practitioners pursue and support the outcomes of such experimentation— even if it means that the current position is left for another—they will be most likely to change nursing's role in society to meet the nursing needs of the nation in the twenty-first century.

PHASE V: INVOLVEMENT (INTIMACY/ISOLATION)

Similar to the sixth stage of human psychological development, during this phase nurses have the potential to develop professional partnerships and affiliations as they become personally concerned for their patients. Commitments to working more closely with other care providers become more easily possible.

In the work setting, all relationships are affected by professional partnerships. A comfort level with self and others develops, leading to mutuality and reciprocity in interpersonal interactions. Personal strengths and talents are utilized for the benefit of the patient.

At the same time, wants and needs are routinely expressed and satisfied. The nurse-patient relationship is more productive in attaining mutually established goals. Patients are able to discuss sensitive issues and personal feelings with their nurse without the fear of rejection or abandonment. In an environment that permits this stage of development to exist, nurses are free to focus more on their relationships with patients rather than on the completion of assigned tasks. With peers, a real sense of collegiality exists. Other nurses' strengths and talents are utilized through consultative and educational processes. Admission and discussion of feelings among peers are expected. A sense of belonging ensues. Identification with nursing as a special community of caregivers unfolds.

Relationships with other health care providers are less competitive, more collaborative. Multidisciplinary discussions can occur to define and explore patient care needs so that the common goals of providing quality patient care can be achieved most effectively and efficiently. Vulnerabilities pose opportunities for interdisciplinary interdependence, since no profession practices in isolation. Valuing, choosing, and committing to the professional nursing practice are the outcomes of this stage. If the nurse is unable to accomplish the tasks of this stage, the practice becomes isolated and sterile.

Knowing that all caregivers are in the common employ of patients increases nurses' sense of connection with their colleagues. The possibility exists to know other caregivers well enough to share common successes and failures. Employers can create the environment that enhances this phase of development by providing opportunities to build collegial relationships and by encouraging interdisciplinary interdependence. Shared mission statements, team-building efforts, shared values clarification, and combined decision making enhance an atmosphere of mutuality and openness. Team building can include negotiating roles and sharing values and visions on a personal level.

Efforts to maintain quality communications among all personnel at every level of the hierarchy are essential. Communications must be clear, honest, direct, and timely. Both senders and receivers must be open to communications flowing in either direction.

In addition to fostering autonomy of practice, the case management delivery system also facilitates intimacy in patient care as well as true collaboration with patients and other caregivers. Patients can view the nurses as their advocates who support their highest level of functioning at a time when they also provide most of their complex care needs. Productivity increases as energies are focused on common goals at communal and/or team activities. An esprit de corps develops during this stage that transcends the provincial view of "we" and "they." There is a realization that the total contributions of all patient caregivers is far greater than what any one professional could ever accomplish singularly. An appreciation and a valuation of other disciplines are reciprocated by the acknowledgment that nursing's contributions are neither more nor less than another profession's—only different.

PHASE VI: PROFESSIONAL MATURITY
(GENERATIVITY/STAGNATION)

This phase of professional maturity is characterized by a concern for establishing and guiding the next generation of nurses. Nurse experts, during this phase of their development, concern themselves with the "larger picture" by making contributions through involvement in professional organizations. The relevance of the nurses' work and its value is questioned and affirmed. Self-preoccupation with one's own career becomes less important than guiding and helping younger members of the profession.[8] Mentoring of others is a natural process during this phase. It creates an opportunity for balance in the career cycle by providing novices with a sense of constancy, direction, and recognition by seasoned, compassionate practitioners. At the same time it provides the mature nurse with the opportunity to teach, role model, and guide the novice.

Unfortunately for the profession, most of the teaching and guiding of new nurses is done by those whose main concern is still their own career development: there are not enough mature nurses to mentor novices of the profession. The ability to care for others, the outcome of this phase of professional development, is provided by too few. This is perhaps one reason why the first phase of development too often ends in lack of trust and confidence. It is the role of the few mature leaders to model the mentoring role to those who might not be quite ready developmentally.

In clinical settings it is a serious problem when the system cannot nurture new graduates adequately to provide needed support and reassurance for the novice nurse. The saying "nurses eat their young" is harsh but not far from the truth, perhaps because of conditions beyond nurses' control. As a profession nursing attracts many persons, yet little attention is paid to the retention of those who are in the first phases of their professional development. Consequently there are too few mature nurses to guide and teach the novice to practice in a reflective manner,[9] rather than depend on procedure book prescriptions for practice. The notion of supervising for retention rather than for evaluation is novel to many a preceptor and supervisor; however, it is the only way to enhance professional development. If nurses never mature or if they succumb to stagnation and accept only those practices that were accepted in the past, then the future of nursing will be uncertain. Characteristics associated with unsuccessful mastery of earlier developmental tasks such as insecurity, devaluation of peers, and destruction competition jeopardize the future of nursing. Even to continue to teach and to practice nursing as it is known today will make nursing obsolete in the twenty-first century. In today's changing world and healthcare economy, mature nurses must guide the future of the profession with confidence, creativity, and leadership.

PHASE VII: PROFESSIONAL WISDOM (INTEGRITY/DESPAIR)

Erikson characterized the last stage of human development as the "acceptance of one's one and only life cycle as something that had to be and that by necessity permitted of no substitution."[10]

It is difficult to examine the last phase of professional development without drawing a parallel with the last stage of human development: during that phase, human development and professional development fuse. Wisdom, the basic virtue of this phase, is expressed by those who can accept who they are within the profession without apologies and without regrets. Nursing leaders such as Virginia Henderson, Hildegard Peplau, Martha Rogers, Rozella Schlotfeldt, and others influence the evolving practice of nursing as strongly as the experienced practitioner who quietly and persistently cares for patients. Similarly, administrators who balance the budget and the grief of the nursing staff with patient care outcomes, and educators who risk rejection because of a novel thought or method of teaching and assume responsibility for allowing their students to experiment with innovative ways of caring for the sick provide the much-needed wisdom for further development of the profession.

Current nursing leaders may be able to preserve some of the traditions, tasks, and values of nursing's past, but nursing is at a crossroad. The potential of nursing may not yet be fully realized. How the nurses of the twenty-first century will practice is still to be determined, in part by today's experts and in part by the vision and creativity of today's novices. How nursing will fit into the shrinking health care economy must be determined by nursing leaders who have professional maturity and wisdom and who wish to bequeath a wealth of practice opportunities to future generations.

CONCLUSION

In order to ensure a future for the profession, today's practitioners of nursing must support and enhance the maturational process of their own practitioners. Nurses in the early phases of their career trajectories deserve the professional and environmental supports necessary to complete successfully the developmental tasks of each phase. If nurses choose to expand their practice or increase their knowledge base in another discipline, they do not necessarily leave nursing, and the profession has not lost a member. Lawyers or politicians with a nursing background view their clients differently from those who do not have a nursing background. Similarly, hospital administrators, health policy planners, or architects who once practiced nursing have a sensitivity for human needs characteristic of professionals called nurses. Thus, there is no need to say that they "left nursing," only that they chose to practice differently.

It is proposed, therefore, that once a person has entered the developmental phases of professional nursing growth, that person's very being is altered. The employment, the task, or the pay is not as significant as the reality that the person is a nurse who practices nursing as a staff nurse, as a mother, as a neighbor, as a health educator, as a lawyer, as a politician, or as a nurse expert. The potential to practice nursing is limited only by each nurse's vision and the profession's tolerance of the varied career paths nursing practitioners follow.

NOTES

1. L.H. Aiken and C.F. Mullinix, "The Nursing Shortage," *New England Journal of Medicine* 317, no. 10 (1987): 641–645.

2. B.J. Kalish, "The Nursing Shortage: Causes, Costs and Cures, in *The Nursing Shortage: You Can't Afford to Lose This Nurse*, American Hospital Association, April 21, 1988.

3. J.C. Hafer and D.M. Ambrose, "Psychographic Analysis of Nursing Students: Implications for the Marketing and Development of the Nursing Profession," *Health Care Management Review* (Summer 1983): 6976.

4. R. Blickendorfer, Teleconference, "Recruiting, Retaining and Reducing Demand: The Nursing Shortage Requires a Comprehensive Approach," American Hospital Association, April 21, 1988.

5. E.H. Erikson, Teleconference, *Childhood and Society*, 2nd ed. (New York: W.W. Norton & Co., 1963), 247–274.

6. J.F. Vogt and B.A. Velthouse, *Retaining Professional Nurses: A Planned Process* (St. Louis: C.V. Mosby Co., 1983), 101.

7. Blickendorfer, "Recruiting, Retaining and Reducing Demand."

8. D.M. Wolfe and D.A. Kolb, *Beyond Specialization: The Quest for Integration in Midcareer*, Unpublished manuscript, Case Western Reserve University, 1980.

9. D.A. Schon, *Educating the Reflective Practitioner* (San Francisco: Jossey-Bass Publishers, 1987).

10. Erikson, *Childhood and Society*, 268.

Chapter 5

Effective Marketing for Nurse Recruitment

John F. Turck III

ATTENTION ALL READERS:
Immediately after reading this chapter, you WILL DO the following:

Return to your homes and pack up all of your belongings.
Cancel any lease or put up your home for sale.
Remove your children from their schools.
Bid farewell to your co-workers, neighbors, friends,
and nearby relatives.
Inform your favorite hair stylist, butcher, auto
mechanic, and all others with whom you have
built a preferred relationship that you won't be needing
their services anymore.
Contact the movers of your choice
AND
You will move to MY town and come to work at MY hospital!

This ultimatum illustrates the vexing nature of our task in nurse recruitment and retention, acute shortage of nurses or not. What power do we have to dislodge others from that comfortable pattern of the status quo, from the security of the known, and to motivate them to make one of the most crucial decisions in their professional and personal lives?

This chapter recommends a power and process any manager can use to recruit and retain nursing staff. That power is called marketing, and healthcare organizations must become increasingly sophisticated in its use to achieve recruitment and retention objectives *and* to provide a satisfying professional experience for the RN—the *R*ecruited or *R*etained *N*urse.

RECRUITMENT AND RETENTION IS MARKETING

One of the first steps toward a successful effort is for an organization's leadership to recognize that the process of recruitment and retention *is* marketing, and that thinking and planning your efforts using a marketing-oriented approach is the key to success.

Regardless of where the nurse recruitment function is housed in your organization—in nursing, personnel, or elsewhere—somebody must bring the marketing perspective and process to the organization's plans and actions.

An effective marketing orientation to recruitment is even more crucial when an acute shortage of nursing resources confronts healthcare organizations. Hospitals nationwide continue to report more than an 11 percent average vacancy rate[1] due to increasing demand and plummeting supply.

The prospects for a quick fix on the supply side are not encouraging. More than half of all first-year college students interested in nursing are leaving for another discipline before graduation.[2] Not surprisingly, the number of RN graduates is expected to plunge from 82,000 in 1985 to 58,000 by the year 2000.[3]

As another facet of the contemporary nursing recruitment challenge, today's college students appear to be less altruistically driven and more oriented toward financial security and careers that yield both professional satisfaction and larger bank accounts or disposable income.[4]

In an era of such scarce resources, there is one dictum, one truism:

THOU SHALL COMPETE!

Actually, a more apt term for the kind of competition you are in would be *battle*. The nature of this battle was best summed up by marketing authorities, Al Ries and Jack Trout, in their book *Marketing Warfare*. According to them, you are fighting your battle

> in a mean and ugly place. A place that's dark and damp, with much unexplored territory and deep pitfalls to trap the unwary.
>
> Marketing battles are fought inside the mind. Inside your own mind and inside the mind of your prospects, every day of the week.
>
> The mind is the battleground. A terrain that is tricky and difficult to understand.
>
> Your entire battleground is just 6 inches wide. This is where the marketing war takes place. You try to outmaneuver and outfight your competitors on a mental mountain about the size of a cantaloupe.[5]

Winner or Loser

Effective managers will join this battle looking for every possible winning edge. These managers are quick to accept a contemporary fact of modern-day healthcare life about nurse recruitment and retention: There are going to be winners and there are going to be losers. The winners will be those effectively using the marketing process.

Some may be uncomfortable in thinking of recruitment as marketing. It may help to realize that a marketing approach has been used by our institutions since they first opened their doors and benefited from the services of the first nurses in return for some form of compensation. The use of the marketing process in most recruitment efforts simply has been done unconsciously, informally, indirectly, and perhaps even poorly.

Today's need for a marketing approach in recruitment simply means that a conscious, formalized, direct effort must be undertaken. Perhaps then, recruitment will be done less poorly.

National Audit Finds Room for Improvement

A comprehensive analysis of recruitment materials from more than 250 hospitals across the nation in response to an inquiry about employment was presented at the May 1988 annual meeting of the American Organization of Nurse Executives. The survey by Connie L. Curran, EdD, RN, FAAN, former vice-president of the American Hospital Association, and this author found that eight out of 10 hospitals responded ineffectively and noncompetitively to an eager inquiry about employment opportunities. Worse yet, one in 10 was actually hurtful to the organization's recruitment goals.

The difference between winners and losers in the mass of mailings was not an expensive print piece or a well-known institutional name or large bed complement or an exotic climate. The big deficit was thought by the hospital's leadership.

Most of the packages, in terms of both their form and content, appeared to be haphazard happenings. The packets betrayed management approaches of a sense of apathy ("Well, that's the way we did it for the last 10 years"); sheer panic ("Let's get something out quick!"); or, most problematically, the "everyone's in charge" syndrome ("I thought upstairs was going to take care of that").

The mailings did not just demonstrate which hospitals were good marketers and which ones were not. They subtly and not so subtly revealed the culture in which the nursing department was either struggling or flourishing.

The hospitals that had the most effective recruitment effort stood out, as winners tend to do. It was apparent that they had brought a systematic process to their effort so that a recruit's attention was gained and sustained. The difference was that somebody was thinking with a marketing mentality.

SIX KEY CONCEPTS FOR AN EFFECTIVE MARKETING APPROACH TO RECRUITMENT

How can you bring a marketing approach to your efforts? It does not have to be difficult. The process is quite manageable. Usually, the barriers are inertia, prejudice, and unwillingness to try another way. Thinking through the recruitment and retention battle requires leadership and perseverance.

The following six key concepts should enable managers to take hold of the marketing process quickly and make it an integral part of recruitment and retention planning and implementation.

Key Concept 1: Marketing Is Not Advertising

Marketing is not (just) advertising or some other highly visible promotional tactic. This common misperception or prejudice hurts both the discipline and those whom it could serve. Although they are part of the marketing process, advertising or other promotional strategies should be the last consideration in most cases. Sometimes your analysis may rule out advertising as a strategy altogether.

Key Concept 2: Marketing Defined

The concept that recruitment is a form of marketing is rooted in marketing's definition. Philip D. Kotler, the Harold T. Martin Professor of Marketing at Northwestern University and one of the nation's respected marketing thinkers, especially in marketing's application to nonprofit organizations, authored one of the most-often cited definitions:

> Marketing is human activity directed at satisfying needs and wants through exchange processes.[6]

In recruitment and retention, do not managers and other leaders (humans) meet their organization's staffing objectives by providing for nurses' (other humans) jobs (needs) that yield income and other financial considerations, and professional satisfaction (wants) in return (exchange) for professional, competent, and caring efforts?

Kotler integrates this basic definition into another that brings us closer to understanding how the various elements or steps in the marketing process are to be managed.

> Marketing management is the analysis, planning, implementation and control of programs designed to bring about desired exchanges with target markets for the purpose of achieving organizational objectives. It relies heavily on designing the organization's offering in terms of the target market's needs and desires and using effective pricing, communications and distribution to inform, motivate, and service the market.[7]

Speaking in plainer terms, Patrick M. Mages, president of The Mages Company, and one of the first individuals to introduce marketing to hospitals around the country, defines marketing and its management this way:

Marketing is the management process by which the changing needs and wants of a market are determined through research and are satisfied by the planning, development, and promotion of products and services in a form and at a location and price acceptable to the market.[8]

Others have defined marketing as "objectivity" or "what you do on the streets" or as "warfare." While these graphically underscore some of the essences of marketing, Kotler and Mages say it most definitively.

Key Concept 3: Marketing As a Business Philosophy

Marketing is a business philosophy—a way of conducting your recruitment and retention operations, which holds that your efforts must
1. Be consumer- or customer-oriented. In building a plan, what the nurse needs and wants must come before what the institution needs and wants.
2. Be quantitatively and qualitatively goal-oriented. Set specific recruitment and retention goals and objectives and then pursue them *aggressively*.
3. Involve everyone in the organization. The marketing mentality must exist and be practiced at all levels, by all personnel—from the chief executive officer to the newest minimum-wage employee. Imagine the impact one inappropriate remark by anyone in an organization can have on a recruit, for example.

Key Concept 4: Take a Ten-Question Market-Planning Test

Your recruitment plans must be built on the honest, objective answers to at least these basic 10 market-planning questions.

1. What Business or Businesses Are We Really In?

In terms of the use of nursing resources, there is an obvious answer to Question 1. But in any organization there are other more subtle, but equally critical, ones to identify and consider in your planning. Yes, nurses are caregivers, but they are also educators, psychologists, managers, and data gatherers as just some general examples. What ones can you think of in terms of the specific nature of your nursing department and hospital? The answers are critical to how you treat your nurses, which ones you seek out, what you say to them in your recruitment process, and more.

2. Who Is the Customer?

Are the customers new graduates, inactives, former employees? Although you can usually think of the recruit as the customer, sometimes it is important to make a distinction between a customer and a consumer. For example, in healthcare service marketing, you may need to think of the customer as the person who makes or directs the purchasing decision (e.g., the admitting physician) while the consumer is the one who actually consumes the service (the patient). In terms of nurse recruitment, you may want to consider spouses, parents, nursing school faculty or guidance counselors, friends, or others as indirect customers or "decision influencers" and the recruit as the consumer.

3. What Does the Customer Need?

Does the customer need a job; income; health insurance and other personal security-related benefits; a new work environment; reliable, up-to-date equipment?

4. What Does the Customer Want?

Does the customer want day care; no rotating shifts; no mandatory overtime; primary nursing; respect from medical, nursing, administrative and other work colleagues?

Consider an interesting corollary to the questions of what the customer needs and wants: *What the customer is buying may not be what you think you are selling.* Theodore Levitt, a Harvard Business School marketing professor whose vision and imagination is helping major portions of the nation's economy compete more successfully by focusing on the customer, cites some classic examples of this concept in his book *The Marketing Imagination.* He points out that Sears, for example, learned a long time ago that its customers are buying ¼-inch holes when it puts ¼-inch drills on its shelves or in its catalogs. Levitt points out how Charles Revson made a key observation about his organization. Although he makes Revlon cosmetics in his factories, he knows that his company is selling hope to customers in the stores.[9] And Kodak knows that it is selling remembrances, not just film or pictures.[10]

Think about your offering from the perspective of new nursing graduates, for example. To them, you are not just offering them a job. You are selling a dream, an opportunity, a future. You are providing the fulfillment of years of hard work, the release of pent-up enthusiasm, the realization of a desire to make a difference—to be a nurse.

What about experienced nurses? They may be buying better working conditions; a chance to start over; or an addition to the house, a sailboat, tuition for children or . . .?

5. Which Markets Will We Target?

Will we target intensive care nurses; rehabilitation or other specialists; nurses with two or three years of experience; supervisors; nurses across town, out of town, out of state; BSNs?

6. What Are Our Strengths?

Are our strengths top pay in the area; effective leadership; longest, most comprehensive orientation? Do we employ the most nurses in the area? Are there excellent relationships and communication between nursing and medical staffs?

7. What Are Our Opportunities?

Do our opportunities include a commercial day care center opening across the street; a student nurse association to hold an annual meeting in town; a new dean at the nursing school; an area plant layoff or closing that may increase chances that some inactive RNs will return to the work force?

8. What Are Our Weaknesses?

Do our weaknesses include inadequate parking; a high-crime area; experienced nurses topping out early; a low pay range; no tuition reimbursement; insufficient inservice time or resources; indifferent shift differentials; lingering misperceptions about how our nurses are treated?

9. What Are the Threats?

Are we threatened by a major competitor on the verge of a big salary increase; area diploma program closing; staff dissension or confusion over major, new nursing policies; a reduction in the supporting work force? Your analysis of this question must be heavily focused on competitors for your nursing resources. Is someone receiving their recruitment materials and seeing how they are positioning their job opportunities and institution and what they are saying about you, directly or indirectly? Remember: the hospital across town is not the only competitor for your nurses.

10. What Is Our Marketing Strategy?

Do we add super bonus incentives for straight nights worked; provide tuition aid for current staff to earn registration; institute a collaborative practice program; create a clinical ladder program; create a nursing administration position or committee of management and front line staff to concentrate solely on retention/turnover issues and solutions; offer intensive care internships to junior students during summer break; switch emphasis from classified to display advertisements?

The sample issues posed within these 10 market-planning questions should not be considered all-inclusive. Every organization's situation will differ in numerous ways and will have a wide range of variables it must or can consider. The main objective is to conduct this analysis on both internal and external markets, be as creative and precise as possible in forming the questions, and not fear the answers. Remember, marketing is objectivity.

Key Concept 5: The Marketing Mix

The marketing mix is a tremendously powerful analytical tool because it identifies the four essential ingredients of any exchange transaction. You can apply the marketing mix to any organizational, professional, or personal situation in which there is an exchange of values desired. Most certainly, it offers a systematic way to analyze your recruitment and retention situation so that you can set priorities for action.

The marketing mix is easy to remember. It is the four Ps of marketing:

PRODUCT
PLACE
PRICE
PROMOTION

Paraphrasing Robin E. MacStravic in an article, "Marketing Health Care Services: The Challenge of Primary Care,"[11] each of the four Ps can be related to a marketing approach to nurse recruitment and retention.

Product

What is the type of job or work being offered: intensive care or rehabilitation, medical-surgical, or flight nurse? What are the opportunities for advancement? What is the usual level of patient contact opportunities? What is the balance between education and experience and what is the balance of responsibility and authority? What is the creative nursing challenge, for example?

Place

How will the job or work be experienced? What is the work environment? What about the location of the facility in terms of ease of access from main traffic routes, or the security of the surrounding area?

"Place" considerations need to go beyond the physical environment. For example, what is the degree of professionalism in the ranks? What is the opportunity for recognition? What are the interpersonal relationships possible at all levels, especially communication? What is the nature of the relationship between the nursing and medical staffs in general?

Of course, the community counts a lot, too. What is the quality of life possible for a new graduate? For an experienced RN with a family? How are the type, supply, and prices of housing? How are the schools rated by the citizenry? What are the recreational and cultural opportunities?

Price

Obviously, what are the salary or wage levels and benefit packages? Are there incentives or bonuses for shifts, for working straight evenings or nights? Bonus points for overtime above a set minimum? How do your financial offerings compare with those of your competitors?

As a separate consideration under price, what are the educational values included in the exchange—orientation, inservice, tuition reimbursement, or payback?

Another set of price considerations has to do with human values more than financial ones. What are the "psychic" prices you make a nurse pay to work for you? Is it an unduly bureaucratic upper or middle management; overdone work rules; long delays for everyday supplies; a dimly lit parking lot?

Promotion

This is part of marketing that most people tend to think of first (see Key Concept 1). It is how and what the job candidate learns about the organization, the community, and the opportunities they offer to the recruit.

Will you use advertising? How much of it will be classified and how much will be display? Will you list all of your nursing positions in one large classified advertisement or will you segment them by specialty or department? What about your direct mail offerings? What will you send out in the first response? Will you establish a system for automatic follow-up and qualifying of an applicant's interest? How fast will you respond to inquiries? How strongly will your communications identify with the recruit's perspective of nursing and life beyond work?

Will you attend career days at colleges? Do you know which ones are likely to yield the best results? Will you have messages and programs targeted at minority applicants?

What you want to plan for in this most visible element of your marketing mix is how the prospect becomes aware, interested, accepts the job offer, keeps it, and even recruits others. Only leadership using a marketing-oriented approach can make this chain of events happen.

A fifth *P* has emerged in marketing recently, again thanks to the thinking and work of Ries and Trout.[12] They have defined a concept closely related to the promotion area: it is called *positioning*. Basically, it is your communications' attempt to find a position or niche in the consumer's mind for your product or service. Translated into nurse recruitment, it means what prospects will think of you when they hear your organization's name mentioned. Will you be known as *the* nurse's hospital in the area with strong nursing leadership supportive of front line staff? Or as a high-technology, research-oriented nursing unit with a strong high-touch emphasis? Or as an organization with a high pay, innovative nursing practice history?

Historically, hospitals in general have tended to try to occupy the "we're the best" position, but it is not always necessary to occupy this position.

Although he was not speaking directly about hospitals or recruitment, Joel Raphaelson, who is quoted in the classic advertising book *Ogilvy on Advertising*, makes a point the overzealous should consider.

It may be sufficient to persuade consumers that your product is POSITIVELY GOOD. If a consumer feels certain that your product is good and feels uncertain about your competitors, they will buy yours.

If you and your competitors all make excellent products, don't try to imply that your product is better. Just say what's good about yours—and do a clearer, more honest, more informative job of saying it.

This approach does not insult the intelligence of consumers. And who can blame you for putting your best foot forward.[13]

Key Concept 6: Develop Your Recruitment and Retention Plans Using the Marketing Model

The marketing model should not be too foreign for hospitals because it is simply another type of planning. The institutional planning model traditionally used by hospitals has a sequential approach of (1) statement of institutional mission, goals, and objectives; (2) strategies, supported by research, perhaps; (3) implementation; and (4) evaluation.[14]

The marketing model contains the same steps essentially, but puts them in a different sequence. It is a significant difference, because with the marketing model, the consumer or customer is considered *first* in the planning process. That is why it is critical to bring a marketing orientation to recruitment. In marketing, you meet your organizational goals by meeting the needs of your customer first.

Adaptation of the market planning model described by Eric Berkowitz and William Flexner[15] will allow an organization to think through its recruitment and retention challenge and position itself for a winning effort. The model has five steps:

1. nurse-oriented situational analysis marketing research
2. segment-specific strategies
3. mission, goals, and objectives
4. implementation
5. evaluation

Again, the marketing model presents a systematic way to think through recruitment and retention issues and plans, and to take action. Whether all steps of this model are conducted by staff or some parts are provided through outside resources, all of the steps need to be followed to ensure effective use of recruitment and retention dollars and efforts.

Nurse-Oriented, Situational Analysis Marketing Research

If you are going to target new graduates, what do you know about nursing students in general? What do you know about the students from the schools with which you have had your most success?

Have you determined from which schools you attract nurses? Are there others which you feel could yield more applicants? Do you know why you are not getting more?

What do you know about the experienced RNs in your primary recruitment area? (Some organizations find that after two years a nurse is most likely to consider a position with another hospital.) Have you tracked graduates and kept in touch with them even though they took their first job somewhere else? Do you know what their wants and needs are *now* after some experience? Which of your strengths may match up with what your research says they are looking for in a position?

Do you know what your geographic pull is? This is important in spending your advertising dollars.

Have you conducted focus group discussions with your current staff? Focus group sessions involve bringing together 10 to 12 persons with an impartial (preferably independent) moderator so that the staff or any other target group you select (student nurses, inactives, competitor's employees) can comfortably discuss their wants and needs, likes and dislikes, and perceptions about your organization as a place to work. You can also use research tools like these sessions to ask which nurses other staff members most respect. Perhaps those model staff members, then, regardless of their standing on the organizational chart, should be key players in your recruitment programs by having them meet with recruits. Focus groups also yield ready-made testimonials that can be used in promotional literature or programs.

Another key market research effort you must conduct is a competitor analysis. What do the opposition's recruitment materials look like? What are they proclaiming as their strengths? What are they implying about your organization? What is the pay level at their institution? What are the fringe benefits? What are they doing about flexible scheduling? Day care? Parking?

Segment-Specific Strategies

"If you don't think in terms of segmenting your markets, you're not thinking," according to Theodore Levitt.[16]

Again, does your market research suggest you should concentrate on new graduates and not aggressively pursue inactive nurses? What can you do to capitalize on the inherent advantage you will have with most former employees?

There are other ways to think about your segments if you have done a good job of analyzing what business you are in. For example, maybe you need to think in terms of nurses who like conducting research or innovating new nursing techniques. Or nurses who like bringing a wellness approach to health care? Or how about thinking in terms of recruiting "adventurers" who will thrive in your corporate culture?

Do not hesitate to segment the segments. You gain both efficiency and effectiveness as a result. For example, you might want to create two levels of intensity in your strategy aimed at the new graduate segment. One level is targeted for an overall effort, while additional tactics are employed on just 10 to 20 key prospects who ranked at the top of their classes.

One last thought on segmenting your markets. The largest, easiest and least costly to reach segment is your current staff. A very fine line exists between recruitment and retention. Be sure to survey this most valuable of all segments and meet their needs and wants in the areas that can have an effect on retention. With all costs of replacing one nurse ranging into the tens of thousands of dollars, retention can be a much more effective, efficient route to go when possible.

Mission, Goals, and Objectives

Now you can quantify your organization's needs and wants as identified in your marketing or institutional planning analysis. Do you need to increase applicants by 50 percent? To increase hire rates by 60 percent? To fill 20 general staff positions and 15 in intensive care in three months so that new beds can be brought on line or existing ones reopened? Do you want to reduce turnover by 75 percent over the next two years? To establish a staff mix of 75 percent BSN and 25 percent all others? To increase the "quality" of your staff by having 25 percent of new hires come from the top 10 percent of their graduating class? To institute a clinical ladder program within 12 months?

Implementation

Implementation is the "doing" stage. You follow through on decisions on such questions whether or not you have a dedicated nurse recruiter. Where should recruitment be based? How will you reach each of your segments? What is going to be the message to each? What will you change first about the working environment based on your market research analysis? How about your pay range and fringe benefits? Are they competitive? Will you establish a day care program?

How will you spend your limited recruitment dollars? How much for classified advertisements? Display advertisements? Advertisements in other towns' newspapers, on their radio stations, or will you rely on advertisements in national nursing journals to reach beyond your town's border? Will you exhibit at student nurse or nurse association conventions? Host a hospitality suite?

What is going to be the style of your recruitment effort? Who is going to meet with new recruits? Will their tour include a moment with the nurse executive? Will they be matched with graduates from their school? From their hometown? Will your model nurses get to spend some time with the recruit? How will you show off the town to them? Will you help them find housing?

Evaluation

Test your assumptions. Count noses. Check which advertisements or media pull the best response from the groups you have targeted. And come back to nurse-oriented situational analysis marketing research. What do the new hires say got their attention. What made them think? Who or what made them feel something? What made them believe? AND what made them act, to make that big decision and exchange values with *your* organization?

TAKING THE BLINDERS OFF FOR THE LONG RUN

By using the marketing model, management will increase an organization's success in recruitment and retention because it allows leadership to remove institutional blinders and do some outside-in type of planning. If you are going to be sincere in your effort to persuade, to motivate, to get a major career and life commitment from a person, you *must place the prospect first in your considerations*.

A caveat: Resolution of nurse recruitment and retention issues usually takes time, especially if your analysis shows that your major problems are found in the *product* or *place* categories of the marketing mix. Longstanding policies and procedures or perceptions about an institution, accurate or not, take more than words and images to change. Behaviors will count the most in the long run. Quick fixes should be tried, but a marketing approach to recruitment should not end with either the first few successes or failures.

Institutions usually take time in changing their behaviors. Because of the continuing acute shortage of nurses, recruitment is not a place to go too slow. Changes should be accelerated as much as possible because demand is heavy. But the good news inherent in the nationwide analysis by Curran and this author is that there is room for more winners.

Will you behave like the California hospital that responded to a blind request for employment information on the same day the letter arrived, or will your organization be like the Maryland hospital that took four months to respond?

Will you be one of the 12 percent of the hospitals that phoned the ersatz applicant of Curran and this author, or the 88 percent that passed up the opportunity to make a direct contact?

Will your organization be one of the 70 percent of hospitals that sent a letter with the mailing, or will it be in the 30 percent group that did not realize the importance of a letter in the package? But be careful what you call a letter. Curran and this author found preprinted, poorly reproduced form letters to be negative influences.

Will you be like one urban Midwestern hospital whose strong nursing leadership effected a "pricing personality" so that the hospital's nurses were always paid at least one cent more than the nurses at any other hospital? Or participate in programs by the area's hospital association to recruit collaboratively outside primary geographic markets? Or support an "earn and learn" degree-completion program at an area nursing school as a means of attracting experienced RNs to the institution or town?

What approach will you take to the nursing recruitment challenge, to this battle? The stakes are high. Losers face revenue losses in the millions of dollars from bed closings or reduced clinic capacity; loss of physician and patient confidence and loyalty because of inadequate staffing levels; a vicious, self-feeding cycle of sagging recruitment results and soaring turnover rates; and even having bonding credit-worthiness threatened.[17]

Winners will enjoy fruitful prospects, on the other hand, for as they adopt an effective marketing approach to nurse recruitment, their organization will have gained an even more commanding power than the one suggested in the ultimatum at the beginning of this chapter.

NOTES

1. *Report of the Hospital Nursing Demand Survey* (Chicago: Center for Nursing, American Hospital Association, 1987).

2. Kenneth Green, "What the Freshmen Tell Us" (based on findings from the Cooperative Institutional Research Program, sponsored by the American Council on Education), *American Journal of Nursing* (December 1987): 1612.

3. *Health United States* (Washington: U.S. Department of Health and Human Services, Public Health Service, 1985), 11.

4. Green, "What the Freshmen Tell Us," 1612.

5. Al Ries and Jack Trout, *Marketing Warfare* (New York: McGraw-Hill Book Co., 1986), 44.

6. Philip D. Kotler, *Marketing Management: Analysis, Planning and Control*, 3rd ed. (Englewood Cliffs, N.J.: Prentice-Hall, Inc., 1976) 5.

7. Ibid., 7.

8. Patrick M. Mages, The Mages Company. Presentation to the Wisconsin Hospital Public Relations Council, April 16, 1981, Germantown, Tennessee.

9. Theodore Levitt, *The Marketing Imagination* (New York: The Free Press, 1986), 128.

10. Ibid., 107.

11. Robin E. MacStravic, "Marketing Health Care Services: The Challenge of Primary Care," in *Health Care Marketing: Issues and Trends*, ed. Philip D. Cooper (Rockville, Md: Aspen Publishers, Inc., 1979).

12. Ries and Trout, *Marketing Warfare*.

13. David Ogilvy, *Ogilvy on Advertising* (New York: Vintage Books, 1985), 19.

14. Eric N. Berkowitz, and William A. Flexner, "The Marketing Audit: A Tool for Health Service Organizations," in *Health Care Marketing: Issues and Trends*, ed. Philip D. Cooper (Rockville, Md.: Aspen Publishers, Inc., 1979).

15. Ibid., 246.

16. Levitt, *The Marketing Imagination*, 128.

17. Suzanne Powills, "Nurses: A Sound Investment for Financial Stability," *Hospitals* (May 5, 1988): 46–50.

Chapter 6

Effective Advertising for Nurse Recruitment

Bernard S. Hodes

Creating a work atmosphere that is attractive to nurses—for both retention and recruitment goals—is part of the challenge. But all the work you may be doing in areas such as maintaining competitive wage scales or building career advancement paths for nurses or accommodating needs for flexible work schedules is lost if the people you want to recruit do not know about it.

When you start considering an approach to nurse recruitment, there are two basic thoughts to keep in mind:

1. *The nurse employment story at your hospital is unique.* No matter how similar you may think the working conditions at your facility are to those of others, there is something special about working at your hospital that is attractive to nurses. If this were not true you would not have the nurses you do have. Nurses have a wide range of employment options. The nurses you have been able to recruit and retain have chosen to work at your facility for some reason.
2. *You cannot assume that anyone knows anything about your nurse employment story.* Just because your facility exists does not mean that people have any idea about what it would be like to work there. In fact, the people you would like to recruit cannot be expected to know that you have job opportunities available unless you make an active effort to reach them with your employment news.

Getting the news out about your unique employment environment is, of course, where recruitment advertising—and other recruitment marketing techniques such as publicity—comes into play. Otherwise you will be dependent on word of mouth to tell your employment story.

BEYOND WORD OF MOUTH

Word of mouth can be a very powerful thing, but any grapevine is inefficient and unreliable. You cannot be certain that the story that is being spread about your hospital is reaching the right people and you cannot be sure that it is being told accurately.

Of all the marketing tools you have available to you to get your employment news to the right people, advertising is the most controllable. With advertising, you can say what you want to say and choose when you want to say it. You can focus your employment story narrowly in order to reach only those people with the specific qualifications that match the job opportunities you have available or expect to have available in the future. You can highlight those specific aspects of the working conditions at your hospital that would be particularly attractive to the people you want to hire.

The ability of advertising to deliver a controllable message comes with a price tag; recruitment advertising costs money. But the costs of an efficient and well-planned advertising program are offset by the returns. Advertising can be very helpful, if not essential, in achieving various recruitment goals:

- *Advertising speeds the flow of applications and lowers the cost of hiring.* Word of mouth is undependable, and using a staffing agency is expensive. Advertising can reach large groups of likely prospects to attract candidates quickly for specific hiring needs. The cost of the advertising and of the processing of replies can be amortized over the number of hires.

- *Advertising can overcome misconceptions about a hospital.* Undeservedly bad word of mouth about a hospital's work environment can keep prospects from applying. Advertising can efficiently counteract this problem by pointing out the positive aspects of the employment situation. It can also be used to announce changes involving a potentially negative past situation—such as a noncompetitive, low pay scale—to a new, positive situation—such as an improved pay scale.

- *Advertising can have a positive effect on retention of current employees.* When current employees see your recruitment advertising it demonstrates to them that you are interested in keeping the facility fully staffed.

- *Advertising helps overcome the effect of competitors' recruitment efforts.* In competitive markets, those hospitals that do the best job in meeting the employment needs of nurses and who aggressively (and consistently) tell their employment stories to nurses will "win." This does not mean that only those hospitals with the largest advertising budgets or best employee benefits will be successful. It does mean, however, that hospitals in competitive markets must maintain a high enough public profile to remind prospects continually not only of the existence of job opportunities but also of the positive aspects of the employment story—whatever they may be. Advertising can help do this.

- *Advertising can create interest in changing jobs among nurses who otherwise would not be contemplating a change.* The people you want to hire are most likely working somewhere else. Most recruitment advertising clustered in the classified sections of newspapers or in professional journals primarily attracts the attention of people actively looking for a job or those who, out of curiosity, are comparing their current situations with available opportunities. In many markets this type of advertising may be enough to fill employment needs, but in highly competitive situations it may not. Through the careful use of nontraditional forms of recruitment advertising—television, radio, outdoor and transit advertising, employee referral programs, and direct mail—a hospital can reach nurses who are not actively looking at traditional recruitment advertisements and actually implant the idea of changing jobs in the minds of nurses who had not been considering it.

These tasks that recruitment advertising can achieve also point out the risks that a hospital—particularly one in a competitive situation—can encounter by *not* maintaining a public profile of its nurse employment history. A hospital with low visibility as an employer can be forgotten by nurses who are considering changing jobs. Also, new nurses entering the field may not consider hospitals with low visibility because these nurses simply will not know about them. Advertising is a powerful communications tool that overcomes this problem by keeping the word out.

Unfortunately, recruitment advertising is often viewed as just another administrative expense, a necessary evil required to fulfill a short-term need. The problem with this point of view is dramatized by the experiences hospitals have had in the last 10 years or so in recruiting nurses. In the late 1970s, when almost all health care facilities were plagued by a nurse shortage, there was a heavy dependence on advertising and other recruitment techniques to answer needs. Then, in the mid-1980s the nurse surplus relieved a lot of the pressure. Many hospitals saw this surplus as a reason to cut recruitment expenses. They stopped advertising, they cut the nurse recruitment staff, and they stopped recruiting trips to nursing schools. Although a few hospitals maintained a recruitment presence even though their recruitment needs were much lower, most hospitals were happy to be "saving money."

Now in the late 1980s we find ourselves with another nurse shortage situation that some experts expect will last through the turn of the century. Once again hospitals are scrambling to recruit.

We have found, however, that the hospitals that maintained some sort of consistent recruitment presence during the surplus years have had a much less difficult recruitment job—although not necessarily an easy one—during this new shortage period. The lesson learned here is that recruitment advertising (along with other recruitment marketing techniques) has a cumulative effect—just as the advertising of consumer products has a cumulative effect on consumer buying patterns. By keeping their employment story public, the hospitals that continued to recruit had a more established image as a desirable place to work than did the hospitals that tried to create that image overnight to meet the new shortage.

"CRISIS" ADVERTISING VERSUS A LONG-TERM CAMPAIGN APPROACH

Most recruitment advertising is done in response to immediate hiring needs. The common scenario goes like this: A job opens and an advertisement is quickly put together to beat the advertising deadline of a local newspaper's Sunday edition. The advertisement is run and the advertiser waits for responses. If the responses do not come in, the advertisement is run again or a new one is quickly created. The process is repeated until the "right" person (or enough of the "right" people) responds.

This pattern usually works well in cases where there are sufficient numbers of qualified prospective applicants looking for jobs or where there is only an occasional hiring need to fill an unexpected or nonrecurring job vacancy. But when there is a continuous need (when, for example, you find that you are looking to fill the same type of job on a monthly basis), this piecemeal approach to advertising will not likely be very successful.

One of the reasons that a piecemeal approach is doomed to failure when trying to overcome a continuous hiring need is that it begins with the mistaken idea that one advertisement will do the job. But experience has shown that one advertisement—no matter how artfully it is written and designed or how large it is or how prestigious the journal in which it appears—will rarely fulfill a large or continuous hiring need. This is so because nurses, like other people, are not always ready to consider a new employment opportunity when they see a recruitment message. When they *do* get to the point of considering new employment they are more likely to look into those situations that they know the most about. Because nurses are bombarded with all kinds of recruitment messages, a single advertisement usually cannot firmly establish a lasting impression of the hospital's employment "image."

Another reason that the piecemeal approach is usually not effective is that it tends to breed an atmosphere of crisis, which in turn creates panic. When the single advertisement (which had been expected to do the job quickly) does not pull enough responses, the first assumption often is that the advertisement was "wrong." It somehow did not carry the right magic words to attract attention, so new advertisements with new messages are quickly created; when they do not pull enough responses, the pattern continues with a never-ending search for the elixir formula. As a result, rather than depending on the cumulative effect of a consistent message to establish the hospital's image as a desirable place of employment, the piecemeal advertising ends up delivering a constantly changing and confused impression.

After some experience in advertising in this piecemeal fashion and not getting the desired results, advertisers often throw up their hands in despair, claiming that advertising "doesn't work," and then turn to staffing agencies to fill their vacant jobs—at a very high cost. But hospitals having a hard time recruiting nurses can learn something from the way staffing agencies gather their pool of qualified people. Employment-related agencies are among the most aggressive and persistent recruitment advertisers. (Of course, you are helping to pay for that advertising through agency fees.) The message that their recruitment advertising effectively sends to nurses is that they can serve efficiently as a clearinghouse for the "best" nursing jobs available. But the question is: If you are able to find a nurse from a staffing agency, why weren't you able to attract that nurse directly through your own recruitment efforts? If the nurse found through a staffing agency finds your hospital a desirable place to work, why didn't that nurse consider you in the first place? One answer is that most likely your advertising (and other recruitment efforts) either did not reach that nurse or your message did not express the desirable aspects of working at your hospital fully enough to motivate that nurse to apply directly. In other words, your recruitment message was not focused in attracting the attention of nurses and appealing to their employment self-interests.

The alternative to trying constantly to come up with new advertising in a crisis atmosphere is the long-term campaign approach. The campaign approach takes a strategic view that recognizes in advance that your hiring needs will remain fairly constant in the future. With this point of view in mind, the campaign approach uses a series of advertisements with a common theme—or an expression of a common and consistent image of the hospital as an employer—to reach nurses at different times and from different angles. This approach starts with the assumption that one advertising message will *not* reach at any particular time enough nurses who are ready to consider a new employment opportunity. It also recognizes that a hospital's employment story will have to be seen or heard many times by a nurse before it can make the impression on that nurse that the hospital is a desirable place to work.

From these basic assumptions, the campaign approach proceeds by determining a strategy that defines the positioning image that the hospital is comfortable in presenting and selecting the media that will be necessary to reach enough nurses to get the message across. Although the campaign approach may not deliver immediate short-term results, its cumulative effect will usually put the hospital that adopts it in a much better position than its competitors.

Perhaps the most difficult—and certainly most frequently encountered—barrier to changing from a piecemeal advertising approach to a campaign approach is budgeting a sufficient amount of money to do the job right. In campaign advertising the expenses anticipated to fulfill the strategy must be budgeted in advance. In general, health care organizations have been hesitant to do this. In other industries where there is a constant need for an influx of new employees—the recruitment of new college graduates at large corporations, for example—the idea of the campaign approach with plans made a year or more in advance is an accepted fact of life, and the budget necessary to carry it out is considered one of the costs of doing business. Most hospitals have not yet come to this point. Perhaps because the nurse shortage of the late 1970s cured itself, the current situation may be thought of as merely a temporary inconvenience. Perhaps there is a reluctance to admit that there is yet another budgetary constant necessary to maintain the smooth operation of the hospital.

Whatever the reason for the unwillingness of many hospitals to budget sufficiently in advance, the surprising experience encountered at hospitals involved in a crisis situation is that somehow the money for recruitment—for both advertising and employment agency fees—becomes available when staff shortages upset things. This crisis situation spending—with all of the scattergun activity inherent in it—is largely wasteful. With a methodical campaign approach the spending can be targeted, which can mean big cost savings over the long run compared with the money spent in a crisis atmosphere. Certainly much less time, energy, and money are spent in maintaining an advertising campaign—even though adjustments may have to be made throughout the campaign to account for changing staff needs— than are spent in constantly trying to create new advertising in a panic atmosphere.

HALLMARKS OF AN EFFECTIVE ADVERTISING CAMPAIGN

You have probably encountered nurse recruitment advertisements something like this: ''NURSING AT XYZ HOSPITAL IS A CARING AND SHARING EXPERIENCE.'' But what does this type of message say? Not much. It certainly does not say anything special about the hospital. It says a great deal about the nursing profession in general. But where is the hospital in which nursing is *not* a ''caring and sharing experience?'' Nurses already know that their jobs involve caring and sharing. That is probably one of the reasons they went into the field in the first place.

The point here is that when you start thinking about the type of message you want your advertising campaign to deliver, or when you are judging the potential strengths and weaknesses of your current advertising, make sure that the advertising is selling your hospital as a place to work, not nursing as a profession. A more effective advertising message using the ''caring and sharing'' theme would be that your doctors and administrators have a caring and sharing attitude about the special employment needs of nurses and have an appreciation of the professional contributions that nurses make. A hospital that can prove that type of claim in a recruitment advertisement will have a pretty good chance of attracting the attention of the many nurses who feel taken for granted or even abused at their current places of work.

When trying to determine the basic concept on which to hinge your advertising campaign's central message, whether you are creating the advertising yourself or with the help of an advertising agency, keep two key factors in mind.

1. *Look at the employment story at your hospital from a nurse's point of view.* Nurses are not volunteer workers who come to your hospital out of purely altruistic motivations. They are doing a job in return for money and the other less tangible aspects that go along with a satisfactory work experience, just as you are. So why would nurses be happy working for you?
2. *Identify the ways in which you are different from other nurse employers.* You will want to emphasize the aspects of the work environment that separate you from competing facilities. Why would nurses be happy working for you *instead* of somewhere else?

It was said earlier in this chapter that the nurses who are currently working at your facility have chosen to work there for some reason. But do you know what those specific reasons are? Have you ever asked your nurses? If not, it would be a good place to start to find out what your employment strengths and weaknesses are. Hospitals that have done this kind of surveying of current employees sometimes come up with some surprising results. Sometimes the most appealing aspect of the work situation is as simple as being located near public transportation. Other times it is more complex: the director of nursing, for example, is considered a particularly admired or effective administrator.

Beyond a survey of currently employed nurses, you need to ask yourself some tough questions to help define who you are as an employer: Who are you competing with in hiring nurses? How does working at your hospital differ from working for your competitors? What are the potentially positive and negative aspects of a nursing job at your hospital as compared with those of competitors? What is your reputation? Is that reputation correct or are there misconceptions that need to be overcome? What are nurses looking for in their jobs? How do the positions available at your hospital fulfill nurse employment needs?

To help you answer these questions, a careful scrutiny of competitors' advertising can tell you what they are claiming as their employment "selling points." The advantages that you have that they are not claiming in their advertising (even though they could) can become your selling points. Also, professional journals continually publish fairly detailed surveys of nurse attitudes about their jobs. These surveys will tell you about nurse employment needs that can then be matched to what you have to offer. Areas where there is a positive match can be another source for identifying your selling points.

Generally, when you have a list of all of the positive reasons that a nurse would want to work at your hospital, the ones you will want to emphasize are those that make you appear to be superior to your competition. If, for example, you have the best compensation plan in town, proclaim it loudly. Or if your hospital has the most advanced technological equipment or is affiliated with a prestigious medical school or has an unusually wide diversity of medical treatment, do not assume that potential new nurses know it. Tell them in your advertising and remind them whenever possible. As mentioned earlier, however, the positive features of working at a hospital are not limited to large, well-known, or prestigious hospitals. A small hospital competing against a large one may have positive work-related features that the larger hospital cannot offer. For example, features such as a small ratio of patients to nurses or the fact that duty specialization is not required may be very attractive to some nurses.

Throughout the whole process of determining what you have to "sell" and what makes your nurse employment story superior to that of others—or at least different—keep in mind that you do not need to appeal to *all* nurses, only those who would be attracted to what you have to offer. The goal is not to attempt to project an image of being the perfect hospital for everyone; instead, the goal is to be able to express truthfully the unique "personality" of your hospital's special employment story. Few hospitals have done the difficult work to get to this point, which is why so much nurse recruitment advertising could be easily interchangeable from one hospital to another.

Determining the image you want to present to prospects and the specific items of information that will sell your employment story is one thing. Getting the message to nurses, both new and experienced, is another.

All types of advertising media—from the traditionally used local newspapers and professional journals to less commonly used media such as radio, television, outdoor and transit advertising, and direct mail—can be (and have been) successfully used for nurse recruitment.

The details of determining which media to use, particularly when it is necessary to advertise beyond a local newspaper's classified section, is best left to professionals such as an advertising agency or a recruitment marketing consultant. A media strategy that a professional can draw up for you will take into consideration the ability of a particular medium—a specific journal or a specific radio station—to reach your most likely prospects efficiently.

While it is impossible here to go into all of the various considerations necessary for selecting appropriate media, there are two important things to remember about media.

First, no single medium can be thought of as being better than all others in every recruitment situation. As your recruitment environment becomes more competitive, it will be necessary to branch out beyond the traditional recruitment media such as newspapers and journals. Actually, the most successful recruitment campaigns use a multipronged approach with a variety of different media in order to reach nurse prospects from different angles.

Second, as mentioned before, a single advertisement—one advertisement in one issue of one professional journal or one broadcast of a single radio commercial—will not accomplish much. Advertising requires sufficient repeated frequency to make the desired impression. If you simply cannot afford to buy enough media frequency to allow it to work properly, it would be best to concentrate your advertising in those media that you *can* afford to use properly. Otherwise, by spreading your dollars too thin, you may end up diluting the effectiveness of your advertising efforts.

WHERE THE MONEY GOES

Media costs account for the bulk of advertising expenditures. In addition, you will usually need to spend some money on producing the advertisements and possibly on consultant fees.

Buying space in a print medium—a newspaper or journal—is very straightforward. The rates they quote are the rates that are charged all advertisers. Rarely will there be any special "hidden" deals that can be arranged to get advertising space less expensively. Broadcast advertising time, however, is almost always negotiated. The rates that broadcast stations quote on their "rate cards" are used as the starting point in determining the cost of any particular time slot. The final rate that a broadcast station charges will depend on how much demand there is for the time slot and on the negotiating skill of the person doing the media buying.

There is little you can do to cut your media costs dramatically without cutting the amount of advertising you do. That is why it is important to focus on the *efficiency* of a particular media vehicle to deliver your advertising to your most likely nurse prospects. Hospitals that try to use the cheapest media are rarely getting a good bargain.

For hospitals that are using a campaign approach with a strategy that is mapped out in advance, there is one cost-cutting technique that you should be aware of. If you advertise with any amount of consistency in certain newspapers or journals, you should look into the publication's discount schedule for frequent advertisers. Very often newspapers and journals will provide rates that are significantly lower than the normal rate for advertisers who place a certain number of lines of advertising or a certain number of advertising insertions within a certain period of time, usually one year. In order to receive this discount rate you (or your advertising agency) must enter into a contract before the advertising is run. The contract specifies that an advertiser expects to run a certain number of lines of advertising or a certain number of different insertions.

The contract serves only as a basis for monthly billings to the advertiser. Subsequent adjustments are made to fit the *actual* number of lines or insertions. If at the end of the contract period you had not used as much space as you had anticipated, you would be billed the difference between the lower rate you had been paying monthly and the actual rate you earned or should have been paying. (You would not be expected to pay for advertising you had expected to run, but did not.) If, however, you used *more* space than the contract called for and therefore may be entitled to an even greater discount because of your higher volume of advertising, the publication would give you a rebate at the end of the contract period for the advertising you ran.

The important thing to remember about contracts is that you will not get any discount rate or rebate if you do not sign a contract *before* placing your advertising. If, for example, you discover after a few months of advertising in a publication that you would have been entitled to a discount rate if you had had a contract, you cannot expect the publication to give you a retroactive discount. The message here is that you will lose nothing by signing a contract—even if it is for the minimum amount allowed by the publication—but you will lose a great deal if you do not have one.

If you do your advertising with the help of an advertising agency, you should also understand how an advertising agency receives compensation for its work. A portion of an agency's income comes in the form of a commission that is provided by the newspaper or journal or broadcast station in which the agency places the advertisement. The media vehicle will bill the agency according to its advertising rates minus a commission of usually 15 percent. The agency in turn will bill the hospital at the gross rate of the cost of running the advertisement and retain the 15 percent difference. For example, if a newspaper advertisement cost $1000, the newspaper would bill the agency for $1000 minus $150 (15 percent) for a total amount of $850. The agency would bill the hospital for $1000; the $150 would be the agency's gross margin for that particular advertisement.

When a media vehicle's advertising rates are commissionable, only recognized advertising agencies are given the 15 percent commission. A hospital placing the advertisement directly would not be given a 15 percent discount. In the example above, if the hospital placed the advertisement directly, rather than through an agency, it would be billed by the newspaper for the full $1000 rate.

The commission that agencies receive from the media covers the work the agency performs in planning, preparing, and placing advertisements, usually including writing copy. However, most agencies charge additionally for creative development and for materials used in the preparation of advertisements, such as typesetting and artwork. If outside sources are used, the suppliers of these materials do not provide commissions to agencies. Therefore, these charges are passed on to the hospital at cost plus a percentage, usually 17.65 percent. For example, if the cost of the typesetting for an advertisement is $85, the agency would add $15 (17.65 percent of $85) and bill the hospital $100, retaining the $15 as its gross margin. The 17.65 percent markup on out-of-pocket expenses is equivalent to a 15 percent commission. The 17.65 percent markup system is also usually used when media vehicles do not provide commissions to agencies. It is also used as the markup on such things as collateral materials (brochures and posters, for example) and on special research projects that the agency may do for a hospital.

SETTING THE BUDGET

How much money should be spent on advertising? As in other aspects of recruitment advertising there is no simple answer that can be applied to all situations.

The question of budgeting is an integral part of the question of what strategy to use. On one hand, the amount of financial support given to advertising will affect strategy decisions. When choosing media, for example, the size of the advertising budget may limit your choices. On the other hand, it is difficult to determine the amount to allocate to advertising before you know what it is you need to accomplish and what strategy would most effectively achieve that goal. Obviously, the decisions about strategy tactics and budgeting cannot be made apart from one another.

Assuming that you are planning to take a long-term campaign approach to advertising, the allocation you need to establish should be made to cover the advertising activities of an extended period of time (usually one year), with specific amounts budgeted to spend on different advertising activities. The total allocation should be flexible enough to meet changing conditions and uncontrollable events.

If you are moving from a piecemeal approach to advertising to a campaign approach, perhaps the best way to come up with a realistic figure is to combine the information you have on your past advertising expenditures with information on the cost of putting together an "ideal" strategy.

With the help of an advertising agency or marketing consultant with experience in nurse recruitment in your area, map out a specific plan that would probably be necessary to meet your anticipated hiring goals for the year. Break that plan down into narrowly defined tactics. For example, if you are planning to recruit nurse graduates in the spring, determine the cost of the advertising necessary to support the effort. If the competitive environment in your area dictates that you must maintain a weekly presence in your local newspaper, determine the year's cost for that. If you decide that journal advertising would be productive, determine how much advertising would give you the exposure to make a meaningful impact on journal readers. Then determine the cost of any other specific tactic—such as a radio campaign, a direct mail campaign, or transit ads—that would be necessary to add to your basic plan, and calculate the expenses on a month-by-month basis.

Then, look at the amount of money you have spent on piecemeal advertising over the past two or three years and average it for a one-year time span. Subtract from that figure the money you spent on advertising to reach the types of people you would now be reaching through your campaign approach. The figure that you have left is the money you had to spend to fill job vacancies that were generally nonrecurring.

The money you spent in the past on those nonrecurring job vacancies, added to the figure you came up with to carry out an ideal campaign strategy (as well as a provision for a contingency fund as a guard against the unexpected), will give you a basic appropriation figure needed for the year. That figure, of course, will have to be tempered with the reality of the availability of funds. But by having planned a year-long strategy—one that identifies *why* specific tactics are deemed necessary—you can look for areas where strategic compromises can be made and at the same time create a fairly well-defined year-long spending path that will help you control costs.

The mistake with this approach is to chip away at that ideal strategy so severely that you are left with no strategy and then find yourself back in a crisis situation. It is much easier to allocate for something closer to the ideal strategy and later cut that strategy back if it proves to be more successful than anticipated than it is to try to find the money to pump up a program that was underfunded initially.

Chapter 7

Nurse Recruitment and Retention from a Nurse Recruiter's Perspective

Kathryn L. Bray

HISTORY

The nursing shortage has been in existence ever since this country stopped training diploma-prepared registered nurses (RNs) and student manpower became unavailable to staff hospitals. There have been periods of abatement over the last 30 years, but they have been brief.

During the early 1970s, people charged with procuring nursing staffs for their respective hospitals found themselves spending much of their time with their competitors at various nursing conventions and job and career fairs. The term *nurse recruitment* became a recognized activity in health care, and these "recruiters" banded together to formalize their function. In 1975 the National Association of Nurse Recruiters (NANR) was formed to promote sound, ethical principles of nurse recruitment.

At that time there were no resources available to teach nurse recruitment. *RN Magazine* was the first organization to provide national recruitment classes; later, NANR assumed that function. A newsletter was developed to share recruitment tips and upcoming recruitment events. The professional journals started publishing articles on interviewing, recruitment, and retention techniques. In 1980, the first book on this subject, *Nurse Recruitment—Strategies for Success,* by Tina Filoromo and Dolores Ziff, was published and became the primer on nurse recruitment.

Nurse recruitment budgets escalated rapidly, recruitment staffs expanded, referral and relocation policies were developed, and overseas and Canadian recruitment ventures were undertaken. Registries and contract nurse employment agencies greatly increased in size, number, and volume. The issues constantly debated during that time were whether or not the recruiter should be a nurse, whether recruitment should reside in personnel or nursing, and where the recruitment budget should best be spent. Recruitment programs were difficult to evaluate because the external and internal environments were constantly in flux and few standards were established.

In 1980, the National Commission on Nursing was established, and public hearings on the nursing shortage were held early the following year. In the initial report, the major issues needing to be addressed at that time were as follows:

- *status and image of nursing*, including changes in the nursing role in response to new variations in health care delivery and professional growth as well as the corresponding changes in interprofessional relationships and public image
- *interface of nursing education and practice*, including current and potential models for basic and graduate education and continuing nursing education to prepare nurses for practice and professional interaction in health care delivery
- *effective management of the nursing resource*, including the mix of organizational factors required for nursing job satisfaction (such as the issues of staffing, scheduling, salary and benefits, support services, modes of care delivery, and career development) as well as manpower planning and recruitment and retention strategies
- *relationships among nursing, medical staff, and hospital administration*, including nurses' ability to participate through organizational structures in decision making as it relates to nursing care, the value and development of collegial relationships among health care professionals, and the development and operation of interdisciplinary patient care teams
- *maturing of nursing as a self-determining profession*, including nursing's right and responsibility to define and determine the nature and scope of its practice, the need for and role of nursing leadership, the potential of collective action to increase decision making in nursing practice, and the need for unity in the nursing profession[1]

In 1982 and 1983, diagnosis-related groups (DRGs) had a profound effect on nurse recruitment efforts. The decreased length of the patient's hospital stay created a climate in which many hospitals seemed to have adequate nursing staffs. Additional economic challenges led to layoffs of employees in ancillary and support services as well as members of middle and higher management. In many cases the nurse recruiter's function ceased to exist or was dramatically altered. Because of their recruitment experience, many nurse recruiters became "health care recruiters" and were charged also to recruit for physical therapists, respiratory therapists, and other allied health professionals. The NANR became the National Association for Health Care Recruitment (NAHCR) in 1984.

It was no surprise to those in nursing circles that nursing shortage issues resurfaced. The only surprise to some was that it happened so quickly. Also, there was a common theme in related conversations that this nursing shortage was "different." The American Hospital Association published a research report in 1987 that summarized some reasons why the current nursing shortage appears to be different:

- the drop in the number of young people in the available college-age pool
- the recently enhanced opportunities for capable women in many formerly male-dominated fields
- public reaction to the extensive publicity (in the years 1983 to 1985) given to hospital closures and contraction in the health care work force
- the ongoing confusion about the outcome of state-by-state legislation affecting changes in entry into professional nursing practice[2]

TODAY

Current and projected RN vacancy statistics are grim. "Trends indicate that, by the year 2000, there will be about one-half as many nurses as needed."[3] Much is in the literature about changing the image of nursing, upgrading compensation packages, and developing nursing career outreach programs for youths, men, and people seeking a second career. The efforts of these programs will not be realized for some years, and clearly there are massive problems facing hospitals today. History indeed does repeat itself and, again, hospital executives are asking the questions: Do I need a nurse recruiter? Should that nurse recruiter reside in the nursing department or human resources? Should the recruiter be an RN? How can we evaluate the effectiveness of our limited recruitment budget?

NURSE RECRUITER

There is an old saying that "you never have a second chance to make a first impression." No matter what the size of the health care organization, there must be someone designated to make the initial contact with any outside candidate (or internal applicant) regarding RN or other hard-to-fill employment opportunities. It is the author's belief that resources are well spent to have a professional recruiter(s) on board to design, implement, evaluate, and manage a recruitment program. In many cases this function may not require a full-time equivalent; in some settings, several recruiters may be needed. However, an individual within the organization must be appointed to manage the function.

In order to manage the professional recruitment program, the ideal nurse recruitment manager needs to have demonstrated the ability to communicate effectively and to command the respect of nursing, human resources, and administration. The nursing shortage often is a very emotional issue and, in order to operate effectively, the nurse recruitment manager must demonstrate maturity, objectivity, and the ability to make many groups of people work together. The nurse recruitment manager must be able to serve as a consultant and facilitator to the appropriate departments and work groups. The nurse recruitment manager must demonstrate the ability to work productively and creatively with the many leadership styles and philosophies typically found in any large department, such as nursing services.

Nurse recruitment is not a clerical function. While many successful and highly regarded professionals came from that background, it is a mistake to think that one who coordinates an efficient hiring program can always develop an aggressive recruitment program. It is also a mistake to think that a nurse recruiter has to be an RN. While the skills inherent in nursing can often be applied to recruitment, an RN lacking management wisdom and experience will find the position difficult. There are those who promote the notion that an effective nurse recruiter must come from human resources, and others argue that human resources departments often do not have the sense of urgency and manpower necessary for immediate action. Some say that the recruiter should come from nursing, as that department has greater financial resources than human resources, yet others say that the recruitment/ employment function clearly belongs in human resources. To avoid all the aforementioned problems, a few have suggested that the nurse recruiter should report directly to hospital administration.

The above debate is at least a decade old, and there are no signs of resolution to this problem—and there is no need for resolution. All of the above scenarios have yielded very successful programs in the past and are continuing to do so today. The key to successful nurse recruitment is *partnership*. Those individuals associated with highly proactive recruitment programs buried turf problems long ago and realized that cooperation and collaboration were the keys to successful recruitment. In order to build or maintain a professional recruitment program, the right person must be charged with the task. Ideally, that person has the academic and service qualifications that command respect from within and outside the organization. While recruitment requires a certain degree of skill in systems analysis and data interpretation, the nurse recruitment manager must give evidence of strong verbal and written skills; be able to coordinate the activities of numerous internal groups (recruitment/retention committees and marketing committees, for example); and demonstrate a thorough understanding of how the nursing department operates. The successful nurse recruiter must know how to use internal resources (public affairs, marketing, volunteer programs, and others) and manage outside vendors, such as advertising agencies. The successful recruiter must be a salesperson for his or her organization. The nurse recruiter must believe in and be enthusiastic about the product (nursing). The recruiter must represent the product honestly, yet be adept in the persuasiveness necessary to excite interest in the product. He or she must be able to follow up the candidate until the sale is closed (the applicant is hired). And last, the recruiter must follow up post-hire to ensure that the proper placement has been made and that the newly hired RN is satisfied with the position.

RECRUITMENT PLAN

There are no secrets for successful nurse recruitment. The success of any program lies in the development and implementation of a detailed recruitment plan. Success lies in the ownership of the recruitment plan by those who have the power to maximize the resources available. Nurse recruitment efforts will succeed for those who are able to quantify their efforts and adjust recruitment directions based on sound data collection and interpretation. Finally, success will be awarded to those who simply follow up repeatedly on all inquiries, interviews, and hires.

Internal Evaluation

The nursing shortage has created a "crisis arena" in many hospitals. The needs are so great that time and attention often are not given to the development of a business plan. This activity, however, must be the foundation of every recruitment effort. It is best to begin by evaluating the product (nursing). What are the strengths and weaknesses of the services that we provide? If we could "wave the magic wand," what would we change? Every hospital has unique offerings and challenges. It is best to be candid about both characteristics and commit to paper those services that demand pride and those that need to be bolstered.

Inherent in the recruitment plan is an analysis of current recruitment and employment practices. What is working well? What is the response time to inquiries? How quickly can interviews be scheduled? How many "layers" must an applicant forge through before offers of employment are made? How quickly do nursing managers respond to applications sent to them?

Most experienced nurse recruiters will agree that their biggest recruitment challenge lies within the very walls of the health care facility for which they are trying to recruit. It is difficult to say succinctly why many of the nursing managers respond sluggishly, but it is a most common practice. Some nurse managers will even assume the role of adversary with the nurse recruiter. This kind of interaction, unfortunately, is also quite common. There is no debate that the first-line manager of a nursing work group is under tremendous pressure. Those nurse managers who have successful recruitment track records have developed a partnership with their nurse recruiters. Applications are reviewed promptly and time is found to interview applicants at the applicant's convenience. Job offers are made and follow-up is conducted in an efficient and timely manner. Frequently, the total process occurs with the initial visit of the RN applicant. The nurse manager who consistently hires successfully realizes that the RN in his or her office needs only literally to go down the street to receive another offer of employment. These nurse managers have developed what recruiters call a "gut response" to the applicant and just about always know whether the applicant is appropriate for the nursing work group. They know the key questions to ask that will elicit any potential problems from the applicant. They also know that, besides the competitor across town, they are also frequently competing with other nurse managers within their own organization. It should be noted that the author does not suggest that every nurse manager assume the style described above, or that references not be checked. Employment offers can be made "pending references." Also, nurse managers should not operate in desperation. If the RN does not fit into the character of the nursing unit, it would be most unwise to hire that applicant. That RN, however, should leave the interview feeling positive about the institution and with some direction of where to go next.

A careful look also needs to be given to the nurse recruiter's activities. Are telephone calls answered promptly? Is there a system for seeing every RN who walks through the door? Are there provisions for backup personnel when the nurse recruiter is at an off-site recruitment event? Are the massive amounts of written communications processed promptly? Before any investments are made in the marketing area, internal systems must be at their optimum. For those experiencing some of the difficulties mentioned above, a dialogue with the nurse executive will be of great benefit. Regardless of the department from which the nurse recruiter operates, the support and advice from the key nursing administrator will benefit all involved in the recruitment-employment cycle.

The greatest sources of recruitment information are the RNs currently employed at the health care facility. An important element of the recruitment plan is provided simply by asking the nurses how they would market their hospital's nursing practice. What are they most proud of? How do they perceive the image of nursing? What advantages do they have that the competing hospitals do not offer? What professional journals do they read? How often do they review the local advertising? How would they recruit future colleagues to their facility? And, most important, how were they referred? Clearly some of the above questions are of a sensitive nature. With expert advice, however, a questionnaire or survey can be constructed to command a good response. One major benefit of this effort is that the nursing staff and management are invited to become partners in the nurse recruitment effort.

External Evaluation

To complement an internal survey, it is most helpful to survey RNs in the community not employed at the facility. With the use of the proper survey techniques, questions can be asked that relate to the outside nursing community's perception of nursing at the hospital. Attitudes can be quite surprising and can be a foundation later for the marketing plan.

A recruitment plan is not complete without addressing the competition. Just as the strengths and weaknesses of one's own facility are analyzed, so too must the competitor come under similar scrutiny. In the past, nursing was somewhat reluctant to undertake this task. Somehow this activity seemed to violate a vague sense of professional ethics. With competition as it is seen today in every health care sector, it is much easier to be objective about what the neighbor has or does not have to offer. It is also very safe to assume that most nurses know what the competitor is offering, if only from the registry pool that works in all of the local hospitals. An unbiased appraisal of the competition is another building block to the marketing plan.

RECRUITMENT/RETENTION COMMITTEE

As plans are being developed to construct nurse recruitment goals and objectives, serious consideration needs to be given to the establishment of a recruitment/ retention committee. Because the shortage of qualified RNs affects so many departments and services, a carefully constructed group of key members of the health care team will ease the burden that generally falls entirely on the shoulders of the nurse recruiter. Membership in this group will vary, but it usually includes representation from nursing (management and staff), human resources, and administration. It is also helpful to include a nursing supporter from the medical staff, public relations, marketing, finance, and other appropriate departments. Most often the person who manages the nurse recruitment function will chair the committee.

The goals and activities of this group can be many. Of the most value is the sharing and dispersing of information critical to the development, implementation, and evaluation of the recruitment program. Because of the potential power held by members of the group, adequate resources may be obtained more easily to ensure success of the recruitment plan. The wide contact base of the membership will also facilitate enlistment of internal, local, and sometimes national experts for specific recruitment/retention projects. This group can assist in establishing organizational priorities, supporting specific recruitment/retention strategies, and creating a climate for innovation. Finally, partnerships will be established between and among departments, and ownership of the recruitment/retention effort will be shared among many.

RECRUITMENT STRATEGIES

The recruitment plan forms the basis from which recruitment strategies can be developed. An initial review of the existing internal and external recruitment systems, materials, environment, and culture provides for problem identification.

It is advisable initially to develop a response to these problems without regard to budgetary constraints. When developing recruitment strategies, innovation and creativity need to be the guiding forces to ensure that all avenues and resources have been considered and maximized. As the recruitment plan develops, financial limitations naturally will lead to the prioritizing of activities.

Advertising

In today's sophisticated marketing environment, it is very common to employ an advertising agency. While some hospitals are very successful in developing advertisements and recruitment materials from internal resources, many hospitals do not have the time, money, and expertise to do so. If a health care facility is in the process of establishing or reevaluating the recruitment plan, it is also a good time to give serious consideration to undergoing an advertising agency review.

The advertising agency review process is similar to any new vendor evaluation procedure. A small group is formed, generally from the nurse recruitment/ retention committee, with the charge of determining which advertising agency has the best "fit" with the health care facility. Most advertising agencies offer similar creative capabilities, charge comparable rates, and very much want the hospital's business. Assuming that past creative campaigns have been excellent and that the agency's financial structure, philosophy, and references are sound, it is the author's opinion that the key decision-making elements lie in who will be in charge of the account and how it will be serviced. The advertising agency's account executive is the one who will capture the uniqueness of the organization and its nursing practice and who will translate that uniqueness to the agency's creative department. The account executive will be sensitive to the limited recruitment budget and give advice about how to maximize that budget with regard to advertising, brochures, and related materials. The account executive will work with the recruitment/retention committee and serve as the media expert and, it is hoped, the public relations expert. The account executive will provide the hospital with useful demographic and other information and suggest methods in which the hospital can explore both traditional and nontraditional recruitment avenues. Finally, the account executive will serve as an extension of the recruitment office and become a valued partner in the recruitment effort.

Classified Advertising

Classified advertising probably captures the largest percentage of any recruitment budget. In addition to announcing new positions and programs, advertisements may demonstrate to current employees that the hospital is "doing something to help them." An experienced nurse recruiter often will know that some classified advertisements will not yield results but will place them for visibility purposes. An experienced nurse recruiter also will know when to refrain from advertising because too-frequent visibility may create the message that his or her hospital is in trouble.

Directory Advertising

There is no simple answer as to how to balance local classified advertising with trade journal advertising. Most hospitals do not have the financial resources to do much, if any, of the latter. However, it is probably money well spent to buy space in the annual nursing career journals that are produced by the major nursing magazines. The distribution of these directories is high and the shelf life is long. With the easy response mechanisms provided by the directories, leads can be responded to quickly and demographics can be established.

Trade Journal Advertising

Trade and specialty nursing journal advertising is very expensive. Most nurse recruiters utilize this strategy to market their hospital's nursing image and programs rather than to find recruits. How much to advertise is determined by the size of the budget and the nurse recruitment marketing philosophy. If the decision is made to establish and maintain a national campaign, it must be done properly. This means that an advertising campaign is developed and advertisements appear on a periodic basis. Inherent in campaign development is a provision for tracking and responding to inquiries resulting from those advertisements.

On-Site Recruitment Strategies

For many hospitals, a significant amount of available resources is spent on open houses, local educational/training programs, employee referral projects, direct-mail campaigns, and other related activities. Many nurse recruiters would support the statement that the return on investment in these areas is significant. Unfortunately, the competitors usually have the same experiences and are vying for the same target audience. The advertising agency or marketing consultant can be of great value in developing a uniquely creative plan to stimulate interest and response to these programs. The most value of on-site recruitment lies in inviting the hospital staff to be partners in an activity that potentially eases the burden of delivering patient/family nursing care.

Off-Site Recruitment Strategies

In the late 1970s and early 1980s, considerable controversy developed about the value of attending job fairs and conventions in key cities throughout the country. In the late 1980s, there are more companies than ever offering meeting sites for employers and applicants to review employment opportunities. These events can be quite costly, particularly when a recruiter has to travel far to attend. The value in attending these job fairs is clouded. Some events have yielded excellent results; for some, these events have been disappointing. It is the author's opinion that the off-site job fairs are of less value today than they were a decade ago. Nurses who once were willing to relocate no longer have to do so because of the development of contract nursing agencies. Nurses now can work in many different parts of the country without a permanent commitment to any hospital or community.

Representation at nursing conventions falls in line with national advertising efforts. Most recruiters go to these conventions expecting not to do heavy recruitment. The visibility factor at these conventions, however, is quite high. It is also most gratifying for employees to see that their hospital is represented at professional meetings and conferences. Representation at these events, again, is determined by philosophy and budget.

Of great value in off-site recruitment is the support and participation of local and regional colleges on career days. The irony of this situation is that many hospitals have restricted the number of newly graduated nurses they are willing to recruit, and this is the most available target population. Clearly there has to be a safe mix of experienced and inexperienced nurses on the nursing units so as not to compromise patient/family care. It is not uncommon for a hospital to restrict the number of new graduates hired in hopes that experienced RNs will fill the vacancies. However, a summer employment program designed for the nursing student is one of the most effective means of nurse recruitment. There is no better way of identifying good employment candidates and easing them into the system. It is in any hospital's best interest to invest heavily in new graduate and summer student programs as well as programs to reward the preceptors who are charged with orienting and mentoring these groups of employees.

One additional consideration to off-site nurse recruitment events: it is wise to include nursing staff, nursing managers, and others when participating in these events. Besides providing for a unique opportunity, bringing others to these events invites partnership on all levels.

Foreign Nurse Recruitment

Foreign nurse recruitment has gained favor by many over the last several years. In some parts of the country, nursing services could not be offered if foreign-trained RNs were not providing nursing care. Most nurse recruiters would agree that this type of recruitment strategy provides a temporary reprieve from the chronic shortage problem. Most would also agree that they would prefer not to invest in foreign recruitment if other immediate solutions were available. Foreign recruitment is very expensive, and the challenge of integrating many of these RNs into the local and professional culture is often difficult. However, because success has been experienced by some, this recruitment strategy should be considered when developing the recruitment plan.

BUDGET

The depth of a nurse recruitment program is a function of how many resources are devoted to the plan and how that plan is managed and evaluated. Few nurse recruitment managers would admit to having an adequate recruitment budget, and most would want the initial investment to be in support of an adequately staffed and maintained recruitment office. Before any monies are spent in advertising or related activities, a mechanism must be in place to track current and future inquiries and applications.

Applicant Tracking

During the last nursing shortage, inquiries were usually tracked by hand, if tracked at all. A number of formats were available that assisted in the tallying of responses to advertisements and other recruitment events. A few hospitals invested in computer programs that assisted in this effort. These programs were generally designed in-house and were predictably expensive.

The advent and evolution of the microcomputer have produced software programs that have revolutionized all areas of business and are now available to recruitment professionals. While data collection activities can still be maintained manually, it does not make sense to do so when both the hardware and the software for such programs are surprisingly inexpensive.

A number of software programs are available that can be custom-designed to capture the unique features of any nursing climate. Most software programs provide word-processing capabilities that allow detailed and painless written follow-up to all inquiries and applications. Some software programs allow the transfer of data to a "hired" file so that the career-planning goals of the new employee can be tracked and supported. A number of programs allow for both generic and custom reports that yield the information necessary for evaluating the recruitment program. A few programs offer a financial component that will provide cost per inquiry, applicant, and hire. Demographics can be tracked and "tickler" files can be automated to ensure that every effort is made to recruit for those hard-to-fill positions. Clinical and subspecialty banks can be developed. Those in college can be tracked throughout their academic careers. Reasons why an applicant rejects an offer of employment or why the hospital rejects an applicant can be collected. The uses of automated applicant-tracking systems are limited only by the recruiter's creativity. Given the above and future capabilities, it is wise to give serious consideration to the purchase and implementation of an automated applicant-tracking system. In many settings an automated applicant-tracking system may equate to up to half of a full-time equivalent.

Other Budgetary Considerations

The amount of money that has been spent on nurse recruitment often comes as a great shock to those joining the nurse recruitment effort. In the last shortage, resources seemed a little easier to come by than in today's arena. No matter how much of an investment is made in nurse recruitment, the real cost of establishing and/or maintaining the recruitment effort should be researched. Where the invest-ment is made is usually determined by the nurse recruitment manager. It is of paramount importance, however, that the actions taken by the manager reflect the philosophy and mission of the recruitment/retention committee. It is vitally important that the nurse recruitment manager has the committee's support at every juncture.

Costs (direct, indirect, and hidden) need to be addressed. Establishing a recruitment program requires startup money that will not need to be invested later in the maintenance of an established program. Retention budgets can range from an annual nurses' day advertisement to sophisticated facility-based newsletters and journals. Scholarships, loan programs, and referral and relocation budgets can be sizable. Personnel replacement costs for internal and external recruitment events cannot be overlooked. It has been the practice of many hospitals to establish a nurse recruitment cost center to assist in tracking costs. It is also wise to establish a nurse retention cost center to accomplish the same purpose. The keys to successful recruitment and retention planning and budget management lie in the abilities of the nurse recruitment manager and the support given by key members of the health care team.

RETENTION PLAN

Recruitment programs and retention programs must be managed in concert with one another. Marketing a hospital's nursing image is based on how that hospital views and supports the professional nurse in his or her clinical or administrative setting. Some health care facilities have initiated one position when an individual manages both recruitment and retention programs. Others have developed the role of retention manager, and that individual works closely with the nurse recruitment manager. Some hospitals have highly defined retention programs; other retention programs are sometimes vague or are dictated, in part, by labor contracts; and some hospitals simply have no retention plans in place. It is of little benefit to develop a recruitment plan if a retention plan is not given equal attention. Where the nurse recruiter fits into retention planning will vary, but as a minimum standard the nurse recruiter must serve as a consultant to nurse retention activities.

Where the nurse recruiter can offer immense service is in the area of interim or retention interviews. After the newly hired RN has been employed for two to three months, the nurse recruiter reinterviews that RN. Questions are asked about the satisfiers and dissatisfiers of the position, work group, and unit/hospital environment. The recruitment process can be evaluated to discover what information was missed or not sufficiently stressed. Questions can be asked as to what works well in the environment, what elements should be incorporated in recruitment/retention planning, and how that RN is interfacing with the philosophy, mission, and vision of the nursing department. Of greatest value is the implied statement that the individual nurse is of great value to the organization and his or her feedback is of importance.

It is suggested that the individual who initially guided the RN through the recruitment-employment process be the one conducting the reinterview. If sensitive employee relations problems arise, they can be channeled to the proper resources. Ideally, the RN should be reinterviewed on a periodic basis to maintain the open dialogue. Later, career-planning issues may be addressed and appropriate referrals can be made. This type of activity is not intended to circumvent the manager of that employee, but to complement the manager's staff development activities.

Exit interviews have long been a part of the personnel process, and many view these interviews as ''too little too late.'' Clearly, much information can be gleaned from exit interviews. However, given the choice, most recruitment professionals would prefer that time and energy be given to retention interviews.

NETWORKING

One of the most interesting ironies in the field of nurse recruitment is that many times a nurse recruiter's fiercest competitor is also that nurse recruiter's closest supporter. In the beginnings of nurse recruitment, an atmosphere was created that encouraged information sharing and promoted ethical recruitment and employment practices. The informal philosophy was that a nurse lost to a competitor was a nurse gained to the community. It was considered good practice to refer actively those RNs for whom there were no openings in the recruiter's facility. Because of chronic cost constraints, joint recruitment ventures were undertaken by some hospitals in order to ensure maximum visibility. Statistics were comfortably shared among nurse recruiters so that local and regional profiles could be established and progress could be measured. Typically, the nurse recruiter was constantly under great pressure to ''get nurses,'' and because nurse recruitment tended to be an isolated function, peer support was sought from other nurse recruiters in the community. The expansion of local chapters of the NANR led to a newly found atmosphere of power and influence in matters affecting the local nurse recruitment community. These groups were not shy about addressing issues that were barriers to ethical nurse recruitment practices.

The events of the mid-1980s led to a hiatus in nurse recruitment activities in some parts of the country. Today, however, the break is over and nurse recruitment is again a hot issue. In many cases, a new generation of nurse recruiters is emerging, and experienced nurse recruiters are highly sought after. The NAHCR has been revitalized, as have local and regional chapters of that organization. Networking is strong and loud and passionate. Community power is again being recognized, and mistakes are being shared.

In order to benefit from the growing available resources, hospitals should support and encourage their nurse recruitment personnel to become involved in the local chapter of the NAHCR. The organization can be contacted at:

National Association for Health Care Recruitment
P.O. Box 5769
Akron, OH 44372
(216)867-3088

SUMMARY

There is no exact formula for successful nurse recruitment. However, if the foundation is properly laid, success will likely follow. The key element is to recruit the best person available to manage the nurse recruitment program. Internal and external assessments need to be made and a recruitment plan developed. A recruitment/retention committee should be formed to advise, monitor, and promote the recruitment program. Cost analyses need to be obtained and strategies developed. Data collection procedures should be in place, and retention planning should be documented. Finally, partnerships should be in place on all levels to ensure that there are no internal obstacles to providing nursing care to patients and their families.

NOTES

1. National Commission on Nursing, *Initial Report and Preliminary Recommendations* (Chicago: Hospital Research and Educational Trust, 1981), 5.

2. American Hospital Association, *The Nursing Shortage: Facts, Figures, and Feelings* (Chicago: American Hospital Association, 1987), 51.

3. Mary D. Naylor and Marian B. Sherman, "Wanted: The Best and the Brightest," *American Journal of Nursing* 87 (December 1987):1601.

Chapter 8

Incentive Programs for Nurse Retention

Donna D. Young

Hospitals and health care facilities cannot operate without nurses. How do you keep a loyal staff content? What keeps nurses on the job? Strategic planning to establish rapport among the professional staff and giving full credit for the professional work they do are crucial. Incentive programs for retention should address respect, responsibility, accountability, recognition, advancement, decision making, education, and environment. Nursing has dealt with many professional issues and dilemmas since the time of the Florence Nightingale crusade. The supply of nursing human resources in the late 1980s is one of the most critical issues the profession has had to face. Quick-fix and short-term solutions are not the answer.

STRATEGIES FOR RETENTION PROGRAMS

Long-term strategic plans are a must. "If the leadership in nursing is strong enough to unite all factions, and if strategic plans are developed to promote nursing, the profession will become stronger. If not, patient care will be performed by less competent people and the profession will deteriorate."[1]

Robert L. Veninga[2] cites four strategies to resolve a crisis, that crisis being nursing human resources:

1. Be truthful about the crisis.
2. Let the staff know that everything possible will be done to protect jobs.
3. Assemble the most talented and creative people, and ask them collectively to address the problems contributing to the crisis.
4. Create a vision. Remember that crises can be the impetus for organizational growth.[3]

Retention of nurses begins at recruitment time. Individual needs and goals are established. Feedback and monitors are used to evaluate the success of the retention. The relationship of recruitment and retention is demonstrated with an interdependent loop.[4] (See Figure 8-1.)

The retention program, interdependent with the recruitment program, requires long-term administrative commitment and support. The outcome of nursing staffing can affect the fiscal position of the hospital, jeopardize the public image for the hospital, and affect medical staff relationships. The hospital administration must have control over the recruitment/retention program, a program based on strategies for long-term results.[5] This is accomplished by direct communications with the manager entrusted to this project. The communication structure model in Figure 8-2 delineates evaluation, feedback, and accountability and depicts the interdependent relationships.[6]

ENVIRONMENT FOR JOB SATISFACTION

A satisfying work environment is the key to the success of an organization and a critical factor in retention. In the health care environment problems have arisen as a result of economic structures, society, women's changing roles, and the nursing profession itself. The environment in the work place must answer the needs of the staff members. Needs that have been identified by professional nurses are:[7]

- rewards of patient care
- possibility of change
- flexibility of the job

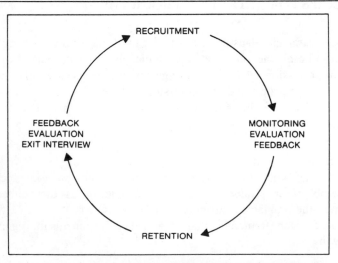

Figure 8-1 Recruitment-Retention Loop. *Source:* Reprinted from "Plan Development for a Nurse Recruitment-Retention Program" by L. Louise Wall in *Journal of Nursing Administration*, Vol. 18, No. 2, p. 21, with permission of J.B. Lippincott Company, © February 1988.

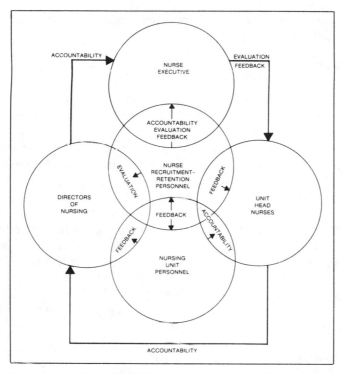

Figure 8-2 Communication Structure Model. *Source:* Reprinted from "Plan Development for a Nurse Recruitment-Retention Program" by L. Louise Wall in *Journal of Nursing Administration*, Vol. 18, No. 2, p. 25, with permission of J.B. Lippincott Company, © February 1988.

- personal enjoyment and fulfillment
- sense of mission
- belief in nursing's possibilities
- pride in the profession

Rewards of Patient Care

A system that recognizes autonomy in decision making, a professional role within the health care team, and opportunity for patient teaching and development of the nursing process promotes rewards from patient care.

Possibility of Change

The nurse executive and the entire administrative staff must introduce, promote, and support positive changes. The administrative staff must support the liaison between the nursing staff and the medical staff. Innovative plans of care delivery, monitoring systems, and entrepreneurships must be encouraged and supported at the administrative level.

Flexibility of the Job

Hospital health care delivery is a 24-hour operation. Patient, family, and physician needs must be met at all times. Flexibility of hours, assignments, and positions meets this need. Managing flexibility can become burdensome, but if goals and objectives are stated and action plans are implemented, job satisfaction is increased and the needs of the patient, family, and physician are met.

Personal Enjoyment and Fulfillment

Health care facilities must provide for the fulfillment that the nurse professional seeks from the job. Nursing is a profession that can offer variety, excitement of pace, and opportunity to care for others. In order to provide for this fulfillment, a facility must have a thorough orientation and/or preceptor program in place. These programs establish the ''feeling of the work place.'' Investment in indoctrination is invaluable. A team effort evident throughout the organization promotes fulfillment of the job as well as personal enjoyment.

Sense of Mission

Health care, as an industry, has established the goal of providing accessible, cost-effective, and high-quality care to the consumer. The nursing staff needs to know the goals and objectives that are in place to meet that mission. Nurses are the deliverers of the care, the product of the health care industry, and must be an integral part of the mission.

Belief in Nursing's Possibilities

The changing roles for women, the technology in health care, research development, and reimbursement programs have opened up vast horizons for nursing professionals. The nurse professional in hospitals is looking for the expanded role and recognition of the expertise achieved through education and experience. Administrative staffs must recognize this need and support programs for the development of role expansion, particularly as it relates to the medical staff.

Pride in the Profession

Pride in the profession has been emphasized over and over in recent years. In their dedication to care delivery, nurses fell behind in the marketing/promotion of the profession. Hospitals can assist this increase in pride by promoting the profession through the media and by utilization of the nurse professional as a valuable resource for any facility project or community effort.

INCENTIVE PROGRAMS FOR RETENTION

The beginning of this chapter was dedicated to an overview of the problem, a strategy guideline, and job satisfaction requirements. The remainder of this chapter discusses specific programs as guidelines for retention. It is important to emphasize that any program adopted by a facility will achieve success only by establishing the mission, goals, and objectives and by involving the nurse professionals in the program from its inception.

The Nurse Entrepreneur

Nurses are developing new careers in nursing. The educational background of the nurse affords preparation in interpersonal and counseling skills. Organizational and cost-control skills are also part of the education and practice of the nurse professional. Research and/or investigations, assessment, and implementation of a plan of care also prepare them for new careers. Nurses are now product managers and developers of revenue sources and are being sought by major industries involved with technology, computers, and personnel management.

A health care facility would be wise to evaluate the entrepreneur value of its nursing staff. Historically, hospitals have looked to the business school graduate for development of products and to the marketer for their promotion. Facilities will enhance retention of nursing staff members by involving nurses in project planning, research and development, and systems implementation. The result is a cohesive health care team, clinically and operationally united and loyal to the facility and its mission.

Recognition Programs for Retention

The section "Environment for Job Satisfaction" referenced personal enjoyment and job fulfillment as strong needs of the nurse professional. Fulfillment and enjoyment are emotions that are best served when shared or recognized. Human resource management studies have proven over and over that more productivity results from positive recognition than from negative criticism.

Performance Appraisal

The most important tool for recognition is the performance appraisal. In a job satisfaction survey conducted by Healthcare Medical Center of Tustin,[8] timely performance appraisals were at the top of the satisfaction criteria perceived by the employee. Performance appraisals require advance preparation by the supervisor administering the appraisal and by the staff member receiving the appraisal. This is an opportune time to evaluate and revise the job description, praise the performance of the individual, and set goals and objectives for future development and contribution to the facility.

Planning the appraisal interview indicates to the employee the importance of his or her role within the team. The human resource is the most valuable asset to any facility, and the performance appraisal is the opportune format for recognition.

Guidelines. The following steps are guidelines to successful appraisal interviews:

- Prepare in advance. Review the facts, give the employee time to prepare, and schedule the appropriate time in advance.
- Put the employee at ease. Explain why you are having the meeting, and ask what the employee hopes to gain from the meeting.
- Conduct the interview. Ask the employee to review his or her performance level during the past year. Compare your views with those of the employee. Keep the meeting positive by being sensitive to self-esteem. Be specific about areas needing improvement, listen sincerely, ask the employee how he or she can improve, mutually agree on objectives for the upcoming year, and end the appraisal on a positive note.

Benefits to the Health Care Facility. The performance appraisal system offers the following benefits to the employer:

- Systematic documentation and monitoring are provided.
- A method of coaching and counseling is achieved.
- Two-way communication is developed.
- Internal improvement is accomplished.
- Employees are motivated toward excellence.
- Positive achievements are rewarded.
- Rewards for nonperformance are minimized.
- High achievers are attracted and retained.
- Returns on compensation dollars are maximized.

Benefits to the Employee. The performance appraisal system provides these benefits to the nurse:

- Job expectations are clarified.
- An opportunity is provided to participate in department planning.
- An opportunity is provided to discuss job performance.

- The individual's importance is reinforced.
- An incentive is given to achieve and improve.
- Employees are recognized.
- Satisfaction is gained about personal achievements.

Letters of Recognition

Letters of recognition from the administrator or corporate official take so little time but can be one of the best methods of recognition to use. Management and supervisory personnel must communicate events or performances by staff members to the administrator or corporate official. Letters should be presented with some ceremony befitting the occasion, such as a staff meeting or a special coffee break set up purposely for the presentation. It is important to note that positive efforts for recognition that will contribute to retention of staff do not always have to be a draw on financial budgets.

Apple Program

In 1985, a peer recognition program to elevate staff morale at Healthcare Medical Center of Tustin was established by Sandy Davidson, human resources director.[9] The program was so successful that it is now a corporate policy, and the program has been implemented in each of the corporation's 23 facilities. The program allows an employee to be recognized for a special deed, a special word, or just "being there." The recognition comes from patients, peers, supervisors, physicians, or staff members from other departments. The recognition is submitted in writing on a simple form. The individual is presented with a red apple pin by the administrative person responsible for the department. After accumulating five red apples, the individual receives a silver apple; after five silver apples, he or she receives a gold apple. The gold apple is presented to the employee by the administrator (chief executive officer [CEO]) at the facility's department managers' meeting. With the implementation of this program, morale stays at a high level. On rare occasions, when times get tough and morale ebbs, the apple program is utilized even more, indicating its value and purpose that recognition is so important to satisfaction and ultimate retention.

Staffing Patterns As a Program for Retention

Staffing patterns are discussed in depth in Chapter 10, but staffing patterns affect retention so strongly that it must be included in the text of this chapter. The nurse professional will remain at the health care facility that provides a staff that renders measurable quality of care. What criteria are used to measure quality? Since care delivery is judged by the consumer, I feel that it is appropriate to cite the criteria of the consumer.

- no complications that might result in death, disability or disfigurement, or a slowed recovery
- improvement in medical condition and ability to function
- improvement in, or at least maintenance of, morale
- a pleasant, comfortable stay[10]

Any nurse professional or staff manager will review these criteria and state that appropriate and safe staffing will meet these quality criteria. Appropriate staff management means incorporating acuity classification systems, skill mix, and the physical plant into the plan. Hours per patient day and full-time equivalents should not be the sole criteria for staffing. A productivity management report is a tool that can be used by nursing management to present a cost-effective staffing pattern to the CEO and chief financial officer (CFO).

Alternative Care Delivery

Alternative care delivery systems are being tested in various parts of the country. Three new models of nursing practice were introduced at Johns Hopkins Hospital, Baltimore, Maryland, in an effort to use personnel more efficiently and address sources of job dissatisfaction contributing to high turnover.[11] All models had three common features: autonomous decision making, decentralized responsibility, and annual salaries instead of hourly wages. All models resulted in increase in job satisfaction; decrease in turnover; decrease in costs associated with recruitment, orientations, and use of registry; and significant increase in productivity.[12]

Another alternative care delivery system, called Primary Practice Partners, is being tested and was summarized in the March 1988 issue of *Nursing Management*.

Flexibility

All hospitals are faced with higher acuity levels, fewer staff resources, increased productivity, and lower budgets for the nursing staff. Variable staffing is a management function of scheduling labor resources to match optimally the work available. Each facility needs to develop flexible, highly trained employees capable of responding to the changing demands of operations.

Computerization

Computerization can enhance significantly the speed, quality, comprehensiveness, and effectiveness of patient-specific care plans.[13] Computerization in the form of order/entry software, pharmacy medication administration records, and computer-printed cumulative laboratory reports assist the nurse in more efficient quality care. Computerization will raise the performance satisfaction of the professional nurse by allowing more direct patient care. Increased performance satisfaction contributes to retention.

Staff Development Effects on Retention

Technological advancements, reimbursement programs, and the extended age of patients are factors nurses must be aware of, as each nurse is continually required to develop new skills, new knowledge, and new terms. The health care facility must be prepared to meet the challenges for staff development.

Continuing education classes must be ongoing and must address all disciplines of nursing personnel. Some facilities may be limited in staff development but should consider a staff development resource pool or access to a consortium. Utilization of in-house staff expertise and recognition of that expertise in a faculty role will enhance the staff development process.

Career ladders for all levels of nursing skills are used in many areas of the country. University hospitals are a good resource for information on clinical ladders, as are the professional journals. Career ladders recognize additional training in a specialized area, recognize years of practice, and recognize achievement and commitment to a facility. Nursing is a profession that has reached a reasonable monetary compensation at the entry level, but compensation has not progressed for additional years of practice. Clinical ladders can assist in meeting the recognition and financial needs of the dedicated, loyal professional.

Advanced degrees for the professional are becoming imperative as the industry changes. Society today is such that work and additional schooling are financially prohibitive to many. Health care facilities should budget monies to be used by the staff for pursuing advanced degrees. Other industries provide this type of reimbursement, and it is time for health care facilities and government programs to meet this need of its professionals.

Through staff development, the nursing staff can promote reentry of nurses into the work force. A pride of ownership is brought out in this type of program and results in retention. Nurse reentry programs at facility levels, apposed to outside colleges, can form a bond with that nurse and meet recruitment needs. This will affect retention, and, as stated earlier, retention starts with recruitment.

Monetary Compensations for Retention

Figure 8-3 gives a summary by percentages of what nurses want most from a job. The survey shows that 51 percent surveyed felt that salary was important. [14]

The crisis of the 1980s has resulted in the most competitive war for wages ever seen in the profession. Salary or monetary compensation is a hotbed for discussion among nurses, managers, CEOs, and CFOs.

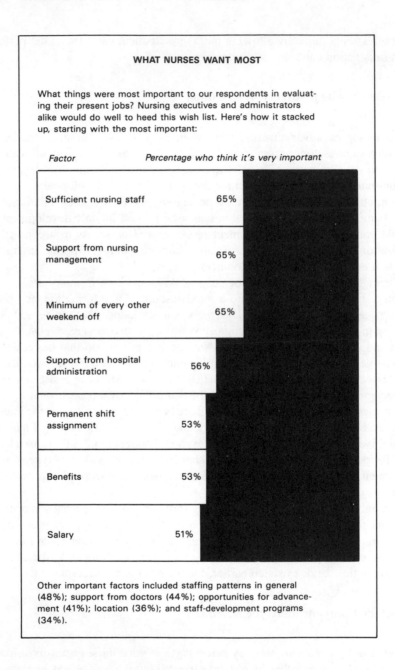

Figure 8-3 What Nurses Want Most from a Job. *Source:* Reprinted from *Nursing 88,* Vol. 18, No. 2, p. 38, with permission of Springhouse Corporation, © February 1988.

Nurse executives are placed in a dual position. On one side, budget constraints and reimbursements do not allow for the salary demands; on the other side, salary compensation is viewed as a factor in elevating the status of the professional nurse.

Career Goals

Career goals are an alternative method of salary compensation. National Medical Enterprises (NME) started a pilot program with employees for career learning with compensation and scholarship support. The program promoted advanced training and education toward a higher skill level, i.e., nurse assistant to registered nurse (RN). The estimated cost to train an aide to be an RN is about $4000. It costs about $2500 to run a classified advertisement for two months in the newspaper.[15]

Cost Savings Incentives

Sharing in savings incentives programs helps employees achieve success. This type of program is set up in a way that the staff shares in the cost savings by improving productivity and efficiency.[16] (See Exhibit 8-1.)

Professional Salaries

In 1986, St. Joseph's Hospital, Atlanta, Georgia,[17] implemented a professional salary system.

- All earnings were stated as annual full-time salaries rather than blue-collar wages per hour.
- Salaries rewarded nurses for past experience and education.
- Salary ranges were created to allow managers to negotiate with candidates.

The results were a reduction of vacancies from 50 to 16 in 3 months, reduced costs of orientation and temporary agencies, and better retention response to competition.

Presenting this type of concept to the board requires planning, background, and financial impact studies to support the proposal.[18]

Differentials, Bonuses, Paid Time Off, Salaried Employees

Hospital facilities offer a variety of financial differentials, bonuses, and incentives to attract and retain staff. The most difficult areas of retention are the critical care units. Historically, critical care staff members have been compensated for the assignment. With the acuity level increasing, the demand for a qualified and competent staff has increased; subsequently, the law of supply and demand is in effect.

Exhibit 8-1 Examples of Hospital Incentive Programs

---

1. Baptist Hospital, Pensacola, Florida
   Department involved: Laundry
   Date: 1963
   Goal: Produce 10 percent more clean laundry with acceptable quality without hiring
               any new personnel.
   Incentive: Employees to receive one-half of the money new people would have been paid if
               they had been hired to handle the increased laundry.

   Results: 1. Production was achieved.
               2. Machine malfunctions diminished.
               3. Employees then earning $225 per month received incentive checks from
                  $35 to $45 per month.
               4. People found joy in achievement.
               5. Other departments expressed interest in becoming involved in an incentive
                  program.
               6. Overtime hours diminished.

2. Holzer Medical Center, Gallipolis, Ohio
   Name of Program: ESP—Employees Saving Plan
   Date: 1977
   Departments involved: Entire hospital
   Goal: Cut hospital costs by minimizing waste and completing assignments more
               efficiently.
   Incentive: Half of savings resulted from contained costs to be divided among the staff
               according to the number of hours worked.
   Results: 1. In 1977, the plan resulted in a bonus of $107.80 per employee.
               2. Employees became more responsible in saving money (i.e., shut off
                  lights, used stairs instead of elevator to save electricity).
               3. Staff initiated money-saving ideas.

   Source: Reprinted with permission from "Incentive Programs: A Way to Cost Containment" by Carol
   Wolmering in *Nursing Management*, pp. 49–51, © September 1987.

The types of differentials that can be offered are percentages over base for the evening and midnight shifts, weekend differential for scheduled weekends, time and a half for part-time employees who work an unscheduled shift, and differentials for relief of a management position or special service.

Because of economics, many salaried employees have been seeking part-time registry work to supplement incomes. Financial impact reports can be done to offer the salaried employee a bonus incentive to work a staff shift in a staffing shortage. (Financial regulations and adherence to labor regulations must be established.)

The issue of wages and working conditions must be addressed. Operational costs put facilities at a disadvantage over agencies that provide manpower alone.

Joint efforts of hospital councils, labor departments, agencies, and nurses need to be made to meet the financial crunch.

Benefits Promote Retention

Benefit packages for employees are at the top of the list of needs when employees are surveyed. Benefits are perceived by staff members as deserved, not earned. Benefits come in all kinds of packages. The most obvious, of course, is health, dental, and eye care. Health care facilities are high users of health care benefits; therefore, premium rates are evident. Some facilities are self-insured; others contract the insurance. Health care facilities can opt to offer a write-off of deductibles based on the directed use of the facility or caregiver.

Retirement programs, particularly with the tax law changes, are of keen interest to staff members and certainly contribute to the retention of the longer-term employee.

Employee assistance programs for the impaired professional are being established more frequently. The profession of nursing and other health care-related professions are high-stress occupations, and facilities need to provide for assistance programs that will keep the staff member in the productive work force.

Employee health programs staffed by physician assistants and/or nurse practitioners can help reduce financial burdens on families and are truly looked upon as benefits. This type of program also reduces the cost of insurance reimbursement for self-insured facilities and provides a more efficient cost-effective utilization of services.

Economic conditions often make it necessary for both parents to be employed. Facilities that can provide on-site child care have a definite advantage. Other facilities should evaluate subsidized programs or child care reimbursements as a tool for retention. Demographic surveys should be conducted to determine the economic feasibility of an off-site-contracted facility.

Vacations, sick time, and/or paid time off are also perceived as deserved, not earned. Paid time off is being used more frequently than sick time. If sick time is accrued as a benefit, some facilities offer a 50 percent pay back for sick time not taken within an appraisal year. The professional nurse is looking for increased vacation time. Financial impacts must be prepared to justify extended time off. This may prove to be a strong retention tool for facilities with high turnovers.

Another financial benefit to the professional nurse is to offer a choice of salary category. The full-time employee receives full benefits; part-time, pro-rated benefits. An alternative would be to offer 20 percent above base and forego accrual of vacation, holiday, sick, and medical benefits. Varied ways of increasing the take-home pay for the individual are all benefits that promote retention by giving the individual control of the choice.

The staff employee responds to the benefits of group social activities or spontaneous treats such as an annual holiday party with dinner and dancing, a family picnic, special ice cream socials, or a pizza night for the midnight shifts. The social events need to put the employee in the limelight, but they should be served by the administration.

Personal recognition of employees by supervisors and administrative staff is beneficial to the facility and promotes the feeling of belonging by the employee. Once an employee feels a part of the organization, retention follows.

Marketing the Nursing Profession Promotes Retention

Nursing services are activities and satisfactions that are provided in the delivery of the health care product. The skillful use of public relations in marketing nursing services will facilitate the goal of retention.

Public relations change the attitudes and the image of the product. Nursing is a profession that needs to change its image from taskmaster to professional caregiver. Marketing is a managerial process of identifying, analyzing, choosing, and exploiting market opportunities to fulfill missions and objectives.[19] Public relations can influence the attitudes of consumers; by promoting the nursing profession, the nurse will be enthusiastic about the job and the institution, producing a high level of satisfaction and ultimate retention.

There are tools to use to implement action after quantitative studies have been carried out to assess the market.

Written Material

Written material must make a statement and be readable, interesting, and professional. The written material must be presented in an aesthetic format.

Audiovisual Material

Audiovisual material can develop effective public relations. It should be prepared with the same professionalism and aesthetics as written material.

Corporate Identity

Corporate identity, logos, signs, uniforms, and the internal feeling of the organization are definite public relation tools. The guest services policy presented at all levels within an organization is a strong corporate identity.

News Releases

News releases are assigned editorial space as opposed to paid advertising space. News releases have high levels of credibility because they are not paid advertisements. They are presented as news and therefore attract the reader who does not respond to advertising. This medium is excellent for marketing services and should be utilized frequently by nurse executives in a cooperative effort with the marketing department.

Speeches

Personal contact is best remembered, and establishing a speakers' bureau as a community resource provides a direct contact method. The nurse executive collaborates with the marketing department to formulate a directory of topics and assemble a roster of nurse presenters who are available to the community. The community then develops an association with the nurse professional through the personal contact. The nurse receives recognition, sells the organization by representation, and feels an integral part of the mission. Buying into an organization is a key factor for retention.

Nursing is a profession that needs to market itself. There needs to be public awareness of the profession and its impact on health care services in the future.

SUMMARY

Incentive programs for retention must be planned with long-term strategies. The positive environment of the work place and communication at all levels are paramount to successful retention programs. Job satisfaction criteria must be supported at administrative levels. Recognition as a professional contributor to the care delivery team results in a satisfaction level that promotes retention. Attention must be given to acuity assessments and assignments of skill levels. Monetary reimbursement changes need to be made to promote the professionalism of the nurse. Benefit packages must be designed to meet the needs of the staff and the organization. Marketing and public relations are key factors to changing the image of the nurse to the nurse professional.

Individual organizations must assess, plan, implement, monitor, and evaluate incentive programs that will lead to retention in the particular facility. There is no set formula, and there are as many variables as there are programs available.

NOTES

1. Editors of *Nursing 88*, "Nursing Shortage Poll Report," *Nursing 88* 18, no. 2 (February 1988): 35.

2. Robert L. Veninga (University of Minnesota, Minneapolis, Minn.), personal communication.

3. Robert L. Veninga, "When Bad Things Happen to Good Nursing Departments," *Journal of Nursing Administration* 17, no. 2 (February 1987): 35–40.

4. L. Louise Wall, "Plan Development for a Nurse Recruitment-Retention Program," *Journal of Nursing Administration* 18, no. 2 (February 1988): 21.

5. Ibid., 21.

6. Ibid., 25.

7. Editors of *Nursing 88*, "Nursing Shortage Poll Report," 41.

8. *Job Satisfaction Survey* (Tustin, Calif.: Healthcare Medical Center of Tustin, September 1987).

9. Sandy Davidson, *Peer Recognition Program* (Tustin, Calif.: Healthcare Medical Center of Tustin, 1985).

10. American Association of Retired Persons, *Exchange* 2, no. 3 (December 1987–January 1988).

11. *Nursing Business News* 3, no. 6 (December 1987/January 1988).

12. "Professional Nursing Practices Models," *Nursing Economic$* (July–August 1987).

13. Shirly Walters, "Computerized Care Plans Help Nurses Achieve Quality Patient Care," *Journal of Nursing Administration* 16, no. 11 (November 1986).

14. Editors of *Nursing 88*, "Nursing Shortage Poll Report," 38.

15. James Brice, "Recruiting, Retaining Nurses Requires Innovative Ideas," *Healthweek* (February 29, 1988).

16. Carolyn Wolmering, "Incentive Programs: A Way to Cost Containment," *Nursing Management* (September 1987): 49–51.

17. Kathy McDonagh, *Professional Salary System* (Atlanta: St. Joseph's Hospital, 1986).

18. *Aspen Advisor for Nurse Executives* 2, no. 7 (April 1987).

19. Caroline Camuna, "Using Public Relations To Market Nursing Services," *Journal of Nursing Administration* 16, no. 10 (October 1986): 26–30.

Chapter 9

Career Ladders for Nurse Retention

Abby M. Heydman and Nancy Madsen

CLINICAL LADDERS IN NURSING PRACTICE

Historical Overview

Planning for one's career advancement is a concept familiar to many businessmen, but it is one that is relatively new to members of the nursing profession. In this predominantly female discipline, the majority of nurses have traditionally viewed their employment as episodic. Some of the factors influencing nurses' decisions to participate in the labor force include level of spousal income, amount of nonemployment income such as inheritance, presence of children, age, and level of nursing education, as well as factors related to the clinical environment.[1] Likewise, until recent years employers have also viewed nurses as a transient work force, and compensation and employment policies have been designed to attract new nurses into the work force rather than to promote retention and advancement of currently employed staff.

The relatively few nurses who in years past made a commitment to nursing as a full-time occupation often received their education in hospital-based diploma programs, and they stayed in their home institution, developing strong institutional loyalties. This loyalty, coupled with clinical expertise, sometimes led to advancement into nursing administration or staff development, which provided the only means of career advancement. Promotions and increase in salary required that nurses leave the bedside and assume administrative or teaching roles. Advancement within clinical practice roles was not available, and differentiation in salary between novice and experienced nurses was minimal.

As cultural values and economic conditions changed in recent years, women have moved into the work force in progressively larger numbers and have

Note: The authors gratefully acknowledge the assistance of Mary M. Karr, who assisted in the literature review for this chapter.

expanded into occupational areas once denied them. For example, women now comprise over 40 percent of business and law school graduates and over 30 percent of medical school graduates.[2] Additionally, women now comprise an ever-increasing proportion of middle management and are beginning to achieve executive-level positions. These and a number of other factors require a new perspective on the role and advancement of women in the work place.

More women are also actively employed in nursing than ever before, and more of these nurses are staying in the work force, although many are doing so on a part-time basis. In years to come, the number of women going into the work force will not change measurably.[3] This factor, coupled with a declining population of high school graduates, will create a labor shortage, not only in nursing, but in most fields. Hospitals and other health care employers will be competing not only to hire, but to retain, well-educated, experienced workers. These shifts indicate that employers must develop employment policies and compensation packages that enhance employee retention and institutional loyalty.

At the same time, nursing has declined as a career choice as evidenced by sharply reduced nursing program enrollments in recent years. A 1986 survey of nursing schools by the National League for Nursing revealed that the number of students graduating declined about 7 percent that year.[4] An increasing demand for registered nurses (RNs), coupled with a decline in the number of RN graduates, has created a nursing shortage that has driven wage rates up, making staff nursing a more attractive option than ever before. Yet nurses remaining in practice are becoming increasingly dissatisfied with the lack of potential gross career earnings in comparison with other occupations and are demanding more opportunity for career progression. McKibbin's 1988 "Analysis of Career Earnings in Nursing and Other Occupations" underscores the severe salary compression in clinical staff nursing positions and the lack of career progression opportunities for nurses as compared with other occupations. For example, chemists' career earning growth equaled 231 percent; engineers, 183 percent; personnel clerks/assistants, 67 percent; general clerks, 84 percent; secretaries, 71 percent; and staff nurses, 36 percent over the course of their careers.[5] Salary compression is likely to be the major issue in nurse-employer negotiations for some time to come. This issue must be addressed if we want to improve recruitment to the field. Studies of college freshmen women indicate that financial reward is far more salient to young adult women than ever before, and this may be a major factor in the rejection of a nursing career by college women.[6]

During the nursing shortages of the 1970s, the issue of inadequate career advancement began to be addressed. More women began staying in the work force for longer periods, and nurses expressed dissatisfaction with the limited career advancement available in clinical settings. This unresolved issue was noted in many nursing studies as a significant impediment to the recruitment and retention of nurses.[7] It was within this climate of rapid social change that clinical ladder advancement programs were initiated. Briefly defined, a clinical ladder advancement program is a system for promotion of nurses, designed to provide rewards for education, experience, and expert clinical skill. Clinical ladder advancement systems include incremental steps in salary related to increasingly comprehensive functions in clinical, administrative, and/or educational roles. These programs are developed within the nursing department's philosophy and goals to accomplish specific departmental objectives, including retention of experienced RN staff. Performance criteria are developed for each step or level on the ladder, and these descriptions are used in the appointment of nurses for each level and for subsequent performance evaluations.[8]

Clinical Ladder Models

Clinical ladders in hospitals were originally designed to increase staff nurse satisfaction and nurse retention by tangibly rewarding staff nurses for clinical skill and judgment developed through experience and education. The design of clinical ladders has taken many forms that have evolved to reward clinical nursing skills in various roles and positions. Initially many institutions developed one-track clinical advancement ladders, primarily in bedside clinical roles within specialties such as critical care, medical-surgical nursing, and perinatal nursing. These institutions developed criteria to delineate clearly the degrees of clinical skill in three to five levels of progressive staff nurse advancement within the clinical area. Stanford University's four-level clinical ladder for staff nurses is typical of this model. Nurse manager and staff development positions are not included in this system.

Other designers attempted to incorporate more than staff nurses in their models by developing multiple-track advancement pathways. For example, the University of California San Francisco nursing department developed a clinical and an administrative track whereby the candidate, having ascended through two preliminary levels of progression, could then choose a clinical or an administrative track for additional advancement. In this model, there are five levels of advancement for clinical staff nurses. The clinical nurse III position is considered a clinical expert on her unit and holds a leadership position. Two higher-level clinical positions, clinical nurse IV and clinical nurse V, are held by clinical specialists with graduate degrees in nursing.[9]

In yet another variation, the Oregon Health Sciences University Hospital developed clinical tracks for almost all nursing positions, including educators, infection control nurses, and quality assurance coordinators, in addition to clinical tracks for staff nurses and administrative tracks for assistant head nurses and head nurses. This career advancement system recognizes the need to correct the problems of salary compression and narrow role development in positions that nurses may hold for many years.

In some instances, clinical ladder designers have added educational components not required for basic or minimal job performance in the clinical role. For example, in some settings such as the University of California San Francisco, advanced educational degrees are required in order to advance through the higher clinical ladder levels. In contrast, at Oregon Health Sciences University Hospital, nurses with baccalaureate and master's degrees receive additional compensation over and above increments for clinical ladder advancement. These variations reflect differing philosophies on the relationship of education and clinical skill development.

In other settings, the clinical ladder proposal specifies that additional professional expectations are included in the clinical ladder levels. For example, Merritt Peralta Medical Center, Stanford University Hospital, the Oregon Health Sciences University Hospital, and others have integrated professional expectations such as community service, clinical inquiry, publication, and participation in professional organizations into performance criteria for each level of advancement. These expectations are included in order to support complete development of the professional role and to enhance professional involvement and commitment. These expectations also embellish institutional reputation, which enhances recruitment potential.

Similarly, the clinical advancement model at Boston's Beth Israel Hospital, one of the hospitals cited as a national model for nurse retention, includes six levels of clinical practice following the entry level. Advancement requires an increase in clinical competence based on accumulated experience *and* willingness to assume increased responsibility within the nursing department. Integration of clinical practice with educational, managerial, and research activities is required for career advancement in this setting.[10]

One interesting departure from these approaches has been the model developed at the New England Medical Center. This institution chose a professional development program to acknowledge and reward nurses who demonstrate excellence in their profession overall, without tying this to the development of additional clinical expertise. This model seeks to acknowledge those nurses who demonstrate the full professional role, including professional behaviors not specific to their job descriptions. Expected outcomes related to research, education, community involvement, and publication are identified in this program, and a bonus system is used to reward these outcomes.[11] A similar program, called the Incentive Career Mobility Plan, was developed at Medical Center Hospital in Odessa, Texas. One advantage of the type of plan is that it can be used to recognize and reward licensed vocational nurses.[12] Although this model appears promising, it does not address the issue of our need to recognize the development of varying degrees of expert nursing practice or salary compression within usual staff nurse roles. Our experience suggests that recognizing a combination of clinical skill and professional activities provides the greatest opportunity for advancement for the largest number of nurses. Not only is clinical expertise rewarded, but standards of care and professional socialization are also achieved. Comprehensive clinical advancement systems appear to provide maximum benefit to the institution.

Effectiveness of Clinical Ladders

Although little program evaluation research has been reported on clinical ladder programs to date, the literature is replete with assertions that clinical ladders have served their intended purpose of retaining nurses. Initial experience in our own setting indicates that one major benefit of the clinical ladder program is that it increases the institutional loyalty and identification of nurses with the employing institution. Nurses in the clinical ladder system adopt a professional identity over and above that of the usual hourly wage employee. Their investment in the clinical ladder program enhances their investment in the institution, thus increasing their length of employment and likelihood of staying, even during difficult periods.

Experience with clinical ladder programs indicates that there are some general guidelines to follow to facilitate successful implementation of a career advancement program. These include the following:

- *Minimize quotas.* Limiting the number of nurses that can advance can sap motivation and discourage participation. Quotas limit the number of nurses who can be promoted, thus diminishing the impact of the clinical ladder system on nurse retention. Some would argue that a unit may need only a few nurses with higher-level skills on a given unit; thus these positions should be limited just as promotional opportunities in the administrative tract should be limited.[13] However, one could argue that the increasing acuity levels of patients and shortened hospital stays indicate that an investment in the highly skilled nurse will produce its own reward by reducing complications that create significant losses over reimbursement. In addition, the highly skilled nurse can far more readily manage the increasingly complex patients who have become the norm on most of our inpatient units.

- *Maximize staff nurse participation.* Many clinical ladder programs developed by nursing administration and educators do not always reflect the complexities of the staff nurse role at the bedside. Staff nurses are more inclined to participate if the expectations are realistic and match their perceptions of the clinical environment. The involvement of staff nurses in the steering committee that develops the clinical ladder proposal will alleviate this problem.

- *Differentiate between the levels through monetary reward.* In many clinical ladders the incremental increase in monetary reimbursement is so small that it appears to the staff nurse to belittle the effort involved for progression. Some individuals have even argued that salary differentiation is not important in a clinical ladder program, suggesting that recognition by title and job description is reward in itself.[14] This position, although attractive in these days of cost containment, simply flies in the face of data on the salience of financial reward to young men and women today. The clinical ladder system is one meaningful way to address the very real problem of salary compression within the field of nursing.

- *Make monetary rewards directly proportional to the need for retention.* The fact remains that administrative advancement is still more lucrative than clinical advancement. A literature review of this subject reveals that discussion about monetary reward as a benefit to the clinical ladder system was noticeably lacking. In contrast, pages and pages have been written about increased status, increased recognition, additional autonomy, and participation in decision making. If nursing is to be perceived as valuable and as a career worth having, financial rewards will have to reflect that value more directly.

- *Design the program so that the criteria are consistent with program goals.* Sometimes clinical ladder programs are too idealistic and heavily weighted toward professional outcomes that are unrealistic for the practice setting (e.g., programs that emphasize research with a predominately diploma education-based work force). In other cases, the criteria are clinically based with too little attention to professional development, as in the case where years of experience are more heavily weighted than educational preparation. In either case, staff nurse participation will not be as meaningful and the desired outcomes will not be achieved.

Other Career Advancement Options

It should be noted that some institutions have improved nursing retention simply by developing restructured salary systems or through long-term clinical pathways that acknowledge years of experience in the field.[15] On the other hand, at least one study suggests that job enrichment with strong task identity are major issues in improving job satisfaction and retention.[16] Regardless of the career advancement program adopted, hospitals must avoid systems that advance nurses through in a few years, quickly reaching a salary peak and a plateau in assumption of clinical responsibility. Career advancement systems must address the concept of a long-term, perhaps a lifetime, career in clinical nursing. A system that recognizes both functional levels of ability and responsibility and length of service will be required to enhance retention of nurses.[17]

Future of Clinical Ladder Systems

Although clinical ladder systems continue to be developed in response to institutional efforts to retain nurses, they are increasingly subject to reevaluation. Sanford, in a provocative article, questions whether clinical ladders benefit the institution or the individual nurse, and in the larger sense whether they benefit only individual institutions or the nursing profession as a whole. She argues that, because most clinical ladders are institution-specific and because program designers do not use a shared developmental theory, the ladders do not have meaning to the nursing profession as a whole. Sanford also suggests that we have not accurately measured or described excellence in professional nursing practice. She suggests that clinical ladders may benefit the institution by increasing retention and may benefit the individual nurse employed in the institution, but more work is needed to develop accurate measures of clinical mastery that will advance the profession and improve the quality of nursing care.[18] One clinical ladder program that is grounded in differentiation of levels of expert nursing practice is based on Benner's research on the nurse's progression from novice to expert practice.[19] Future research must seek to validate the benefit of experience and expertise to hospitals as they struggle to provide excellent and affordable patient care.

It is true that much more work needs to be done on describing expert nursing practice in order to improve our ability to reward and support these behaviors in the care of patients. On the other hand, our experience with clinical ladder programs in a variety of settings over the past 10 years has helped us to improve career advancement opportunities for increasing numbers of nurses. The next task is to articulate this development to the public and to prospective nurses in order to enhance recruitment to the profession.

CAREER LADDERS IN NURSING EDUCATION

Historical Overview

Career ladders in nursing education are pathways that facilitate upward mobility from one level of nursing education and practice to another. Hypothetically, the student can progress from the level of nurse aide or orderly to licensed vocational nurse (LVN), to RN prepared with an associate degree or diploma in nursing, and on further to baccalaureate, master's, and doctoral degrees in the field. The educational career ladder enables the nurse to move from the bottom level of the hospital nursing hierarchy (nurse aide or orderly) to the top of the hierarchy (nursing chief executive officer [CEO]).

A diagram of this concept would look something like Figure 9-1.

The career ladder concept has been embroiled in controversy within the profession almost from the time it was first suggested. Historically, concerns about a career ladder in nursing emerged as diploma nursing education began to decline as the predominant educational pattern for nurses. The gradual development of baccalaureate nursing programs, along with a growing acceptance of college education for women began highlighting the need for clear patterns of educational advancement for nurses by the early 1950s. The exponential expansion of community and junior college programs further fueled these discussions.

One of the earliest published references to the concept of career ladders in nursing was made by Lassar Gotkin in Mildred Montag's seminal work, *Community College Education for Nursing*. He wrote:

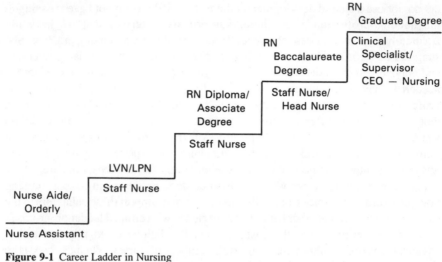

Figure 9-1 Career Ladder in Nursing

Still another proposal is made which is commonly referred to as the "ladder concept." This plan would make it possible for students to enter programs designed to permit the completion of one year with employment possible thereafter as practical nurses; the completion of two years permitting licensure as a registered nurse; an additional two years providing for courses in management and teaching. There is in this plan considerable confusion about the objectives and methodology of technical and professional education.[20]

Although Montag and her associates in the early community college movement were strong advocates of the development of associate degree nursing programs, they had a clear vision about the complementary but differentiated nature of technical and professional education. Her colleague, Louise McManus, in the foreword to the same book noted, "Will not the difference in the fundamental sciences required for professional functions present in nursing the same barriers to progression from technical to professional roles without considerable retraining that it has in engineering?"[21] A similar sentiment was also expressed by Bernice Anderson for the Four State Associate Degree Nursing Project, a Kellogg Foundation project for the development of associate degree programs in California, Texas, Florida, and New York:

> There is no barrier to seeking further education if one is eligible. However, a change in occupational goals does necessitate spending time that may appear to be overlapping. . . . One can move from one educational level to another but "at a price."[22]

Now more than 30 years after Montag's book was published, and 20 years after Anderson's book, we can say without hesitation that nurses who are graduates of diploma and associate degree nursing programs have indeed encountered many barriers and have "paid a price" in seeking advancement in nursing education. The controversy about technical versus professional education for RN licensure continues unabated, and the issue of upward mobility for technical graduates is a major one within the profession. On the one hand, there has not been wide acceptance in baccalaureate education that technical education provides the appropriate foundation for professional practice and education. On the other hand, few associate degree or diploma nurse educators are in agreement with Montag's notion that technical education is an end in itself. Many would argue that diploma or associate degree education is the first (or even the second) rung on a career ladder leading to professional nursing practice.

Nursing and other female-dominated, largely undergraduate, health occupations such as medical records have shared this preoccupation about students' rights to direct articulation and upward mobility to professional-level programs. Yet there is little discussion or acceptance of the notion that paralegal training is the first rung on the ladder to law school. Even less consideration is given of the notion that physicians' assistant training is a step on the rung to medical school. Of course, both of these professions require preparation at the graduate level, a significant distinction over nursing and medical records administration.

One of the interesting and unique features of American higher education is its egalitarian emphasis. This is no more apparent than in the shift from mass education to nearly universal higher education that occurred in the United States during the period from the 1950s to the present. Within this social environment, it has been very difficult to support the notion that any technical program is "terminal" in nature. Moreover, historically nursing has always been a source of upward mobility for women. Complex advanced placement procedures and frustrations in moving from a technical level of nursing to the baccalaureate degree have led to charges of elitism in baccalaureate education. Dissension over articulation between technical and professional programs has been aggravated by the fact that these undergraduate programs are poorly differentiated. They prepare students for the same RN license, have similar curricula, and accept the same types of students. This is not to say that there are not differences between technical and professional programs, but rather that there has been inadequate differentiation between them. This may be one reason for the growing support for nursing programs that offer the first professional degree in master's or doctoral degree curricula. To highlight this problem, findings in a recent survey of associate degree nursing (ADN) programs in California demonstrate that ADN programs in that state tend to require three years of college because of prerequisites required for admission, extensive general education requirements on local campuses, and units related to articulation between LVN and RN career ladder options. The articulated LVN-ADN options required the most units, but many traditional ADN programs required well above the 60–70 semester units typical of associate degree curricula.[23]

As ADN programs evolved through the 1960s and 1970s, they began to be developed in senior colleges and universities in states that did not initially create a system of community or junior colleges. Consequently, in these settings, ADN students were very often enrolled in the same foundation science courses as the baccalaureate nursing students and other preprofessional students. Rena Boyle, then dean at the University of Nebraska Medical Center School of Nursing, encountered this problem in her school. In response, she and her faculty developed a unique 2 + 2 + 2 career ladder model in which students could progress through the associate to the baccalaureate and master's degree in nursing.[24] One drawback in this innovative program was that the proportion of students who went on to complete the baccalaureate degree program, in spite of complete articulation between the curricula, did not meet expectations. The ratio of baccalaureate degree to associate degree graduates was inadequate in relation to state and local needs for professional nurses.

Career Ladder Models

Articulation is a term that denotes the formal linking of one educational program to another. Some nursing programs provide this educational pattern when their primary purpose is to provide upward mobility for students. Articulation between educational programs is more difficult in those settings where academic policies differ, where similar courses are offered for lower or upper division credit, and where institutional philosophies differ. In general, associate degree and diploma nurse educators are more favorable to models that permit their students to move directly into the next level program through formal transfer of credit rather than through validation of prior learning in challenge examinations, portfolio evaluation, or other academic assessment measures. Nonetheless, many senior colleges and universities have rather definitive procedures that nursing programs must follow in order to admit and advance-place nurses into their curricula.

Several career ladder models exist in nursing education. A few, as was once true at the University of Nebraska Medical Center, offer 2 + 2 options (associate plus baccalaureate degree) programs or 2 + 2 + 2 options (through the master's degree). These comprehensive career model programs require a major commitment to the career ladder philosophy. More common among career ladder programs are "capstone" or "second-step" programs for RNs. These two-year curricular options usually represent the only nursing curriculum at the undergraduate level offered by the parent institution, and frequently they are designed to meet the needs of several "feeder" community college or diploma nursing programs. These upper-division curricula are designed specifically to meet the educational needs of the RN adult learner and are probably most successful at acknowledging the prior learning of these students. However, not uncommonly these programs actually require more units in nursing in residence to meet degree requirements.[25]

Traditional four-year baccalaureate programs that are designed for prelicensure students also offer options for the RN student. Advanced placement procedures, including assessment measures, are used to determine the appropriate degree plan for the individual student. Once rather inflexible and not particularly hospitable to RNs, these programs now offer a host of advanced placement options not available just a few years ago. The decline in enrollment of traditional students has made the RN and LVN student a popular marketing target for these schools of nursing.

RNs who want a master's degree in nursing should be encouraged to investigate the availability of BS/MS articulated programs in their area. These programs are designed specifically for nurses whose academic ability and career interest make them good candidates for graduate study. The University of California San Francisco offers a model of this type. The BS/MS option provides a more direct route to the graduate degree and should be explained in career counseling options for RNs.

RNs who have BA or BS degrees in other fields often express an interest in baccalaureate or graduate nursing education. Because of their prior investment in other degree programs, these students are not interested in another lengthy educational program. These students, who frequently want the BS degree in order to meet admission requirements for a nurse practitioner or graduate program, should be encouraged to seek admission directly to a graduate program. More graduate schools are accepting these nontraditional students directly into their graduate programs and are providing them with opportunities to make up baccalaureate level deficiencies while in the master's degree program.

Career ladder opportunities have also improved for LVNs. As hospitals began to employ more RNs and to reduce their vocational nurse staffs in the 1980s, community colleges and senior colleges initiated advanced placement options for these students. Vocational nurses, who know what the work of nursing involves and who have already made a commitment to that work, have been considered good candidates for career ladder programs.

Advantages and Disadvantages of Career Ladder Programs

For many students, incremental education is a logical and worthwhile, albeit somewhat inefficient, way of achieving their career goals. Some students feel confident that they are prepared both economically and psychologically for the short-term investment made at the initial rung of the ladder. Education in increments simply appears more feasible for these students, many of whom may be first-generation college students or nontraditional students in terms of academic background and life experience. For these students, the achievement of a baccalaureate or higher degree may seem to be dependent upon their ability to become self-supporting quickly. Among the significant advantages to the career ladder approach to nursing education is the relatively short time frame to licensure as either an LVN or RN. Employment at this point enables the student to use earnings to pay for continuing education up the career ladder. Remedial course work and academic support services may also be more readily available to students in community or junior colleges. Success at this level, along with maturation, may enable some students to reach the BSN or higher degree goal, whereas their unreadiness for the senior college setting may have made this outcome less certain at an earlier point in their lives.

The disadvantages of the career ladder approach are time, money, and inconvenience. There is little doubt that most students experience some delay in moving from one rung on the ladder to another. Schools often require that students moving from one level of licensure to another have at least one year of work experience before admission to the second-step program. Directly articulated programs are few in number. For this reason, although it would normally take a student about two years of study to achieve the associate degree, it may take an LVN approximately three years or more to achieve the same goal. Similarly, the associate degree graduate may find that it takes a total of five years of college to attain the BSN degree. This system is obviously inefficient; thus career ladder programs should be designed to meet needs where they exist but should not become the predominant model of education in nursing, as has been suggested on occasion.

There is some evidence that career ladder programs may be more costly to both the schools and the students. Although students in career ladder programs can step out to earn money along the way to their final goal, they must take into account lost earnings that would have been received if they had attained the goal earlier. At least one recent study indicated that it is a good investment to complete the BSN degree in a timely fashion when earnings of BSN nurses from four-year programs are compared with those of RNs from two- and three-year programs who have later received the degree.[26] Increased cost is also incurred by the schools that support career ladder programs. Since these programs are often longer and require additional instructional units, educational costs are higher.

Although upward mobility options have improved dramatically in recent years, finding a program that facilitates advanced placement with a minimum of delay is a significant challenge. Once students become LVNs or RNs, they tend to initiate a standard of living that is difficult to maintain without full-time work. This relegates educational options to limited hours and days, necessitating a long-term plan to achieve the next rung on the ladder.

Advanced Placement Procedures

Nursing programs use a variety of means for career ladder students to validate prior learning for purposes of advanced placement within a nursing program. Direct transfer of credit is done for courses from regionally accredited colleges and universities according to policies developed between these institutions. Nursing courses may not be directly transferable in those cases where similar courses are designed as upper division in senior college nursing programs whose curriculum is exclusively at the upper-division level. In these cases, senior colleges offer a number of mechanisms for establishing credit for prior learning. Among the most commonly used mechanisms are standardized tests offered by such groups as the College Level Exam Program (CLEP), American College Testing Service (ACT-PEP), and National League for Nursing Mobility Examinations. Unfortunately, many nursing programs continue to use teacher-made tests for assessment purposes. Since a minority of nursing faculties has preparation in test construction, these examinations tend to be idiosyncratic to a particular program.[27]

Special Course Scheduling

Nurses can expect to see more options and special course scheduling designed to meet the needs of the upwardly mobile LVN and RN. Enrollment decline nationwide has provided a strong incentive for schools of nursing to create new marketing strategies for these students. The weekend college, off-campus centers, evening, and block scheduling will continue to emerge in more communities in the years to come as the population of high school graduates continues to decline and the interest in nursing among young college-age students wanes. One recent nursing article described a pilot program designed to bring baccalaureate nursing education into a community where access to that level of education was limited. Program designers used the local community college as the site for instruction and for library and bookstore materials, a creative way to enhance convenience for working students.[28]

Educational Benefits As a Recruitment/Retention Strategy

Educational benefits as a recruitment/retention strategy are growing in popularity, although there are virtually no research or program evaluation data published to demonstrate the effectiveness of these benefits. The investment in these benefits does appear to offer a certain value-added connotation that may be effective in both recruitment and retention. Certainly, once a nurse is enrolled in an educational program, there would be a good reason to stay with an employer at least through program completion. It has also been shown that baccalaureate-prepared nurses do stay in clinical nursing, so that, despite opinions to the contrary, nurses are not likely to opt out of hospital nursing just because they have completed the baccalaureate degree. Tuition remission and other educational benefit programs help an institution to meet a commitment to internal promotion. This investment, which demonstrates the employer's willingness to assist employees in raising the level of their education, enhances the institution's ability to live up to this commitment to internal promotion. In institutions that have a significant imbalance of technical versus professional nurses, a program of educational benefits will aid the nurse executive with moving more of his or her staff from technical (LVN and ADN) to professional competency.

Career Counseling in Nursing

Career counseling of young men and women interested in a career in nursing, as well as for those individuals already in the field, should be encouraged. Students should be referred to resources available in local colleges and universities that have career counseling and placement centers. On the one hand, students who indicate the ability and interest to pursue directly an associate or baccalaureate degree should be advised on admission procedures and financial aid for these schools. Career ladder options should be explored with students who are less certain about their long-term commitment to school or who may need more academic support services and maturation before moving into professional education. Nurses may also need recurrent counseling throughout their careers. Burnout, physical injury, and a desire for change are just a few of the reasons nurses might be referred to counseling services. Retention of nurses in years to come may well require recruitment from within. The availability of career counseling may be one way to help nurses reevaluate their careers and to move from one position within the hospital to another.

Career Pathways in Nursing

Perhaps the most poorly marketed aspect of nursing as a career is the enormous opportunity that licensure as an RN offers. Few occupations or professions offer as many full-time or part-time options to the working adult. Variety in nursing positions, opportunity for lateral or vertical career changes, and national and international mobility are significant assets in a nursing career. Careful career planning enables nurses to take advantage of these options. Career planning also helps the individual to avoid the frustrating delays and expense that occur when poor choices are made about educational programs or nursing positions.

New Career Options

Entrepreneurship seems to be the latest byword in nursing success stories today. Nurses are actively developing businesses and products for marketing. Continuing education providers, home health care agencies, sick child care services, and medical product lines are just a few of the businesses developed by nurses. An abundance of new publications is available on this topic and should be reviewed by nurses who are interested in establishing their own business.

Although more nurses are employed by hospitals than ever before, new opportunities for nurses also abound in ambulatory treatment centers. Dialysis units, home care, ambulatory surgical centers, specialty clinics for seniors and the disabled, cruise ship clinics, oil rig health services, school nursing, industrial nursing, and Planned Parenthood are just a few of the out-of-hospital options for nurses.

Case management by professional nurses is the newest focus of attention in hospital nursing circles. Modified from the case management concept in social work, this model offers the opportunity for job enrichment and better utilization of professional nurses, while assisting hospitals in providing managed care in a cost-effective manner. Our capitated system of reimbursement for health care has helped to push this concept forward. Assisted by a technician who handles secretarial and technical functions, the RN case manager assumes responsibility for coordination of care to enable the patient to meet discharge goals. Further elaboration of case management models may create yet another interesting career option for nurses.

SUMMARY

Career ladder systems, in both the clinical and educational setting, are likely to remain high-visibility items on the nursing and hospital agenda for the foreseeable future. The current nursing shortage is likely to be exacerbated by other labor shortages in the 1990s as the numbers of educated and skilled workers entering the work force decline. In the face of high demand for nurses and continued weak enrollments in nursing programs, additional efforts are likely to be made to enhance career ladder clinical and educational models to recruit, retain, and recognize nurses.

NOTES

1. Peter I. Buerhaus, "Not Just Another Nursing Shortage," *Nursing Economics* 5, no. 6 (1987): 267–279.

2. Ibid.

3. Bill Clinton, "On Rebuilding the Nation," *American Association of Higher Education Bulletin*, 40 (May–June 1988): 4–7.

4. "Latest NLN Data Shows Alarming Drop in R.N. Graduations," *Nursing and Health Care* 8 (November 1987): 530.

5. Richard C. McKibbin, "Analysis of Career Earnings in Nursing and Other Occupations," Memo to State Nurse Association Presidents and State Nurse Association Executive Directors, March 11, 1988.

6. K.C. Green, "The Educational Pipeline in Nursing," *Journal of Professional Nursing* (July/August 1987): 247–257.

7. Jerome P. Lysaught, *An Abstract for Action* (New York: McGraw-Hill Book Co., 1970).

8. American Hospital Association Division of Nursing, "Career Advancement for R.N.'s in Hospitals," *Nurse Executive Management Strategies* 6 (1985): 1–12.

9. Jane Hirsch et al., "On the Scene—Section II—University of California, San Francisco," *Nursing Administration Quarterly* 11, no. 4 (Summer 1987): 47–61.

10. Beth Israel Hospital's Division of Nursing Services, Human Resources and Public Affairs, *Professional Nursing Practice at Boston's Beth Israel Hospital* (Boston: Beth Israel Hospital), 5.

11. Karyl Woldum et al., "The Professional Development Program: An Alternative to Clinical Ladders," *Nursing Administration Quarterly* (Spring 1983): 87–93.

12. Jeanne Phillips Campbell and Trudy Williams, "Marketing to Nurses through an Incentive Program," *Journal of Nursing Administration* (October 1983): 9–12.

13. Florence L. Huey, "Looking at Ladders," *American Journal of Nursing* 82, no. 10 (October 1982): 1520–1526.

14. American Hospital Association Division of Nursing, "Career Advancement for R.N.'s in Hospitals," *Nurse Executive Management Strategies* (1985): 1–12.

15. Kathryn McDonough and Mary Ann Sorenson, "Restructuring Nursing Salaries," *Nursing Management* 19 (February 1988): 39–41.

16. Rita R. Roedel and Paul Nystrom, "Clinical Ladders and Job Enrichment," *Hospital Topics* 65 (March/April 1987): 22–24.

17. Carol S. Weisman, "Recruitment from Within," *Journal of Nursing Administration* (May 1987): 24–31.

18. Rhea Sanford, "Clinical Ladders: Do They Serve Their Purpose?" *Journal of Nursing Administration* 17 (May 1987): 34–37.

19. Ann Hunstman, J. Lederer, and E. Peterman, "Implementation of Staff Nurse III at El Camino Hospital," in *From Novice to Expert*, ed. Patricia Benner (Reading, Mass.: Addison-Wesley Publishing Co., 1980).

20. Lassar Gotkin, "Part II," in *Community College Education for Nursing*, ed. Mildred Montag (New York: McGraw-Hill Book Co., 1959), 343–344.

21. Louise McManus, "Foreword," in *Community College Education for Nurses*, ed. Mildred Montag (New York: McGraw-Hill Book Co., 1959), xi.

22. Bernice Anderson, *Nursing Education in Community Junior Colleges* (Philadelphia: J.B. Lippincott Co., 1966), 277.

23. Helen A. Hanson, "Survey of California Associate Degree Nursing Curricula," for the Articulation Committee of the California Association of Colleges of Nursing and Associate Degree Directors of Northern and Southern California, January 1988.

24. Rena Boyle, "Articulation: From Associate Degree through Masters," *Nursing Outlook* 20 (October 1972): 670–672.

25. Donna M. Arlton and Marie E. Miller, "RN to BSN: Advanced Placement Policies," *Nurse Educator* 12 (November/December, 1987): 11–14.

26. Seigina M. Frik, "Which Route to Nursing Is Most Cost Effective?" *American Journal of Nursing* 88 (June 1988): 880–884.

27. Donna M. Arlton and Marie E. Miller, "RN to BSN: Advanced Placement Policies," 11–14.

28. Marilyn L. Rotnert et al., "Joining Forces To Meet the Needs of the RN Learner," *Nursing and Health Care* 9 (May 1988): 261–262.

Chapter 10

Nurse Staffing Determination: A Merging of Ethics, Standards, Quality, and Costs

Joanne Olsen and Jean C. Lyon

Staffing determinations can present truly ulcer-producing dilemmas for the nurse executive. The nurse executive is frequently alone at budget defense, and during the process is often seen as "protecting nursing." The nurse executive is frequently placed in a position where the chief executive officer believes that the nurse executive is a nurse first and an administrator second, and often presumes an inflexibility on the part of the nurse executive to alter the nursing hours per patient day because, after all, she or he is a *nurse*. The nursing staff tends to feel that the nurse executive has deserted the nurse at the bedside. The staff views the nurse executive "as one of them now," who is unable to identify with the realities of being staffed with two regular nurses, two floating nurses, two registry nurses, and one nursing student for 12 open-heart surgery patients, 4 of whom are new postoperative patients. The nurse executive frequently stands alone in her or his efforts to balance the quality equals cost plus patient outcome equation ($Q = C + Pt. O$).

Staff determination has always been the responsibility of the nurse executive, but the current changes in health care have broadened the role into that of resource allocator. The role of resource allocator is now competing with two other long-recognized functions of the nurse executive: determination of the standards of care and development, and implementation and evaluation of the quality assurance program.[1] The nurse executive is being asked daily to balance the cost/quality equation. Some nurse executives are being asked to utilize fewer resources by reducing the standards of care and decreasing the amount of nursing care provided. The current economic constraints in health care are placing incredible strain on the nurse executive and challenging her or his moral judgments and decisions.[2] The nurse executive must act as the moral conscience of the organization, guiding the organization through a decision-making process regarding cost/quality as well as conveying the outcome of decisions to the administrative team, the medical staff, and the board of trustees. The once-mundane function of staffing determination is now far more complex and encompasses ethics, standards, quality, and cost issues.

The nurse executive is uniquely qualified to understand the components of the cost/quality equation. However, the nurse executive may have difficulty in being perceived by others as being objective in viewing the equation. Quality is usually presented as a perception or feeling, and the nurse executive is frequently placed in the position of defending quality without being able to quantify and define quality.

The purpose of this chapter is to examine the nurse executive's role as resource allocator, including facilitation of the evaluation of standards of care and utilization of an ethical framework in adjusting standards of care. The chapter also addresses the need to link cost of care with quality and the importance of communicating changes in patient care delivery standards and of obtaining agreement with the changes among the nursing and administrative teams.

This chapter does not address the mathematical formulas used to calculate staffing needs. (For this information, the reader is referred elsewhere.[3])

STANDARDS OF CARE

Standards of care are written statements reflecting what is valued. Standards are developed by an authority or general concensus of opinion to be used as a model against which quality is measured. Standards of care are *value statements* about practice and are statements used to assess the practice.[4] A nursing standard provides a definition of quality of care that includes quantitative criteria for evaluation. Nursing care delivered according to the established criteria must result in positive outcomes for the client.[5] Standards of care are generally related to the process and outcome of practice. Standards provide the practitioner with statements about what the practitioner is to do and the anticipated or expected outcome. Standards are written statements about the components of care delivery that influence nurse staffing determinations.

Standards of care directly influence workload measurement systems (acuity) and as a result the nursing unit staffing determination. An example of this is provided in Exhibit 10-1 for an infant receiving phototherapy. Each of the indica-

Exhibit 10-1 Patient Classification Worksheet

Patient Name _____Room _____ Shift D E N			
Diet	I	II	III
Bottle-feeding—by nurse			(X)
Breast-feeding—instrument assist		(X)	
Bottle-feeding—instrument 1st time	(X)		
Treatment			
Phototherapy—set up and monitor		(X)	
Blood transfusion			(X)

tors of care in Exhibit 10-1 have associated standards of care. The standards associated for a patient with phototherapy describe the nursing practices that should take place in relationship to phototherapy.

Table 10-1 depicts the standards of care and nursing time required for a newborn receiving phototherapy. These standards are converted through the application of industrial engineering methodologies into workload measurements.

The time to complete each step in the standard and the frequency in 24 hours with which the standard is to be carried out are determined. Workload measurements are then assessed on all patients, as illustrated in Table 10-2. The sum of the measurement is used to assess the number of personnel required to deliver care to the predetermined standard.

As the nurse executive looks for ways in which to allocate resources strategically, standards of care must remain an important area of focus. As the nurse executive considers altering standards, the expertise of the appropriate nursing groups in the organization must be obtained. Never lose sight of the objective of providing positive outcomes for clients.

The need to allocate resources presents an opportunity for the nurse executive to address practices in health care that have become rituals rather than validated practices. It also provides an opportunity for the nurse executive to emphasize practices that are beneficial yet frequently ignored by the nursing staff.

IMPLICATIONS OF ALTERING STANDARDS

Cost-containment efforts have focused the nurse executive on evaluating the organization's standards of care delivery. As health care organizations are chal-

---

Table 10-1 Care Standard—Newborn Phototherapy

Normal Newborn Phototherapy	Time (min)	Frequency (per 24 hr)	Min in 24 hr
1. Initial assessment each shift to include documentation	7	3	21
2 Eye patches in place during phototherapy session; eyes are examined for discharge every shift and patches changed as necessary; include documentation every 4 hr with vital signs	5	6	30
3. Bililight radiance is assessed and documented between 6012 nm (white light) every 8 hr	2	3	6
4. Distance between lights and newborn is measured and documented every 8 hr (distance between 14 and 16 inches)	4	1	4
			61

(61 ÷ 3 = 20 min per shift)

Table 10-2 Workload Assessment

Total Minutes Required		Total Minutes Available per Care Provider		Total Staff Required
1920	÷	480	=	4

lenged in the cost-containment environment to reduce costs, the nurse executive may be asked to adjust standards of care to a minimum safe level.

In considering altering standards, it is important for the nurse executive to be conscious of whose values the original standards address.[6] Were the standards written based on the values of the patient and/or family, the physician, the nursing staff, the institution's executive team, or the institution's board of trustees?

As standards of care are altered, the nurse executive must obtain the approval and commitment of the medical staff, the organization's executive team, and the board of trustees. For example, if the schedule for linen changes is altered from daily and as needed to a Monday-Wednesday-Friday schedule, all of the parties involved need to agree.

A nurse executive who alters care delivery standards without the endorsement of the appropriate groups runs the risk of unilaterally altering the values of the organization. Conversely, the nurse executive who changes care delivery standards by processing the decisions with the affected groups systemically brings the organization through a decision-making process that balances cost and quality. The nurse executive, in taking affected groups through this process, is able further to convey clearly the consequences of actions.

Crisham[7] recommends the use of a decision matrix model when evaluating decisions regarding standards of care (see Exhibit 10-2, for example). As the nurse executive reflects on care delivery standards as a means of adjusting staffing levels, she or he must balance the benefits of such actions against the harm. Making judgments about care delivery standards involves a person's moral principles or ethics.

Ethics

Ethics is defined as "the discipline of philosophy dealing with what is good and evil and with moral duty and obligation."[8] In staffing determinations, the nurse executive must determine the standards of care for nursing, the levels of patient outcome that are acceptable, and the allocation of nursing resources. All of these decisions involve right and wrong decisions.[9] Each ethical dilemma confronting the nurse executive "is a combination of choice between what 'should' or 'ought to' be done (theory of obligation) and judgment about the value of the chosen action (theory of value)."[10]

Exhibit 10-2 A Decision Matrix*

	MORAL PRINCIPLES				PRACTICAL CONSIDERATIONS		
Problem: Post-open heart surgery patient resource consumption. Open heart patients are cost outliers.	Stress & anxiety patient/family neutral or decrease	Stress & anxiety care givers neutral or decrease	Provide necessary resources to the most seriously ill	No increased mortality	Remodeling necessary to handle ventilators in step-down unit	Cost of care decrease	Discharge to home remains at ALOS 7 days
A L T E R N A T I V E S							
Refuse high risk patients for open heart surgery	−	0	−	+	0	+	0
Discharge patients to step-down area 48 hours post-surgery (0 arrhythmias, 0 vasopressor w/in 36 resting b.p.m. 60–100)	+	+	+	+	0	+	+
Alter staffing to 1:1 for first 4 hours post-open heart only	0	−	+	−	0	+	−
Transfer patients on ventilator to step-down unit if unable to wean w/in 72 hours post-op	−	−	−	+	+	+	−

*The diagram, although not practical in the numerous ethical decisions that are made daily by the nurse executive, would certainly be useful for the nurse executive as a tool to use in a group process situation. + = criterion met; − = criterion not met; 0 = not applicable.

Source: Adapted from *Journal of Nursing Quality Assurance,* Vol. 1, No. 1, p. 31, Aspen Publishers, Inc., © November 1986.

Crisham's decision matrix[11] is used to illustrate the evaluation of alternatives in care delivery issues to determine an alternative that meets or most closely supports the nurse executive's ethical principles. In identifying alternatives consistent with established moral criteria, the integrity of self, health care providers, and the health care institution is maintained. Exhibit 10-2 assumes that the moral principles for all groups involved in evaluating and selecting alternatives are congruent. Moral principles are beliefs developed from our experiences that guide our actions. Moral principles are convictions about right and wrong that guide our judgments. If the underlying moral principles were not congruent, a separate matrix would be completed for the group. The nurse executive who finds herself or himself drawing up numerous separate matrix diagrams may need to determine whether her or his underlying moral principles are concordant overall with those of the institution.

The ethical principles used to select alternatives are developed from the union of the theory of obligation and the theory of value.[12] The nurse executive may explore and develop an ethical framework by completing the statement "I ought to (the action) or ought not to (the action) because. . . ."[13] The nurse can then explore her or his moral principles in view of ethical theories.

In making decisions regarding health care, the nurse executive must balance the benefits of actions against the harm. Determining the criteria against which to evaluate alternatives is an ethical decision that involves the moral principles of the nurse executive. The "balancing of benefits and harms" helps "establish standards against which quality will be measured."[14]

Quality

Before it can be determined that quality patient care is being delivered, the term *quality* must be defined within each health care organization. *Webster's New World Dictionary* defines *quality* as "the degree of excellence which a thing possesses; excellence; superiority."[15]

Quality has also been defined as conformance to requirements.[16] Donabedian has said that quality of care depends on the appropriate objectives of care and then on ways to attain them.[17] A frequent occurrence in health care has been a lack of definition of quality and separate evaluations of the costs and quality of care.[18]

Many factors comprise the concept of quality care. As depicted in Figure 10-1, these factors include the following: standards of care, ethics and values, safety, prevention, risk management, costs, intervention, patient care, critical thinking or reasoning, utilization patterns, outcomes, and monitoring. All of these factors fall within the umbrella or scope of the quality assurance (QA) program. The amount of influence placed on any section of the quality assurance program is determined by administration, nursing, medical staff, and patient input.

Each acute care institution must make a decision to define the standards of care and the level of quality to be achieved, with a clearly defined acceptable range of

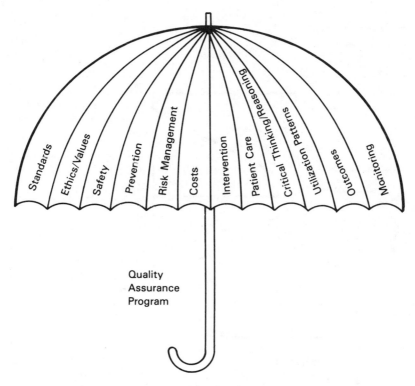

Figure 10-1 Quality of Care

deviation. The quality measures utilized must be accurate, should incorporate a comprehensive quality assurance program, and should have a solid risk management program in place. Examples of specific quality measurements within the risk management program include the number and severity of medication errors, the number of successful malpractice suits, patient complication rate and resulting increase in patient length of stay due to complications, and patient satisfaction.

Nurses who are dissatisfied with the patient care that is delivered are at high risk for leaving the institution to work in a more desirable environment. The institution then must incur the cost of recruitment and orientation for a replacement nurse, if a replacement can be found. The institution that provides less than quality care also is at risk for the development of a reputation in the community among nurses and patients for providing inferior care.

THE NURSE EXECUTIVE'S ROLE IN QA

The nurse executive plays a critical, pivotal role in the organization's QA/risk management program. Figure 10-2 provides a visual interpretation of the nurse

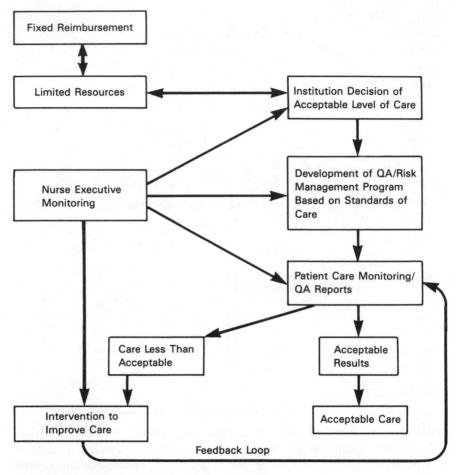

Figure 10-2 Nurse Executive Role in QA/Risk Management

executive's role in QA. The nurse executive provides input into the institution's decision of what comprises an acceptable level of care, assists with the development of the QA/risk management program based on standards of care, reviews patient care monitors and QA reports, and intervenes if necessary to improve patient care. A major function of the nurse executive's role is monitoring.

Monitoring

The QA/risk management plan should have clearly delineated steps for intervention and action in the event that the QA indicators fall outside the acceptable range of excellence. As Donabedian has stated regarding quality assurance, "In the final analysis, there is no substitute for professional commitment and accountability.'' [19] There is no individual in the institution more capable of monitoring the results of the QA program than the nurse executive.

Beyers observed that QA professionals are being asked to serve as health care's conscience, the mediator between administrative and clinical goals. [20] But it is the nurse executive, as part of the administrative team, who has been empowered to maintain quality patient care, to be the voice of the patient and the nurse, assessing and retaining resources at the bedside. *Monitoring*, which is defined as the process of watching or checking on a person or thing, [21] is a critical part of the nurse executive's role in maintaining quality in patient care.

Open communication between the nurse executive and other administrators and nurses in the organization is necessary to ensure that quality continues to be defined consistently by everyone. Quality should not be defined as ''goodness, or luxury, or shininess,'' because these are vague terms that imply that ''quality is merely goodness that always costs more.''[22]

Cost of Quality

The cost of quality, according to Crosby, [23] is the cost of doing things wrong. The institution's costs increase from errors that are made because of a nursing staff insufficient to provide the quality that is needed to prevent mistakes and resulting complications. Repeated cuts in staffing on a continual basis will result in nurses' being required to cut corners and provide unacceptable care. [24] Nurses who continue to work in an environment where the care is not acceptable will suffer low morale and will make mistakes. The cost of mistakes made can be measured quantitatively in dollars and then converted to full-time equivalents (FTEs).

It takes few mistakes due to cost cutting in nursing to exceed the cost of increasing nurse staffing. It is easier to recruit and retain nurses in an environment that consciously monitors quality indicators and patient outcomes and intervenes to improve quality as needed.

Quality is equal to cost and patient outcome. Quality must start at the top administrative levels in an organization and be maintained at that level. Maintenance of quality standards will reduce overall costs and optimize patient outcomes (Q = C + Pt. O).

Cost Equation

The advent of prospective reimbursement in the 1980s caused the health care industry to look closely at ways to reduce the total costs of providing care. Nursing service departments, by nature of their size and overall budgets, are frequently targeted for major budgetary cuts. Nursing executives, now more than ever, need to develop methodologies to balance the quality/cost equation.

Costs of Patient Care

Cost-effectiveness and cost/benefit analysis are two analytical techniques used frequently in the determination of how resources will be allocated. Cost/benefit analysis provides information on the positive and negative consequences of directing resources for provision of a specific service or activity. The decision maker is able to determine whether the allocation of resources enhance (1) the value of goods and services provided and (2) the general social welfare.[25] A monetary value must be assigned to all outcomes under cost/benefit analysis. Cost-effectiveness requires that outcomes be expressed in commensurate units.[26] The goal of cost-effectiveness is to maximize the total benefits for the resources allocated.

Ehrat recommends a model for quantifying quality and measuring quality efficiency.[27] She maintains that "quality care effectiveness and efficiency will need to be projected and monitored in much the same fashion as the overall budget." Ehrat describes a methodology for determining the cost of meeting predetermined standards of care and recommends that each nursing unit review the unit-based quality review audit criteria and quantify the expected quality outcome.[28] She proposes a quality measurement system, as reflected in Table 10-3. The standards have a total possible point score (a). Each standard also has total possible point score (b) and is assigned a weight in percent (c) [$C = b/a$] under column 1. Looking at the first standard, if all 10 charts were in compliance, a score of 18 would be assigned under the fourth column (Total Score). To achieve a quality rating of 100 percent, the unit must achieve 144 out of 144 points. To determine the percent compliance, the sum of the total score under Column 4 is divided by the total number of possible points multiplied by 100.

$$\text{Quality effectiveness} = \frac{\text{sum of Column 4}}{\text{maximum possible score}} \quad \frac{120 \, d}{144 \, a} \times 100 = 83.3\%$$

An efficiency performance ratio is then identified that compares inputs with outputs. Outputs are a measure of production (patient days, laboratory tests) and inputs are a measure of resources consumed in the production of the outputs (labor rates, labor hours, quantity of materials).

$$\begin{matrix} \text{Performance ratio} \\ \text{(patient days/worked hrs)} \end{matrix} = \begin{matrix} \text{output} \\ \hline \text{input} \end{matrix} \begin{matrix} \text{(patient days)} \\ \text{(productive hrs worked)} \end{matrix}$$

Hospital outputs are usually patient days, which are a unit of measure equal to one patient in the system for 24 hours.

If a nursing unit had in 1 month 100 patient admissions with a length of stay of 3 days, the unit had a census of 300 days. If the patient days are compared with the

Table 10-3 Nursing Unit: Normal Newborn Phototherapy (Length of Treatment Three Days) (Nine Shifts)

Month:
No. of Charts Reviewed: 10

Standards	Weight	Points per Compliance	No. in Compliance	Total Score
1. Newborn state of undress documented during each shift's initial assessment [standard = 9×] 2 points	12.5% (c) (18 pts) (b)	2	5	10
2. Eye patches in place during phototherapy session documented every 4 hr with vital signs [standard = 18×] 4 points	50% (c)	4	6	24
3. Bililight light radiance documented between 6–12 nm (white light) every 8 hr [standard = 9×] 2 points	12.5% (c) (18 pts) (b)	2	8	16
4. Distance between lights and newborn documented as 14–16 inches every shift [standard = 9×] 2 points	12.5% (c) (18 pts) (b)	2	8	16
5. Serum bilirubin tested and results documented a minimum of every 24 hr [standard = 3×] 2 points	4.2% (c) (6 pts) (b)	2	9	18
6. Nurses' notes reflect negative monitoring of trends in serum bilirubin with documented treatment adjustments as indicated every 24 hr [standard = 3×] 4 points	8.3% (c) (12 pts) (b)	4	9	36
	100% 144(a)			120(d)

actual productive hours worked for the same unit, an efficiency or performance ratio calculation is established.

$$\text{Patient days/worked hr} \quad 0.172 \quad = \frac{300 \text{ patient days}}{1740 \text{ productive hr}}$$

For every hour worked the nursing unit produced 0.172 patient day of care. Increasing the unit's efficiency in producing patient days is achievable either by increasing output while maintaining or decreasing inputs:

$$\frac{\uparrow \text{Outputs}}{\downarrow \longleftrightarrow \text{Inputs}} = \frac{325 \text{ patient days}}{1740 \text{ productive hr}} = 0.186 \text{ patient day/worked hr}$$

or by maintaining or increasing outputs while decreasing inputs

$$\frac{\uparrow \longleftrightarrow \text{Outputs}}{\downarrow \text{Inputs}} = \frac{300 \text{ patient days}}{1640 \text{ productive hr}} = 0.182 \text{ patient day/worked hr}$$

Ehrat's next step is to determine a quality efficiency calculation.[29] The calculation, again, is a performance ratio comparing input with output.

$$\text{Performance ratio (quality days/worked hr)} = \frac{\text{output} = [\text{quality days}]}{\text{input} = [\text{productive hr}]} = \frac{\text{Quality effectiveness} \times \text{patient days}}{\text{productive hr}}$$

$$250 \text{ quality patient days} = \frac{(0.833 \times 300)}{1740}$$

The input factor of nursing productive hours worked is used in recognition of nursing's role as a direct influence on the quality of care provided. Again, quality efficiency scores can be increased by increasing the sum of the raw total score and maintaining or increasing the patient days while at the same time maintaining or decreasing productive hours worked.

$$\frac{\text{Quality days} \uparrow}{\text{Productive hr} \longleftrightarrow} \qquad \text{OR} \qquad \frac{\text{Quality days} \longleftrightarrow}{\text{Productive hr} \downarrow}$$

Ehrat provides a means to relate quality, patient volumes, and nursing resource utilization.[30] Outputs are easily adjusted to take into consideration patient acuity by multiplying the patient days by the average patient acuity. This number then replaces the patient days as the output measurement throughout the formulas.

Trending data on the monthly quality efficiency may then be tracked for changes in patient volume, patient acuity, and quality compliance with established standards or productive hours. Finding the cost/quality connection is accomplished by multiplying the productive hours worked times the average hourly rate on the unit.

$$\text{Quality days/paid dollar} = \frac{\text{Quality days}}{\substack{(\text{productive hr}) \times \\ (\text{avg. hourly salary}) \\ 1740 \quad \times \quad 17.00}} = \frac{250}{(1740)(17.00)} = 0.008$$

The data can then be used over time to trend changes in cost/quality efficiency. The cost/quality relationship can be altered by manipulating variables in the formula.

Favorably altering the formula occurs by increasing quality compliance while maintaining or increasing patient days and maintaining or lowering labor costs.

Labor costs might be decreased further by reducing the average hourly wage or total productive hours.

The calculation of the cost/quality equation allows for a determination of the costs of 100 percent compliance to the standards through a simple algebraic equation.

$$\frac{\text{Quality days}}{\substack{\text{Labor costs associated} \\ \text{with the quality costs}}} \times \frac{\text{perfect quality days}}{X}$$

$$\frac{250}{29,580} \times \frac{300}{X} = \begin{array}{l} \$35,496.00 \\ \text{cost of 100\% compliance} \end{array}$$

The calculations as presented by Ehrat assume that the nursing staff is working at maximum quality productivity while delivering care.

In the cost and quality of patient care delivery theory, two rational propositions are identified. The first proposition states that if financial resources for providing patient care decrease, the quality of care will decrease. If fewer nurses are providing direct care to patients because of budgetary cuts, patients will be compromised. This axiom, although frequently stated by the nurse executive, remains difficult to substantiate.

The study of cost and quality issues in patient care must continue to take place in order to guide the nurse executive in making critical decisions regarding the allocation of resources.

The second relationship proposition states that a decrease in nurse executive monitoring and intervention in the QA program at the top administrative level will yield a decrease in the standards and quality of care provided. The nurse executive must, along with the nursing staff, establish the standards of care that will be provided to patients, monitor the results through a QA program, and interrelate the cost/quality connection. The nurse executive must then intervene to make any necessary changes, based on the results.

Implementation: Exemplar

The executive team is meeting and a determination has been made that costs must be cut. Even you, the nurse executive, agree the figures do not lie. All eyes turn to the nurse executive, and why not? Nursing service, by the nature of its size, is usually the first target for budget cuts. The chief financial officer (CFO) offers, helpfully, that over at Community Hospital their CFO is forcing a change in staff mix to save money. The personnel director indicates that a recent study of the hours per patient day places your facility in the upper 65th percentile for staffing. The vice-president over purchasing states that a proposal has been received to go to all 2020 electric beds at a savings as calculated by the vendor of 1.2 FTEs per nursing unit.

The chief executive officer (CEO) then leans forward in the chair and looks directly at you before stating, "Can we reduce the nursing hours per patient day?" Quickly you scan the room and note that your colleagues' body language reflects a preparation for your usual "No, because . . ." response. You, yourself, feel the release of your catecholamine stores as you prepare to fight (flight is not part of the nurse executive's innate makeup).

You are ready to say "No, because . . ."; however, you open your mouth and out pops "Yes, the nursing budget can be cut." Everyone is caught off guard. Your colleagues, who also had a catecholamine release and were ready to fight when you stated your usual "No, because . . . ," have the wind taken out of their sails.

The CEO approaches with trepidation: "O.K., how many FTEs?" This is the time to request a two-week period to study the numbers and report back. You will be given the usual three days. At this point you must get down to serious business. You need to call upon your colleagues in other institutions to identify truly workable cost-reduction strategies in patient care delivery. You also must get the nursing administrative team together to identify cost-reduction strategies. All standards of care must be reviewed and adjusted to a new level. For example, if phototherapy measurements were being done and documented every four hours, consider going to every eight hours and after any adjustment due to serum bilirubin results trending. If patients currently receive p.r.n. medications within 15 minutes after a legitimate request, change the standard to 25 minutes. It is understood that there will be certain standards of care that cannot be adjusted.

The next step is to quantify the savings in terms of nursing productive hours worked. After a determination regarding the standards alteration has been made and quantified, the nurse executive is in a position to make a presentation to the CEO or administrative team.

The nurse executive needs to be prepared to take the executive officer or team through the decision-making process on actions that result in a staff reduction yet remain consistent with the moral principles of the institution. The nurse executive should consider using the matrix diagram as developed by Crisham[31] (Exhibit 10-2). The diagram allows the executive group to agree/discuss the moral principles underlying each decision. After a group consensus has been reached on the care delivery, the nurse executive should insist that a similar presentation occur with the board and medical staff leadership. The three-legged stool of board, executive management team, and medical staff leadership must be on a level plane with equal understanding of the manner in which cost reductions will affect patient care. One cannot overemphasize the need for the moral principle of honesty in presenting alterations in the standards of care. Standards cannot be altered that are ridiculous even to the casual observer. The credibility of the nurse executive would be in serious question if she or he recommended that standards be adjusted to an unsafe level.

Before any standards changes are implemented there must be administrative commitment to the project. A strategic plan should be developed to clarify expectations and develop a project plan. An example of a strategic plan is shown in Figure 10-3.

In helping the institution identify the risks involved in altering standards of care, the nurse executive must use all means available to quantify the impact. The administrative team must be given a means to assess the risk in quantifiable terms.

SUMMARY

Determining optimal staffing levels for optimal patient care outcomes at optimal costs requires the interrelationship of ethics, standards, costs, and quality. The role of the nurse executive is to balance the equation of quality against costs. Decisions regarding resource allocation are becoming a major area of function for the nurse executive.

The judgments the nurse executive makes on standards of care involve the moral principles of the nurse executive and those of the facility as influenced by the board, the executive management team, and the medical staff. Standards of care directly influence the cost and quality of care delivery. Standards of care also have an impact on the message of the facility regarding quality. Institutions that place a high value on quality are able to recruit nurses and reduce the nursing costs associated with employee turnover and care delivery errors. The nurse executive must work toward demonstrating that the cost of high quality is not nearly as expensive as the cost of poor quality. An institution that struggles to provide adequate care incurs costs in employee orientation, recruitment, patient care delivery errors, systems errors, registry fees, decreased productivity, decreased employee morale, and loss of physician satisfaction and patient satisfaction.

The nurse executive must consistently seek ways to express in quantifiable terms the costs of failure to meet quality standards. The nurse executive is the conscience of the institution. The nurse executive has been empowered to monitor quality of care and to facilitate the clinical needs of the patients and the administrative needs of the facility. The nurse executive consistently assesses the environment for quality of care indicators. Patient outcomes from care providers must remain a primary focus of the institution, and it is the nursing executive who must consistently voice and refocus the institution in its role of providing quality patient care.

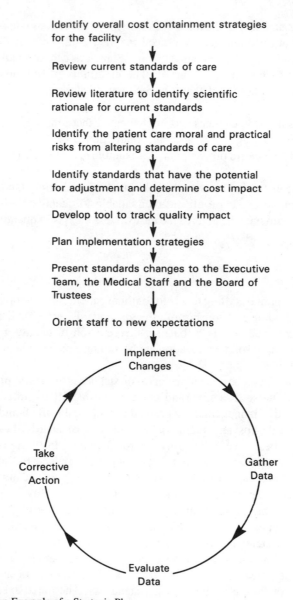

Figure 10-3 An Example of a Strategic Plan

NOTES

1. L. Simms, S. Price, and S. Pfoutz, ''Nursing Executives: Functions and Priorities,'' *Nursing Economic$* 3, no. 4 (1985): 238–244.

2. Patricia Crisham, "Ethics, Economics and Quality," *Journal of Nursing Quality Assurance* 1, no. 1 (1986): 26–35.

3. R. Kirk, *Nurse Staffing and Budgeting: Practical Management Tools* (Rockville, Md.: Aspen Publishers, Inc., 1986).

4. J. Beckman, "What Is a Standard of Practice?" *Journal of Quality Assurance* 1, no. 2 (1987): 1–6.

5. E.J. Mason, *How To Write Meaningful Nursing Standards* (New York: John Wiley & Sons, Inc., 1984).

6. Beckman, "What Is a Standard of Practice?" 1–6.

7. Crisham, "Ethics, Economics and Quality," 26–35.

8. D.B. Guralnik, ed., *Webster's New World Dictionary* (New York: Simon & Schuster, 1984).

9. Crisham, "Ethics, Economics and Quality," 26–35.

10. P. Sigman, "Ethical Choices in Nursing," *Advances in Nursing Science* 1, no. 3 (1979): 44.

11. Crisham, "Ethics, Economics and Quality," 31.

12. Sigman, "Ethical Choices in Nursing," 37–52.

13. Crisham, "Ethics, Economics and Quality," 26–35.

14. S.T. Fry, "Moral Values and Ethical Decisions in a Constrained Economic Environment," *Nursing Economic$* 4, no. 4 (1986): 161.

15. Guralnik, *Webster's New World Dictionary,* 1161.

16. K.F. Gross, "A Quality and Cost Control Model for Managing Nursing Utilization," *Journal of Nursing Quality Assurance* 1, no. 1 (1986): 36–46.

17. A. Donabedian, "Quality, Cost, and Cost Containment," *Nursing Outlook* 32, no. 3 (1984): 142–145.

18. E.L. Larson and D.A. Peters, "Integrating Cost Analyses in Quality Assurance," *Journal of Nursing Quality Assurance* 1, no. 1 (1986): 1–7.

19. Donabedian, "Quality, Cost, and Cost Containment," 145.

20. M. Beyers, "Cost and Quality: Balancing the Issues through Management," *Journal of Nursing Quality Assurance* 1, no. 1 (1986): 47–54.

21. Guralnik, *Webster's New World Dictionary*.

22. P.B. Crosby, *Quality Is Free* (New York: McGraw-Hill Book Co., 1979), 14.

23. Ibid.

24. V.L. Strong, "Nursing Products: Primary Components of Health Care," *Nursing Economic$* 3, no. 1 (1985): 60–61.

25. L.G. Anderson and R.F. Sottle, *Benefit-Cost Analysis: A Practical Guide* (Lexington, Mass.: DC Heath Company, 1977).

26. Ibid.

27. K.S. Ehrat, "The Cost-Quality Balance: An Analysis of Quality, Effectiveness, Efficiency, and Cost," *Journal of Nursing Administration* 17, no. 5 (1987): 6–13.

28. Ibid., 6–13.

29. Ibid.

30. Ibid.

31. Crisham, "Ethics, Economics and Quality," 31.

Chapter 11

The Medical Staff's Influence in Nurse Recruitment and Retention

Terence F. Moore and Carolyn E. Fraser

Physicians can play a very positive or very negative role in the recruitment of nurses and especially in their retention. To understand the physician's role in recruitment and retention it is important that we understand the various physician personality types that work in a hospital setting.

PHYSICIAN PERSONALITY TYPES

There are essentially four types of physicians, based on their interrelationships with the hospital and its staff. Please keep these types in mind when choosing physicians to participate either formally or informally in your recruitment and retention activities. We have developed a matrix that was originally designed to select effective medical staff leadership, but the model is appropriate for nurse recruitment and retention.[1]

The matrix shown in Figure 11-1 measures two qualities: the physician's attitude toward the institution and whether or not he or she is a high-action or a low-action oriented physician.

The position shown in the lower left-hand corner of the matrix could just as well be called the "Scrooge" type of physician. This type of physician might also be called an "isolationist." "Isolationists" are people who state, usually to their close professional friends or others in the community, that the "sky is falling" or everything is getting worse. Their major consistency is that they are almost always negative toward any progressive action that is not in some way self-serving. Their negative mumblings are usually restricted to private conversations, and therefore they are easier to tolerate than some other types. However, they can be a drain on nurses and damning to the morale of the staff as a whole because they tend to verbalize in negative terms. They are ineffective in nurse retention and should not be used for nurse recruitment.

The dependent/bureaucrat shown in the upper left-hand corner of the matrix has a positive outlook on life but often fails to act. Particularly, this type fails to act to

150

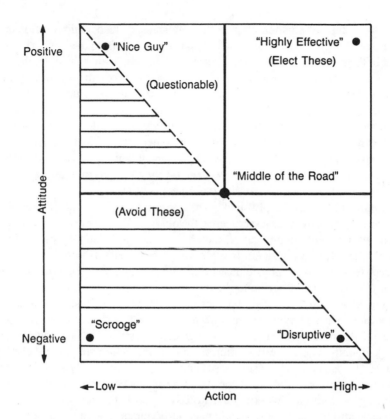

Figure 11-1 Matrix for Measuring Physicians' Personality Types. *Source:* Reprinted from *Organizational Burnout in Health Care Facilities: Strategies for Prevention and Change* by E.A. Simendinger and T.F. Moore, p. 88, Aspen Publishers, Inc., © 1985.

help nurses solve many of their problems or advance the profession of nursing. We refer to them as bureaucrats because they actually find comfort in an organizational setting, especially one in which decisions can be deferred to someone else or made by a group. They can be identified by such comments as "we are lucky to have things the way they are," "have a nice day," and "I really like _____." Seldom do you hear them make any action-oriented statement such as "Let's move on this project." They often wait until a crisis develops, and even then they usually manage to skirt it. They are definitely not the type to involve in projects in which you expect action. These physicians will not actively or publicly support change if it is controversial or critical. They like to be involved but not accountable. However, they will make supportive statements regarding hospital and nursing staff and can be used for initial one-on-one recruitment efforts—not retention.

The worst type of personality in both a medical staff leadership position and on the nursing floor is the disrupter/vitriolic physician shown in the lower right-hand corner of the matrix. Unfortunately, because these people are so visible, they often become elected to positions of responsibility and, even though they may be a vocal minority, tend to turn otherwise positive forums into an opportunity for tantrums. Too late, people realize that these physicians do not represent anything but their own vested interests. Even those who are truly concerned about the quality of patient care have little concern for nurses and other paramedical specialists within the organization. They often create an environment that is almost intolerable. Do not use these people on committees, because they require time and attention to contain damage. In fact, do not use these people at all.

Sometimes the vitriolic physicians are referred to as "ceiling shooters." The name derives from the characters seen in the old John Wayne movies who rode into saloons without bothering to get off their horses and then fired their pistols into the ceiling. The vitriolic physician is often seen "firing pistols into the air" for no apparent reason. These physicians are the responsibility of the chief executive officer (CEO), as we describe later.

It is interesting to note the similarities that exist between physicians' attitudes in patient care areas and their actions within the committee structure of a hospital. A middle-of-the-road physician, as the name suggests, is rather neutral and is average in both his or her orientation toward taking action and his or her general attitude. This is not a style of rule or personality type, but merely a compromise of the various extremes. Middle-of-the-road physicians border on being suitable for leadership positions or working constructively with the nursing staff, have a reasonable attitude, and are somewhat action-oriented. You might hear them say, "I may vote no on this proposal, but wonder what other alternatives are available to us."

The high-action, positive-oriented person shown in the upper right-hand corner of the matrix, whom we label a "developer/benevolent autocrat," can wield tremendous influence at the board level, with administration, and with the nursing staff. This action-oriented person is well-thought-of and has usually taken the time to analyze any potential counterarguments. He or she is in great demand. Be supportive of them in terms of helping them be aware of details, summaries, and follow-up. If at all possible, try to involve these people in nurse recruitment and retention activities. If a committee is being formed to retain nurses, tap these types of individuals.

An example of the difference between the effective physician leader and the dependent/bureaucrat is that the dependent/bureaucrat mentions that there is a hole in front of the hospital that has caused two broken legs, but that it is to be expected because of recent construction. The effective leader calls the appropriate person in administration; if the hole is not corrected, the developer/benevolent autocrat again asks the administrator or takes it to the appropriate subcommittee of the board if necessary. The drifter/passive physician, or "Scrooge," mumbles that the hole is to be expected because administration is incompetent and the whole organization is in disrepair. The disrupter/vitriolic physician contacts a member of the board and demands that the wrong hole be filled.

Mandell describes the type of physician who is essentially disruptive, but focuses on the physician's actions in patient care areas.

> Who are these bad boys wreaking such havoc on the patient floors? Often, but by no means always, naughty boy is a surgeon or member of a mutilating specialty. I know of no psychiatrist who has ever thrown a Kelly clamp against the wall or threatened an LPN with excommunication.[2]

Mandell's description, of course, is exaggerated because many surgeons are pleasures to work with.

POSITIVE CONTRIBUTIONS PHYSICIANS CAN MAKE TO THE RECRUITMENT/RETENTION PROCESS

Some of the specific contributions physicians can and should make to the recruitment process are worthwhile noting.

Physicians Should Help with Education

Physicians sometimes complain about the lack of nursing skills, but the good physicians—the really good ones—work with nursing supervision in conducting nursing seminars and informal training. Such training can assist in the development of a better rapport between nurses and physicians. Some physicians even sponsor educational awards that recognize outstanding employees. These physicians support and encourage the continual development of nurses.

In one hospital, which developed a service line approach to managing the neurological services, the department chairman said that he was very willing to meet with the director of the nursing education program to review and make suggestions about the types of educational programs that would be most beneficial to the patients and staff of that unit. More important, he volunteered to conduct a series of educational seminars for the entire nursing staff. Eventually, all physician members of the neuroscience department taught these courses, and the nursing staff responded by holding a special reception in recognition of the physician's efforts.

Physicians Must Be Supportive of Nurses with Both the Families and the Patients

Physicians who criticize nurses to other members of the staff, family, and patients can do much to demoralize the staff. When this occurs repeatedly it is supervision's responsibility to review it with the offending physicians. It should be explained that the hospital does not condone the staff's making derogatory, nonsupportive comments to patients and families regarding physicians and they should refrain from similar behavior. If the behavior continues, the hospital administration, nurse manager, or senior-level manager should be involved. In most instances, things will not get better unless there is an intervention of some kind.

The first step in this type of intervention is to identify exactly what the situation is. Second, it is important to document the situation and almost always discuss it with the particular physician before introducing it into a wider forum. Sometimes it can be useful to keep the discussion generic and not label any particular physician as disruptive or negative. For example, at one of the departmental meetings concern might be expressed because some of the members of the nursing staff believe that certain physicians are exhibiting disruptive behavior. Then cite specific examples of this type of behavior without naming the physicians.

Physicians must understand that negative comments they might make about the staff to families and patients can only harm themselves if some type of legal action results from the patients. The physicians would not tolerate having the nursing staff make derogatory observations about their inabilities, and nursing has the same right to expect that negative comments about their conduct will be made to them in private.

Physicians Should Have Realistic Expectations of Nurses

The transition many hospitals have gone through in recent years, the transition of having to do more with less, has not been acknowledged by many physicians. The cutback in nurse staffing created by poor reimbursement rates and reduced staffing created by the nursing shortage have had a compounding effect on the inability of nurses to "do all things for all people," and that includes physicians. It is no longer possible for nurses to follow physicians around and wait on them while they engage in social conversations with others on a particular nursing unit. Certain standards of what is an acceptable expectation of nurses' time must be agreed upon by nurse management and the medical staff.

We anticipate that the demands on nurses' time will be further exacerbated because of the reduction in nursing supervision at many hospitals that will most assuredly occur during the next few years.

Problems with Nurses Should Be Handled First before Going to Someone in Administration

The most appropriate method for a physician to communicate a problem for any area, whether it is the operating room or the emergency room, is directly with the nurse(s) involved. The next step is with the nursing supervisor of that particular unit. If it is a managerial problem—for example, inadequate supplies—the physician should begin with the nursing manager. Physicians should then move up the chain of command if the problem is not resolved.

Unfortunately, the lower-level employees and supervision are often bypassed, and a problem is taken directly to senior management or even the board. Administration is sometimes guilty of fostering this situation because it responds to physicians, fails to inform them of the proper communication channels, and does not involve the appropriate paramedical staff in the problem-solving process.

A physician often stopped by the office of an associate administrator and complained about the incompetence of a particular nurse in the operating room. The associate administrator unwittingly responded to the physician's concerns by calling the operating room supervisor and further compounded the problem because he bypassed the director for nursing. The situation was finally rectified when the director of nursing told the CEO about what had occurred. The CEO wisely put a stop to this two-way "leap frog management."

Outstanding Performance Should Be Recognized

The opposite situation occurs when physicians fail to recognize nurses for what they do, particularly when they are outstanding. One major hospital chain instituted a program to recognize all employees, including nurses, who went above and beyond the normal call of duty. This program is described in Chapter 8, but it merits a more detailed outline. The program uses a simple form or a three-by-five-inch index card. Anyone can recommend someone for an award. These nominations are reviewed every week by a committee of top management, and those who are deemed appropriate (about 90 percent are approved) receive a pin (an enamel apple). The award is always made by the person nominating the particular employee, and physicians often nominate others for the awards as well as receive them. When a person accumulates five apples, their fifth apple is a silver apple. When they have accumulated five silver apples, they are awarded a gold apple. Hospitals have also attached $100.00 to a silver apple and $500.00 to a gold apple. The program has proven successful in fostering more positive relationships among employees and between employees and physicians.

Accept the Nurse As a Colleague

Some physicians cannot accept the nurse as a professional colleague. One physician we know always refers to the medical staff as the professional staff—the inference is that nurses and other paramedical personnel are not professional. Physicians who cannot accept the nurse as a professional colleague are not much different from senior administrators who cannot accept lower-level supervisors as professionals.

NEGATIVE PHYSICIAN TRAITS THAT DETRACT FROM NURSE RECRUITMENT AND RETENTION

Many of the negative actions of physicians are simply the opposite of some of the positive contributions already noted; they include the following:

Intimidation and Bullying Behavior by Physicians. Intimidation and bullying are detrimental to nurse retention. Although it may not be cited as a high priority in many surveys, such behavior is widely acknowledged in candid conversations with nurses as sometimes being the factor that caused them to leave nursing. A physician with a condescending attitude toward nursing is a liability in today's environment of nursing shortages and should be treated as a liability.

Unavailability. Not being available is also a negative factor in nurse-physician relationships. It is frustrating to be responsible for a physician's patient when the physician is unwilling to be available either via telephone or in person on a timely basis.

Making Negative Comments about Nurses to Others. Physicians sometimes "run down" various members of the nursing staff in informal conversations and even in formal committee meetings. Furthermore, their comments are often not restricted to nursing and some physicians can always be counted upon to make disparaging remarks about the hospital staff.

Failing To Recognize Nurses Who Do a Good Job. Some people have a mental block about recognizing and extending their appreciation to others who do a good job. Although this trait is not as detrimental as always being negative, it leads to apathy on the part of the staff toward doing a good job.

Technical Incompetence. It is annoying to work for someone who is incompetent. It is equally frustrating to take orders from a physician who is technically incompetent or at least not as proficient as he or she should be. That type of mediocrity breeds mediocrity at the paramedical levels too. Good people will not work in this type of environment for very long.

Not Taking Suggestions about Patient Care from Nurses. Physicians are only with patients a relatively short time during the day. Nurses are usually with patients from 8 to 12 hours. Physicians who consistently ignore suggestions from the nursing staff about their patients do a disservice to both the nursing staff and their patients.

INCORPORATE PHYSICIANS INTO YOUR ORGANIZATIONAL STRUCTURE

One of the keys to having physicians involved in nurse recruitment and retention is to involve them in the organizational structure of the hospital. All of this sounds like a "motherhood statement," because most physicians are already given some opportunity to input in the decision-making process. However, more can be done to involve them.

The more modern service line approach to organizing the hospital fosters physician involvement. In these models, human and other resources are focused on various specialties such as neurosciences, women's health, and oncology, rather than functional departments such as the radiology, laboratory, or house-keeping departments. A major advantage of the service line approach is that physicians can be easily involved within the structure of their particular service line. They should be involved in all major decisions (marketing, capital expenditures and planning, and human resources).

One area that should be an integral part of these organizational discussions is nurse recruitment and retention. Every opportunity should be taken to review the nurse staffing situation and how physicians can assist in the recruitment and retention process.

If a hospital does not have a fully developed service line organizational structure, it may wish to involve a physician in a nurse recruitment and retention committee. Other members of the committee could be residents, someone from personnel, education, and/or other members of nursing.

As a minimum, nurse recruitment and retention should be reviewed on an ongoing basis at various standing committees of both the medical staff and board to keep them apprised of the staffing situation and to get their input. Open, frequent communication between medical staff leadership and nursing leadership is essential if good relations are to be maintained.

In summation, no nurse recruitment and retention program can be totally complete unless there is a concerted effort to involve the physicians in the process.

CHIEF EXECUTIVES ARE RESPONSIBLE FOR PHYSICIANS' ACTIONS

The ultimate responsibility for assuring that physicians are not a disruptive force with the nursing staff is clearly the responsibility of the CEO of a health care institution. The CEO cannot assure that a physician will be a positive influence on the nursing staff and, therefore, nurse recruitment and retention, but he or she can assure that the negative actions of physicians are kept within reasonable bounds. Nurses should not feel that their jobs are threatened simply because a physician is unhappy with their performance on a particular day or week or because a physician is abusive. Administration has a duty to assure that physicians are counseled if they exhibit disruptive behavior that in any way threatens the hospital's para-medical work force.

Many hospitals have a clause in their bylaws that specifically states that a physician's privileges may be withdrawn if they exhibit behavior disruptive to the institution's mission. If such a clause is not in effect, it should be incorporated into the bylaws of the hospital.

It is probably fair to say that some CEOs do not correct disruptive physician behavior for a number of reasons—mostly because of fear. It is easier to ignore their behavior than to correct it. If this is a problem within a hospital, the director of nursing has the responsibility to bring it continually to his or her supervisor. This should be done through carefully documented accounts of abusive behavior by physicians.

In a survey of 3,500 nurses, the nurses were divided into two groups: those who were dissatisfied and those who were satisfied with nursing as a profession.[3] Of the top 10 dissatisfiers, both groups listed lack of support of hospital administrators the second highest. The lack of support from nurse administrators was listed as the fourth highest dissatisfier, followed by salary.[4]

Support from senior management is absolutely essential to nurse retention. If a situation is to be improved, it is up to the nurse administrator to assure that top management is continually aware of the situation. In one hospital, a general surgeon continually berated nurses in both the intensive care unit and the operating room. It was felt that one of the major reasons for the high turnover rate of nurses was this particular surgeon's ongoing tantrums. The disruptive behavior stopped abruptly when the surgeon was called into the CEO's office and told that detailed accounts of his actions would be kept whenever his behavior became excessive and that these accounts would begin to be reviewed with the medical executive committee after they were discussed with him.

Without the support of top administration, the nurse manager is powerless in eliminating and even reducing negative behavior by members of the medical staff.

The opposite situation occurs when a physician becomes overly affectionate toward members of the nursing staff. Huge lawsuits in recent years over sexual harassment have been awarded to plaintiffs, and most CEOs are keenly aware of this liability on the part of other hospital employees and usually act swiftly. However, CEOs also need to be aware that sexual harassment by physicians can have an equally devastating effect on nursing morale and potentially can create the same kinds of lawsuits as have been awarded to other employees.

A nurse dreaded working alone with a particular physician because of his sexually suggestive remarks and innuendoes. The CEO called the physician into his office and reviewed the situation with him. The CEO also mentioned that the matter would appear in the formal minutes of the joint conference committee distributed to the members of the board if the behavior happened again. The physician terminated his amorous advances.

In conclusion, even though physician attitudes are not often cited as a key factor in nurse satisfaction or dissatisfaction, they can be a major detractor in other attempts to improve nurse recruitment and certainly in nurse retention. Therefore, every attempt should be made to assure that physicians are a positive, integral part of any nurse recruitment and retention program.

NOTES

1. Earl A. Simendinger and Terence F. Moore, *Organizational Burnout in Healthcare Facilities: Strategies for Prevention and Change* (Rockville, Md.: Aspen Publishers, Inc., 1985), 85–116.

2. Harvey N. Mandell, "Staff's Naughty Boy," *Postgraduate Medicine* 6 (June 1980): 39.

3. Florence L. Huey and Susan Hartley, "What Keeps Nurses in Nursing," *American Journal of Nursing* 88 (February 1988): 181–188.

4. Ibid., 183.

Chapter 12

Select To Search and Sell: Strategies for Recruitment of Students into Nursing by Nurse Educators

Fay L. Bower

The task of educating nurses has changed a great deal in the last 50 years. We no longer sequester young women in hospital dormitories while using them for free labor. Classes, for the most part, are scheduled at colleges and universities and not in hospital classrooms. The faculty is university-prepared and is composed of duly recognized academicians. Student rights are as important as faculty rights. Teaching strategies are varied, and testing has become a scientific endeavor. Virtually every aspect of nursing education has changed. However, the operation that has most recently changed is the way in which we acquire enrollments into the schools of nursing. For many years freshman classes were admitted after a rigorous and lengthy selection process. Even during times of war, when applications for nursing school dipped, the process of filling the first class of the nursing program was a matter of selecting the best persons from a pool of applicants. Classes were just smaller.

Today, for most schools, the process of acquiring a new class of students is quite different. We have moved from a "select mode" to a "search mode" as we recruit men and women into nursing. We use sophisticated techniques to interest people in nursing and into our specific schools. As in all other aspects of nursing education, recruitment and retention of nursing students are very different today than they were years ago.

In the early 1980s, applications to nursing schools and the pool of interested potential nurses began to decrease. We cited the recession as the reason (and it probably was one of the reasons) and believed that we could continue to operate under the status quo as we had weathered other applicant drops before. We knew that nursing enrollments were cyclical and that ultimately there would be an upswing and young women and some men would return to school once the recession was turned around. History was our barometer. In the past, when we faced a shortage of qualified applicants we simply waited until whatever caused the situation changed. We continued to select from the pool we had. In retrospect, we should have paid much more attention to the situation, for we were in the early phases of the most devastating shortage nursing and health care has ever encountered.

There were many indicators we failed to note. We know them all today. It was not until we acknowledged the severity of the situation that we were able to shift the way we acquire new enrollments. Once it was clear that women (and they are the predominant group of nurses and those interested in nursing) were interested in moving into other careers did it become abundantly obvious that we had a serious and irreversible condition. Figure 12-1 illustrates this point.

The reasons for the shortages are varied and many: the options for women—who traditionally have been attracted to nursing—far outweigh what nursing can offer. High school graduates seek careers that have status, pay well, and provide advancement, and without night hours, high risk, or stressful environments. There are fewer college-bound women now that the "baby boom" is over, and nursing has a poor image (it is usually seen as a service job equal to that of a motel maid).

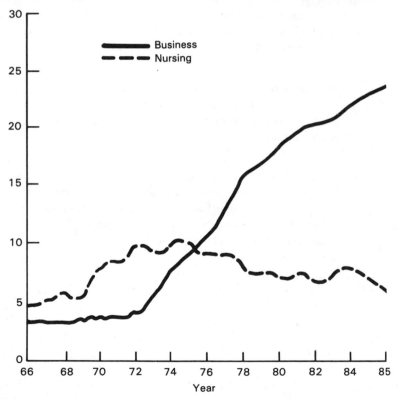

Figure 12-1 Career Preferences among Full-Time College Freshman Women, 1966–1985. *Source:* Reprinted with permission from *The New England Journal of Medicine*, Vol. 317, No. 10, p. 644, © September 1987.

At one time when a nurse was asked what she or he did, people responded to the reply with "Oh, I admire you, nursing is such a noble vocation." Today, the response is very different. Now they say, "Why do that? You could be a doctor," or "Oh, yuck—the job is so terrible." It is clearly evident that the image of nursing is poor; when this poor image is coupled with the competing options, it is obvious that the shortage of applicants is not going to change—not without a lot of effort.

Sometime in early 1983 I realized that we had a serious enrollment problem. I did not have it all nicely conceptualized, but I knew that we had to do something. As I look back now I realize I was entering a new era of nursing education and a new venture for the school and me. I was to become very knowledgeable about "marketing," "recruiting," and "image building."

Until 1983 I thought that marketing was what you did when you went to the store to select food. I knew that business schools used the term, but I thought it was a fancy way to describe advertising. I now know that recruitment is a marketing process and that image building is the way to recruit. Every once and awhile I reflect on the past and on Florence Nightingale's work and writings, and I realize that she, too, was using marketing strategies, but she probably did not know it.

According to Mentzer and Schwartz,

> Marketing consists of the activities performed by individuals or organizations for commercial or noncommercial objectives aimed at satisfaction through the exchange process of buyers' demand for products, services, people and ideas.[1]

I did not know when I asked my associate dean to find out what high school graduates, registered nurses (RNs), and transfer students expected of the educational experience at the university that I was in the first phase of marketing. I did not know when I asked the associate dean to survey the local career counselors to determine the reasons students were selecting other majors that we were doing one of the most important activities of marketing. By the time I had planned a faculty/dean retreat to discuss the strategies for reaching our objectives related to the direction of the school, I was totally involved with marketing. I finally knew when we were designing flyers and brochures that depicted nurses in "high technology" and "caring" poses that we were looking for ways to excite the reader, to sell the product, and to create an interest in an exchange of something we had to offer for something the buyer wanted. We were using marketing strategies to sell our product—education.

Nursing care shortages and declining enrollments forced us into marketing modes because we began to see that the preparation of nurses is an exchange process. We had the programs that prepared people to provide health care to others, but there were limited numbers of persons interested in our product (and many product makers); so we learned quickly to develop strategies to encourage others to seek what we had to offer.

All over the U.S., schools of nursing are marketing their programs. We have all discovered that there are several aspects of marketing and that we must use them if we are to turn the nursing care shortage and enrollment declines around.

An important concept of marketing is image making. It is very difficult to sell a product if it is not what the buyer wants. In 1957, the president of General Electric, John B. McKitterick, formally defined the marketing concept as "a consumer-oriented, integrated, profit-oriented philosophy or business."[2] The marketing concept includes gathering information from consumers, then using it to develop the company's product/service offerings. We now know that generally the public does not want what we have to offer, so recruitment for nursing schools means more than selling. It means that we (educators and hospitals, as the employers of most nurses) must change the nurses' role so that it is what the student-to-be wants. The change has already begun, but much more is needed.

There are four major components of marketing: product, distribution, promotion, and price (see Figure 12-2). These concepts are called marketing decision variables, and they set the direction for what we did to increase our enrollment.

PRODUCT

The actual production, in this case the education of student nurses, is not a marketing activity.[3] However, marketers study the consumers' product wants and design a product to achieve the desired characteristics. Product variable decisions and related activities are important because they are directly involved with creating "want-satisfying" products. Our task in nursing is to create the kind of job environment and career options that the student wants. We need to do far more research to determine exactly what kinds of changes in nursing would make nursing more attractive. However, empirical data indicate that the nurses' role must be more autonomous, less stressful, and perceived as more important. This is the image-making aspect of marketing.

For us nurse educators it was important to create an image that would make nursing an attractive career. We did this by focusing on the appealing aspects of the role. We do not deny that there are problem areas; however, we decided to highlight those aspects of the nurse role that throughout history have lured nurses to the profession. We formed focus groups of nursing students, nurses, and ex-nurses and asked them to tell us why they entered nursing. All of the groups said that they were drawn to nursing because they wanted to help others, that they cared for others, and that they wanted to see the sick well and to keep the well from becoming sick.

Thus caring, comfort, and cure became the theme of our image building of nursing. Of course we highlighted the beginning salaries and pointed out that no

Marketing Environment

Political Forces   Legal Forces   Regulatory Forces

Product

Price   Buyer   Distribution

Promotion

Technological Forces   Economic Forces   Societal Forces

Marketing Environment

Figure 12-2 Variables of the Marketing Mix and the Marketing Environment. *Source:* William M. Pride and O.C. Ferrell *Marketing: Basic Concepts & Decisions*, 5th ed. Copyright © 1987 by Houghton Mifflin Company. Used with permission.

other graduate with a baccalaureate degree could enter a field with a starting salary of $32,000.

At the same time we began to work closely with local hospitals to discuss ways in which the nurse role could be improved so that the issues of status and autonomy could be a part of the role.

DISTRIBUTION

To satisfy consumers, products must be available at the right time in a convenient and accessible location.[4] The marketing manager attempts to make products available in the quantities desired to as many customers as possible and to hold the total inventory, transportation, and storage costs as low as possible. Nursing educators can do a great deal to address these distribution variables. Holding classes at times and in places that students want them is really possible. At the university level, classes are offered on weekends and in the late afternoon so students can work during the day and all week. Scheduling students so they can have clinical courses close to their homes is one way of keeping transportation costs down. Providing outreach off-campus programs is another way to improve distribution. In the fall of 1988 the university offered the baccalaureate program at one off-campus site. As surveys are completed we may expand to other sites.

Distribution of the product also involves the distribution of information, both about nursing and about the program for the preparation of nurses. This led us to the development of colorful, artistic, appealing brochures, advertisements, and flyers. Much of the story line was about the career and its appeal for those who wanted to care and comfort and use their knowledge to make a difference in someone else's life.

This leads me to the third aspect of marketing—promotion.

PROMOTION

Promotion facilitates exchanges by informing people about the organization and its products. Promotion is used for several reasons. For example, it might be used to increase public awareness of an organization or a new product or branch. In addition, promotion is used to educate consumers about product features or to urge people to adopt a particular position. It may also be used to renew interest in a product where popularity is waning. This is currently very true of nursing. Given the sudden change in patient acuity and thus the demands on nurses and the high-risk nature of the health problems of today (acquired immune deficiency syndrome, for example), many people have lost interest in a career in nursing. Promotion is necessary to rekindle interest. Most schools promote nursing as well as themselves. Promotional activities for nursing's image include more than brochures and advertisements. Personal announcements at gatherings of students, informational meetings at the university, video "spots," radio announcements, and "nurse day" activities are just a few of the ways we have promoted nursing and our program. Again, focus groups of students helped us to determine what prospective students wanted to hear about the job/career. We used their comments, we photographed their activities in clinical settings, and we used these pictures in our promotional materials.

We promote the university school of nursing as a community where each student is treated as an individual and is part of a culture that cares. We focus on the values of education (excellence, education of the whole being, and service to others) and how a university education can help the student in the nurses' role. We tell the students that an education at the university prepares them for a very important role where they can use their intellect *and* their caring abilities. Our promotional materials highlight the importance of nursing as an intellectual process—that the decisions nurses make are critical to the patient's progress. At the same time we picture nurses doing caring activities—comforting the aged, positioning the bedridden, rocking babies.

Since our focus groups told us that they were interested in careers that would make them feel important and where they could do important work, we focused our informational meetings on how the nurse is involved in hospital management, decisions, and in physician-nurse collaborative decisions about the treatment plan for the patient.

The informational meetings, where interested persons are invited to meet at the university to hear about nursing and our program, have increased in attendance and have provided one of the best means for the distribution of knowledge. Once an inquiry comes to our office (either by mail or a telephone call) we follow up with a one-page flyer that invites the inquirer to an informational meeting. We do this because we discovered that personal contact with us and a view of the university were good ways to capture the inquirer's interest. Our enthusiasm about nursing and an opportunity to see the university environment promoted nursing and our program better than written materials. Those who voiced continued interest left with an application and information about financial aid, housing, and who to contact if they had additional questions. Within a week these prospective students received a follow-up letter that thanked them for their interest in nursing and our program.

Once we receive an application to the nursing program, our efforts to "get an enrollee" increase. The application is reviewed, an entering grade point average (GPA) is calculated, transfer courses are evaluated, and a phone call is made so the applicant will know quickly the status of the application. This process of evaluation often recruits a student for the future, since some applicants are not able to meet the entrance requirements. The phone discussion alerts the student to what needs to be completed and where to obtain the course work. This is where articulation agreements with community colleges and other universities are critical. Because we have articulation agreements with all of the local colleges and universities, we can make a recommendation to the applicant that is to his or her advantage and that demonstrates our interest in the student rather than in enrollments for us. Ultimately, this process brings us an enrollment into nursing but at this point it is directed more at what the student needs; we do not care where it is acquired.

During the informational meeting, the issue of cost is discussed. Cost is the fourth aspect of marketing, and in marketing language it is known as *price*.

PRICE

Consumers are interested in a product's price because they are concerned about the value obtained in an exchange. Because price is so important to consumers, it is a critical component of the marketing plan. It often is used as a competitive tool by the marketer.

In nursing education price is not a promotional tool because the cost of education is more a part of the kind of education (private or public) the students desire. However, scholarships and loans are offered and used as promotion to demonstrate the potential for accessibility to a program.

Financial assistance is a major issue in private education and one we had to address early in our marketing plan. In the past, the university's tuition was affordable by nearly everyone. But as inflation rose and salaries were adjusted to meet market value, tuition rose. A great disparity occurred as we tried to compete for students when the public programs essentially were free.

In order to keep our price competitive, we had to locate additional sources of support. Traditional grants in aid, federal student guaranteed loans, and university-supported need-based scholarships were not enough. We developed two other options that have helped price us right.

The first option was based on linking the service agency recruitment efforts with ours. We wrote to local hospitals and asked them to use the money for one Sunday full-page advertisement to support one student in our accelerated second-baccalaureate option (a 15-month learning experience). A $14,000 investment to locate nurses guaranteed one nurse in 15 months who would repay the support by guaranteeing two years in the agency. Our research on retention demonstrated that a nurse who stayed for two years usually stayed beyond five years. Our offer was both a recruitment investment for the hospitals and a retention mechanism for them. The hospitals' advertisements had not been very successful, so our offer was appealing. In addition, it provided new linkages for us and them as we together tried to address the nursing care shortage. A side effect of this alliance was that it created new interest in each other and new commitments to work together.

The second option to help price the experience within reach was also a joint service-education venture. The university agreed to reduce tuition in exchange for faculty and space. Many of the nurses in the hospital had the qualifications for university appointment and had in the past taught part-time for us. We offered to hire the nurses who could meet the university appointment criteria and could teach the course work we offered in exchange for reduced tuition for a limited number of qualified applicants. On-site education for these nurses who wanted a baccalaureate degree would be provided. Our faculty would go to the agency, and their faculty appointments would come to the campus and teach our generic students. This option appealed to the agency because it helped them retain nurses who otherwise probably would have left, as they were restless and wanted advanced degrees. We also offered scholarship money for those nurses who met merit criteria. Clinical excellence (as documented by the nurse manager who supervised the applicant) and scholarly achievement (as measured by the GPA earned in the basic program) were the criteria. The response to this option has been surprising. Thirty-five RNs are expected to begin classes in the fall.

The most important idea to extract from this discussion is that recruitment of individuals to nursing school must include the ability to provide what the buyer (student) wants. Schools must be able to interest prospective students in a career that offers attractive job opportunities, salary, and advancement. Schools cannot simply advertise, nor can they survive using old methods. We can no longer select the best from a pool of applicants; we now must promote nursing and persuade individuals to enter the profession. Above all, we must develop programs and career options that students want. Although we at the university ''backed into'' the use of marketing strategies, as did others, we all know much more about what it means to market a program.

The profession must use all of the technology available in order to assure that nursing grows and thrives. We have through history faced many threats and hurdled many obstacles, but none quite like the one we face today. We can gain new knowledge and use modern business practices such as marketing to reverse the nursing care shortage, but we must work together (education and practice) to accomplish our goal. With one participatory effort we can solve this nursing care shortage problem.

NOTES

1. J. Mentzer and D.J. Schwartz, *Marketing Today*, 4th ed. (New York: Harcourt Brace Jovanovich, 1985).

2. Ibid.

3. W.M. Pride and O.C. Ferrell, *Marketing: Basic Concepts and Decisions*, 4th ed. (Boston: Houghton Mifflin, 1985).

4. Ibid.

Chapter 13

Nurse Recruitment and Retention in Smaller Hospitals: A Unique Challenge

Joseph M. Smith

Discussions of the impact of the nursing shortage are taking place in hospitals all over the country. For some facilities the problem borders on a crisis severe enough to threaten the very existence of the organization. Consider the plight of the smaller rural hospital, which operates with only enough professional staff to meet the patient care needs for its normal average daily census.

The crisis can begin quickly and may deteriorate to a situation where the hospital can no longer admit additional patients because the nursing staff is insufficient for the patient load. Even one unfilled nursing position combined with a call-off due to illness, coupled with three or four unplanned admissions, can force administrators to make difficult choices.

Should admissions be limited with the obvious effect of reducing the income to the facility, or should they take a chance and attempt to deliver care with less than the minimum nursing staff? How will the community react when a patient is sent to another facility some distance away when it is generally known that the local hospital is not full? Clearly the above scenario describes a no-win situation for administrators and patients alike. The solution to the problem is an elusive one, but one that demands the attention of every smaller hospital administrator and nursing executive. Advanced planning and innovative programs may help minimize the frequency of such occurrences.

Recruitment and retention of nurses in smaller and rural hospitals present a unique challenge and many opportunities for administration and nursing executives. The projected nursing shortage clearly will affect these facilities more seriously than larger institutions. The strategies that smaller hospitals will have to employ are somewhat different, however, because there are a number of factors in recruitment and retention that are different from those experienced in hospitals larger than a 100-bed capacity.

Factors affecting recruitment and retention of nurses in smaller institutions are as follows:

- nursing leadership
- lack of diversity in nursing
- limited career ladder
- fewer continuing education opportunities
- inability to compete financially
- physician attitudes and actions

By exploring how each of these factors operates to limit the supply of nurses and by proposing some solutions for each, nursing executives will be provided with opportunities to help ensure a supply of registered nurses (RNs) needed to maintain quality of care and compete effectively in today's health care marketplace.

NURSING LEADERSHIP

Rural facilities must be able to attract professional nurses from a wide geographic area, yet the hospital may not be well known outside its immediate service area. Placing advertisements in newspapers in larger cities generally produces disappointing results, and the expense can be substantial. Job fairs and recruitment seminars are often dominated by the major health care providers who offer enormous recruitment incentives and make showy presentations. The standard methods of recruitment just do not work for isolated hospitals. The challenge of overcoming these hurdles falls on the nursing executive, who must possess the ability and the resources to recruit effectively. A weak nursing executive will not be a good salesperson or ambassador for the hospital.

If the smaller or rural hospital is to compete effectively for the diminishing pool of professional nurses, it must recognize that the role of the nursing executive is more than that of just a firefighter who keeps nursing under control and schedules the staff to meet patient care demands. The position must be a prominent one and should be compensated accordingly. I recommend placing the nursing executive at the same level as the chief financial officer and including him or her in all high-level committees and strategy sessions. The nursing executive must be a team player who shares the vision of the board and chief executive officer (CEO). Only under these circumstances will he or she be able to sell opportunities effectively to prospective nurses. Effective personal selling by the nursing executive may be the most important recruitment tool available to the smaller institution.

Arousing the initial interest of prospective candidates requires an organized approach to presenting the opportunities available.

Make the Community Aware That Positions Are Available. The nursing executive should be an excellent public speaker who routinely makes presentations to clubs, organizations, and special interest groups. If enthusiasm is evident, attendees will be encouraged to communicate with potential candidates in their circles of friends and relatives.

Forge Relationships with Local Businesses and Industries. Recruiting for business managers in rural areas can be as difficult as recruiting nurses for hospitals. Provide local businesses with a list of opportunities at the hospital; these can be used to attract candidates for the positions who may also have spouses who are professional nurses.

Provide a Direct Path to the Nursing Executive. Occasionally a prospective candidate will call a personnel department about potential nursing opportunities. An effective recruiting strategy will include expediting information to the nursing executive, who makes immediate contact and sets up an initial meeting. Avoid all of the bureaucratic procedures, such as filling out forms, until a strong interest is developed. Make time for a meeting that fits the candidate's schedule, and pamper the candidate. Include an introduction to the CEO on the first visit. These steps will make the candidate feel important and needed.

Establish the Nursing Executive As a Role Model. Future nurses begin to show interest in a nursing career in high school. The nursing executive should present opportunities frequently to juniors and seniors at local schools. High school counselors should feel free to direct an interested student to the nursing executive so that selling a nursing career can be done by the person most qualified to cultivate enthusiasm for that career.

Let the Public See Your Nurses. A good leader will try to direct public attention toward the people who really perform the work. In a nursing career there are few opportunities to be recognized for a job well done. A nursing executive should routinely seek out and high-profile the individual, both internally and to the public. Small newspapers are often willing to run human interest stories or short articles about the accomplishments of an individual nurse. Do not forget to include a picture. This is an excellent forum to help the hospital to communicate its message and to focus attention on its nursing staff. It is a low-cost method of rewarding high performance and telling the nurse that he or she is important to you and to the community. If the local paper is reluctant to run the article, take out a paid advertisement. The cost will be greatly outweighed by the benefits that accrue to the institution. In summary, the leadership qualities of the nursing executive will be important factors in nursing recruitment. The roles of salesperson, counselor, and ambassador may be as important as skills in nursing management.

LACK OF DIVERSITY IN NURSING

The smaller hospital traditionally combines the various types of nursing services into one unit. Specialty nursing opportunities are usually limited by the number of patients, the size of the staff, and financial resources. A medical/

surgical unit may contain patients who would be separated in larger institutions. Prospective nursing candidates from larger facilities often have a preference for a specific area of nursing, such as the emergency room, intensive care unit, oncology, coronary care, or surgical care. As nursing skills become more specialized, nurses will be increasingly reluctant to embrace a position that is perceived as general duty nursing. How does a small facility that combines patients for efficiency attract nurses who are increasingly specialized?

Implement a Case Management Approach. Instead of assigning nurses to a section of a unit containing a variety of patients, assign them to patients whose conditions are consistent with their area of specialization. Encourage a case management approach such that the nurse can function as the expert in that area of nursing. Encourage physicians to look to the specialized nurse as an assistant or consultant for their patient's specific needs. Include patient education in the nurse's responsibilities and encourage them to help train other staff members such as licensed practical nurses (LPNs) and aides in the care of that disease entity.

Market the Advantage of a General Nursing Practice. When case management is not practical, it will be necessary to encourage the specialized nurse to embrace a position that contains a variety of nursing responsibilities. The organization should develop a package of information that demonstrates the positive aspects of a general nursing practice. Provide a range of continuing education opportunities that help the specialized nurse feel more comfortable in other areas of nursing practice. Ensure that proper orientation with an experienced nurse is made available. There is nothing more intimidating than to be thrown into a nursing situation where skill levels have not been attained or where past skills have become rusty because of lack of recent exposure. Reassurance that an effective system of retraining is in place will allay any fears that a candidate may have about a general nursing practice.

LIMITED CAREER LADDER

Opportunities to advance one's nursing career in smaller hospitals appear limited if traditional nursing roles are perpetuated. Prospective candidates will want to know what opportunities exist and will attempt to identify a career path for themselves. They will shun an organization that demonstrates a pattern of professional stagnation. Smaller hospitals have more opportunities than they think. Creative use of nursing personnel can provide challenging positions that serve to create an effective career ladder.

Identify the Traditional Nursing Career Ladder. The hospital should be prepared to commit to a well-defined career ladder in the interview stage. Organizational charts with positions identified should be combined with position descriptions for each step in the career ladder. Descriptions should include the requirements and responsibilities for each position. Give the candidate a complete set to study at leisure. A candidate will then be able to determine the extent of opportunities that exist and to project his or her future growth in the organization.

Identify Nontraditional Nursing Opportunities. While many nurses prefer traditional nursing roles, some highly qualified individuals will be searching for opportunities on the fringe or outside of nursing itself. These candidates will be attracted to an organization that subscribes to a philosophy of personal growth, even if it means eventually losing a nurse to a position in the organization that takes him or her away from direct patient care. The nursing executive should be able to identify candidates who wish to practice nursing for a period of time and eventually grow into a position that is outside nursing services. Examples of such opportunities include positions in the management of outpatient services, utilization review, personnel administration, and outreach community health education. Position descriptions for these opportunities should also be given to prospective candidates. This strategy will encourage the professional nurse to join the organization as a stepping stone to other career opportunities. A supply of RNs in nontraditional positions also provides an immediate source of staff during peak census periods or temporary vacancies. Additionally, these options serve to attract professional nurses who may otherwise shy away from the smaller organization and serve as a key retention strategy for qualified individuals.

Involve Nurses in Hospital Decision Making. Progressive organizations recognize the tremendous pool of talent that exists within the ranks of the nursing professionals. Many nurses are creative thinkers with substantial experience in areas not involving nursing directly. Smaller hospitals can enrich the jobs of their nursing personnel by including them on *ad hoc* committees and task forces dealing with a variety of operational issues. For example, an RN may be particularly talented in interior decorating. Include that nurse on a hospital beautification task force. Similarly, there may be a nurse interested in joining a committee that is exploring the feasibility of an outpatient women's health center.

Finding the potential individuals to serve on these groups can be a simple task. Ask the personnel manager to review the files of all nurses for past experience, and identify areas of interest by sending out a brief survey. When an opportunity presents itself, the CEO or assistant administrator personally should invite the nurse to participate. Make sure the nursing department frees time so the nurse can be an active participant on the committee. Even if the nurse declines to join the committee, the ego boost created by asking can have a substantial impact on nursing morale and may eventually effect retention of the individual.

The adoption of creative policies for advancement will enhance recruitment efforts. Market your organization as a progressive institution that recognizes the individual's desire to grow through traditional and nontraditional routes.

FEWER CONTINUING EDUCATION OPPORTUNITIES

The financial vise continues to tighten on smaller hospitals, which are repeatedly squeezed to provide more services with fewer resources. Cost-reduction opportunities are becoming more limited, and administrators are forced to reduce programs that do not generate revenue. Continuing education is a favorite target in difficult times. Cutting the education budget is the equivalent of organizational suicide. An organization cannot expect to attract and retain skilled professionals if it obstructs the road to professional development. Progressive organizations recognize the need to upgrade individual skills constantly and will provide the necessary resources to offer high-quality educational opportunities. Progressive organizations will tie professional continuing education closely to future viability. Nurses who are provided with opportunities to enhance their skills will be attracted to the organization initially and likely will remain in the organization for longer periods.

Effective continuing education strategies that facilitate recruitment include the following:

- Provide candidates with a comprehensive list of programs that demonstrate the organization's commitment to continuing education.
- Develop a relationship with local colleges and universities and initiate programs with them that meet the continuing education needs of the nursing staff. Encourage the development of programs that help LPNs progress to RN status. The hospital should have a tuition reimbursement program tailored to the professional nurse. Additionally, scheduling flexibility should be allowed to facilitate ongoing education.
- Make arrangements with larger institutions to borrow continuing education programs in videocassette format and make them available around the clock to all nurses. This is a lower cost alternative to continuing education outside the organization. Ready access to a videocassette recorder at convenient times will encourage participation.
- Reward nurses who make continuing education a priority. A well-trained, up-to-date nurse is more valuable to the organization, and efforts should be made to demonstrate that such initiative is valued.

INABILITY TO COMPETE FINANCIALLY

Wages for RNs are clearly escalating at larger institutions, and tremendous incentives are offered for recruitment. The smaller facilities cannot compete directly in this arena. Attracting registered professionals from larger institutions whose salary structures are substantially higher is very difficult, yet there are methods that can be employed to become more competitive.

Utilize Appropriate Levels of Caregivers. Many organizations have joined the crusade for an all-professional staff. In the process they have strained the supply of RNs and escalated the cost per discharge. Many tasks now performed by RNs can be performed effectively by other caregivers, such as LPNs and nurse's aides. In other industries, management is careful to utilize highly skilled individuals only in areas where their expertise and training are needed. Lesser-trained individuals are assigned to perform the more routine tasks. By evaluating which caregivers are best suited to the tasks and assigning them appropriately, fewer RNs may be needed; the financial resources then can be put into RN salaries to make them more competitive with those of larger institutions while maintaining the appropriate nursing budget.

Implement Appropriate Compensation Programs. An organization that simply increases the hourly rates for RNs could run the risk of increasing costs for overtime. Instead, the organization should adopt programs that add to the RN's compensation without affecting the base rate. Differentials for shift work, team leader, charge nurse, and the like can be generous and increase substantially the effective hourly rate. A thorough explanation of these programs along with a sample yearly earnings chart should be provided to each prospective candidate.

Provide Seed Money for Nursing Students. Although finances are frequently tight in smaller hospitals, a proactive recruitment program that costs money can actually save money in future years. Estimates for recruiting nurses range as high as $20,000 per nurse when the direct costs of recruitment are coupled with the cost of orientation and lost productivity. Assuming that one-half of that cost is related to direct expenses for recruitment, smaller hospitals with a creative program can reduce that cost drastically by a few simple measures.

- Offer small scholarships to graduating high school students who have been accepted in an accredited school of nursing. Scholarship size can vary, but a sum of about $500 per student is recommended. There should be no strings attached to this grant. One can ask how the hospital benefits from such a program. The benefits are twofold. Primarily, young people are encouraged to enter nursing as a career, and the hospital does its part by stimulating interest in the profession with the long-term benefit of increasing the pool of available nurses. In other words, the hospital will be doing its part to reduce the nursing shortage. The second advantage is perhaps more subtle. By advertising that the hospital offers these scholarships and by attaching importance to the award process, the community image of the hospital is enhanced. The organization will be perceived as a proactive one, and one that is interested in the welfare of young adults in the community.
- Develop a scholarship for students in their final year of nursing school. These scholarships should be substantial and should cover the majority of the cost

for tuition and books for the final year. In return for the scholarship, the student signs an agreement to work for two years at the hospital or repay a pro rata share for any period less than two years. Fully document the program, including the agreement forms. Do not forget to add the criteria for qualification. If you want the best and the brightest students as employees later on, attach a required grade point average qualification. Once the program is developed, personally meet with the financial aid officers at local schools of nursing and explain it. Encourage them to recruit candidates for you. Once they are identified, have the candidates screened and interviewed by the nursing executive just as if they were seeking employment. Once the scholarship is awarded, use the opportunity to highlight the program by submitting information to the local newspaper.

By comparing the annual cost of the two scholarship programs with that of conventional recruitment methods, one can easily see the tremendous advantage to smaller hospitals. The following illustrates the impact:

	Cost per Nurse	Annual Cost*
Conventional recruitment programs	$10,000	$30,000
Scholarship program	2,666	8,000
Cost difference	$ 7,344	$22,000

*Assumes three nurses are recruited each year and scholarships amount to $2,000 for a full year scholarship.

Besides the financial advantages, these programs offer the additional benefit of having a supply of graduate nurses always on hand. Nursing executives can count on replacement nurses for those who leave during the year. Even though they are not experienced nurses when they arrive at your facility they eventually will join the ranks of fully qualified practitioners. Nursing turnover is a fact of life in small hospitals in spite of aggressive retention efforts. Only by assuring a continuous replenishment process will such facilities have an adequate supply in the future.

PHYSICIAN ATTITUDES AND ACTIONS

The quality of the work environment for RNs in any hospital is heavily dependent on the attitude of physicians toward nurses. In organizations where physician/nurse teamwork is prevalent, RNs enjoy higher status and a more satisfying work experience. If nurses are perceived as mere handmaidens, professional resentment will lead to unacceptable nursing turnover. Additionally, an organization's reputation for a less-than-ideal environment between physicians and nurses can seriously impede recruitment efforts. The smaller institution must actively work to create a positive relationship between physicians and nurses.

Fostering a good professional environment will require a strong commitment and heavy involvement by physicians. Some suggested strategies are outlined.

Involve Physicians in Nursing Manpower Planning. A medical staff that understands the need for nurses and appreciates the difficulty of recruiting will be more sensitive to the environment created by them.

Introduce Prospective Candidates to Key Medical Staff Members. As part of the interview process include a few minutes with physicians who are supportive of nurses and who are perceived by their peers as leaders. They will convey the message that RNs are valuable and welcome in the organization.

Include Physicians in RN Meetings. Greater appreciation of the role of the RN will be achieved if a doctor receives firsthand information about problems between nurses and physicians. Physicians must be made aware of their impact on the nursing environment.

Appropriately Discipline Abusive Physicians. Administration and the medical staff should develop a policy jointly that clearly outlines the hospital's expectations of physicians with regard to their relationships with hospital staff. Policy violations should be dealt with appropriately and expeditiously. Prospective candidates should be made aware of the organization's commitment to maintaining a professional atmosphere at all times.

SUMMARY

While the nursing shortage is expected to continue, smaller and rural hospitals can ensure a continued supply of RNs if their recruitment and retention programs are aggressive. Recognition of the organization's limitations, and highlighting its unique characteristics, actually may give many smaller hospitals an edge over their larger competitors. There must be organizational commitment to recruiting high-quality, skilled professionals that must be endorsed and supported at all levels within the organization. Through creative methods the smaller facility will be able to identify potential candidates and successfully recruit them to its staff. Smaller hospitals that adopt a wait-and-see attitude will find themselves without an appropriate number of RNs, and eventually that shortage could affect their ability to meet the patient care demands.

Chapter 14

Nurse Recruitment and Retention in an Urban Hospital

Catherine DeVet

Recruitment and retention are often treated as separate entities. However, they are a continuous process used by hospitals to assure that a resource of sufficient quality and quantity is available to meet the nursing care needs of their patient clientele (Figure 14-1). This process can be unique for each institution because of differences in philosophy, services, case mix, complexion of the medical staff, and whether it is a profit-making or not-for-profit organization. Hospitals also may find they have very different access to financial resources that can be used for the recruitment and retention of staff. For example, by virtue of the philosophy and/or the location of the facility, it may treat a larger number of indigent patients for whom limited, if any, reimbursement may be available. The "profit" of the institution may be slim, and no substantial amount can be budgeted for recruitment and retention activities.

Urban hospitals share special challenges in the recruitment and retention of nurses. Within any urban area, a number of facilities exists. Therefore, urban hospitals are likely to be competing for the same nursing resources within a restricted geographical area. At times this proximity of institutions may be as close as across the street or on the same block.

Nurses in an urban market often have a choice of a variety of acute care institutions. One or more facilities may be university-affiliated settings that serve as major tertiary care centers. Others may be more community- or specialty-focused. In addition to the number and variety of acute care settings, nurses also have many other health care agencies in an urban area for whom they can work. These can include extended care, public health care, community and visiting nurse agencies, home health care, industries, and nursing personnel agencies. Therefore, the urban hospital finds that the market for nursing expertise is broad and very competitive.

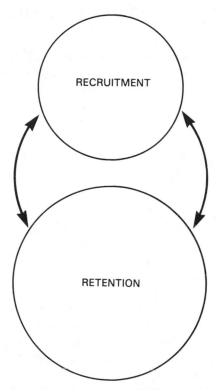

Note: Recruitment and retention are not separate entities but parts of a continuous process. Of the two, retention should be the larger focus of the urban hospital.

Figure 14-1 Recruitment and Retention: A Continuous Process

DIFFERENTIATION AS A KEY TO SUCCESS

Because of the special challenges urban hospitals face in the recruitment and retention of a qualified nursing staff, they must evaluate continually their approaches to this process and compare their efforts with those of their competitors locally, regionally, and nationally. Urban hospitals must match the opportunities offered by other facilities while constantly striving to create unique niches that will differentiate them from others. The ultimate goal is to convince nurses that employment at this specific institution offers something special that is valuable to them. The opportunity an urban hospital may offer nurses may be completely different from that offered by other organizations or it may be a different twist to a common benefit. For example, a hospital may be the first in the urban area to offer a profit-sharing method of reimbursement to nurses or it may offer a creative committee structure to enhance the participation of nurses in controlling nursing practice in the institution.

STRATEGIES FOR RECRUITMENT

Recruitment of nurses often is viewed as the responsibility of a designated nurse recruiter or the human resources department within the hospital. However, successful recruitment is the responsibility of *all* employees of the hospital. What employees say about their place of employment in the community influences the attitude of potential recruits. An institution whose own staff enthusiastically markets it to others as the best place to work will have greater success in recruitment than an institution that relies primarily on a designated few in the personnel department to do the recruiting.

Employees: The Major Nurse Recruiters

Research has shown that nurses view group cohesion and positive affiliation among their work group as being important facets of job satisfaction.[1] If a nurse believes that an institution offers such an environment, she or he is more inclined to seek a position in that environment. Employees of a hospital, especially the nursing staff, can influence nurses to seek employment within an organization by depicting the work climate as supportive, collaborative, and employee-oriented. Employees equally can diminish the effectiveness of a personnel department's recruitment effort by making disparaging remarks about the work environment of their institution to others in the community.

Because of the significant influence of employees' word-of-mouth advertising, the hospital must focus on developing its own work force as a powerful marketing tool to attract nurses. This includes training employees in marketing behaviors and then reinforcing this behavior with feedback on the results of the recruitment effort. If the effort of a particular employee was instrumental in recruiting a nurse, this could be highlighted in the internal newsletter of the organization. Institutions also have offered employees a "finder's" bonus to stimulate employee participation in the recruitment effort. The bonus is usually a prorated sum based on the number of hours the recruit will be working and is paid in increments over the first 6–12 months of employment to assure that the new recruit stays a sufficient period of time to make the bonus economically useful.

The existing nursing staff within a hospital is instrumental in a successful recruitment strategy. All nurses are potential marketers to student nurses and other nurses who come to the institution, such as agency nurses and nurses who are seeking positions and touring the institution. These potential recruits have ample opportunity to observe how nurses treat each other, what type of nursing care delivery system is actually practiced, and the relationships nurses have with administration and physicians. In their busy work schedule, nurses may forget that there are potential recruits constantly in their environment. Frequent, repeated coaching to enhance the nursing staff members' ability to market their institution positively while conducting their normal work duties is an imperative part of any hospital's strategy for recruiting nurses.

Compensation: A Major Issue of Recruitment

Salary has emerged as a most significant factor in both the recruitment and retention of nurses.[2-4] The ''new'' nursing work force is no longer oriented to the altruistic values of the past, when the opportunity to serve others was the highest priority in choosing nursing and concern for compensation was considered inappropriate. While research indicates that factors other than pay contribute to the job satisfaction of nurses, salary and benefits have emerged among the top issues in the current nursing shortage.[5,6]

In order for a hospital to compete for nurses in an urban area, it must offer a salary that is competitive with that of other hospitals in that area. Also, because the shortage of nurses is a national phenomenon, the need to be competitive on a regional and national level is becoming more important in attracting both experienced nurses and newly graduated nurses from other communities to one's own urban area.

Providing competitive salaries is a significant challenge for many urban hospitals with fixed reimbursement systems and a large number of indigent patients, whom they may treat because of their philosophy, types of services, and geographical location. Creativity in salary structures and benefit packages may mean the difference between a successful recruitment strategy and a continuing loss of recruits and turnover of existing staff.

Package Compensation Attractively

Urban hospitals should package the entire scope of their financial supports to present an optimal picture of what the institution can offer to potential recruits. This is especially important for hospitals that cannot afford a starting salary that matches or exceeds that of the wage leader in the area. Another strategy to compete with the wage leader would be to offer a benefit that appeals to nurses but is not offered by other institutions in the area. This may be a child care program, moving expenses, life insurance, or a flexible benefits package that offers employees a choice of benefits from which they can select. A hospital may offer a lower starting salary but a wider salary range, so the nursing salary is less compressed than that of other institutions. This would have the added benefit of rewarding nurses who are retained in the hospital for a number of years.

An institution that cannot compete with the top salary offered by others should take extra care to stress in its advertising and interviewing process those non-economic factors it offers that are significant to the job satisfaction of nurses. For many recruits, these nonmonetary benefits may be sufficient to offset the difference in salary that may exist. The factors might include the opportunity for career development within the organization, decentralized nursing organization, participation in practice decisions via participatory management or joint practice committees, autonomy in patient care practice via a primary or case management nursing care delivery system, and recognition programs supported by nursing and hospital administration.

Salary will remain an important issue in the recruitment of nurses in an increasingly tight market. Urban hospitals will need to plan continually for ways in which financial resources that may have been used for other services or programs can be diverted to support a stronger salary program for nurses. Also, nursing and hospital executives will need to work proactively with legislators and third-party payers to reevaluate the information on which reimbursement levels are set, since it did not include significant attention to the salaries of nursing personnel, the largest group of employees in the hospital.

Benefits As a Competitive Edge

The benefits provided to employees can be the distinguishing factor used to recruit nurses in an urban area where many health care institutions are competing for the same resource. Child care has been mentioned as a potentially significant benefit for nurses, a predominantly female work force. Before instituting this benefit, the institution should closely evaluate the potential nurse recruits, since some institutions may not hire a sufficient number of mothers with young children to make child care a cost-effective benefit. A related benefit that will become more popular with the aging of the population is adult care, in which care for the parent of the nurse will be provided if needed. Child/adult care programs offer significant financial risk to the organization and should be evaluated carefully and planned prior to their implementation.

Retirement programs will become a more popular benefit as the nursing work force ages and new nurses come from a group of "second-career" individuals who will be older and interested in retirement benefits. Retirement programs may also be used by hospitals as part of creating a "career" environment for nursing personnel that fosters long-term employment and institutional loyalty.

A cafeteria-like benefits package may be more attractive than the fixed benefits package that many organizations currently offer. In this new approach, employees are able to select the benefits they desire, within certain parameters. This prevents duplication of benefits that already may be available to the nurse through a spouse. This benefits package thus becomes more valuable to the nurse as part of the total financial incentives the organization has to offer.

Other financial rewards that nurses seeking employment may expect include compensation for education as well as experience and a more attractive wage range. The creative use of bonuses or a profit-sharing program can be used to decrease the compression of wage ranges in the hospital's salary schedules and make the total compensation package more attractive for nurses.

Relationships with Nursing Schools: A Critical Factor

Since a major source of nurses for urban hospitals may be new graduates from nursing programs in the area, it is imperative that the urban hospital establish and maintain close and continuing positive relationships with the area's nursing schools. The hospital should form relationships with as many institutions as possible, using as many methods as possible. The closer and more enduring the relationship, the greater the opportunity to recruit from the program.

Techniques used to establish a relationship between the hospital and the nursing school can foster loyalty on the part of both faculty and students. A loyal faculty member can serve as an excellent marketer for the institution as well as for potential recruits if the faculty member decides to make a career change. One mechanism to secure a relationship with the faculty is the use of shared or joint positions in which the hospital and the school of nursing contract so that faculty members have clinical positions in the hospital. In addition, the faculty and the nursing staff from the hospital may serve as members on one another's committees, particularly those that affect the clinical environment in which the students practice. A hospital can cooperate with schools of nursing in providing continuing education programs or innovative programs that facilitate the matriculation of nurses from the hospital into undergraduate and graduate programs.

While the relationship with the faculty is important, the relationship the organization can establish with student nurses is crucial. A hospital should provide clinical practice areas for as many student groups as possible. When the students come to the institution, every effort should be made to make them feel welcome and establish an identity with the hospital.

Student nurses should be recruited actively for employment in the hospital during their student experience to increase the students' familiarity and comfort in the hospital's environment. This can be done through the use of student employee positions in which the student acts in the role of a nurse's aide or in a more advanced technician role, depending on the student's level of program completion. Student extern programs can provide a unique educational experience for students while simultaneously orienting the student to the facility with the expectation that the student return to the organization after graduation. Certain programs pay for the student's tuition in the senior year of the program with the student's commitment to remain employed at the hospital for a designated period of time after graduation.[7] Hospitals can also offer student loans and scholarships with or without stipulations that the student either work for a specific time at the organization after graduation or pay the money back.

Hospitals should be sure to offer recruitment information to students at the local schools of nursing early, since students often are making choices for employment prior to their final semester. The manner in which the hospital offers its recruitment materials can influence the success of its efforts. Having pizza parties or special events at the school or hospital may be the way that one hospital successfully differentiates itself from other health care agencies in the recruitment effort. One institution sponsored an entire week of events highlighting nursing in which many programs were specifically targeted for student nurses and new graduates.[8]

Many hospitals currently are using monetary incentives to recruit nurses. The urban hospital that is competing for nurses must seriously consider matching such an incentive, particularly in the recruitment of nurses who are not from the area and have no other criteria on which to judge the work environment in the various urban hospitals. However, bonuses for signing on carry questionable value beyond initial employment. Institutions that do not deliver a satisfying environment for the new employee will experience high turnover and little return on the investment the bonus represents.

As institutions become more sophisticated in their recruitment efforts and nurses become more discerning in their job search, the activities that differentiate an organization will be the key to success. Urban hospitals constantly must fine-tune the total recruitment effort to maintain a competitive edge over other health care institutions in the same area. In order to do this, the hospital should create a specific position or committee to oversee the total nurse recruitment program and provide the ongoing focus to the important details that can mean the difference in an institution's successfully recruiting a nurse who is "shopping." A nurse as manager of recruitment and retention who is knowledgeable about the institution and the field of recruitment can be an invaluable resource. Often, the fact that recruits have one person who coordinates the employment process and keeps them informed throughout the interview process can project a "caring" image that is significant to many nurse applicants, particularly new graduates. The nurse recruiter (or designated committee if a recruiter is not available) also should keep statistics such as turnover, exit interview information, and the success of different advertising techniques, which can be important in the evaluation of the total recruitment program.

Untapped Markets in the Urban Area

One source of nurses that an urban hospital will need to evaluate is the pool of inactive nurses in the area. Urban areas may have a significant number of such nurses who would be willing to return to the work place with sufficient support and orientation. Refresher programs in the past have had an inconsistent return on the investment, and a hospital will want to evaluate carefully the best method to attract "refresher" nurses to its organization. Ideally the refresher program will be based in, and financially supported by, the hospital so identification and loyalty are established with the nurse from the outset. However, the hospital may not have sufficient resources to offer a refresher course but may be able to offer itself as a clinical site for nurses in a program sponsored by a community college or other community education agency. It is important that the hospital involve itself in any program that offers a potential supply of nurses.

A source of nurses that is often overlooked is the existing pool of untapped resources in the institution's own part-time nursing staff. The institution should evaluate its full-time incentive programs to assure that they are as appealing to its part-time staff as possible and market these incentives to that group.

Marketing the Niche That Differentiates

To recruit successfully, an urban hospital must have the same characteristics as the other hospitals in the area plus a niche that differentiates it from the others. This niche must be advertised effectively and will need constant change because others are bound to copy a successful strategy. Recruitment factors that offer an urban hospital opportunities to differentiate itself successfully from others include an individualized orientation program, support for continuing education, opportunity for advancement within the organization, support for nursing research, opportunity for participation in making decisions related to nursing practice in the organization, flexible staffing schedules, and supportive ancillary departments. The key to using these characteristics as successful recruiting tools is to convince the recruit that your program is *the best* in at least one characteristic while the other areas are equal in quality to competing institutions.

Having excellent programs within an organization is ineffective without a first-rate marketing and advertising program. A hospital must advertise at least as much as its competitors to sustain name recognition. Also, an urban hospital must advertise differently to attract different types of nurses. For example, what appeals to new graduates is often different from that which appeals to experienced nurses, second-career nurses, or nurses returning to practice after a stopout. Assessment of the needs of the organization can serve as a basis to identify the types of nurses needed and direct the thrust of the marketing and advertisement effort.

While the hospitals within an urban area compete for the nursing resources available, cooperation may be an effective strategy to attract nurses who are able to relocate to the area. The goal of the cooperative effort is to concentrate resources regionally and nationally to market the urban area as a center of excellence for nursing. Rather than recruiting for a specific institution, this strategy seeks to increase the overall nursing resource available for employment in the urban area. The strategy is in its infancy, and specific guidelines have yet to be developed on how nurses who are attracted to the area through this marketing technique would then be recruited to different institutions.

An urban hospital can market itself nationally by using a marketing firm with an established reputation for representing excellent hospitals. The firm contracts with the urban hospital to represent it in a national market. The firm is able to use its pooled resources from many organizations to reduce the cost of such national exposure and thus can be a cost-effective mechanism for an institution to advertise on a national level.

In summary, recruitment is part of a total process by which a hospital obtains a nursing work force of sufficient quantity and quality to meet the patient care needs of the client population. The keys to successful recruitment are to match adequately the incentives offered by competing health care agencies and to market aggressively a valued incentive that differentiates oneself from other organizations.

Recruitment of an adequate pool of nurses will require hospitals to offer nurses competitive salaries and benefits, a significant challenge in this era of cost containment. Hospitals, as well as all health care agencies, also must become involved in activities focused on attracting more individuals to choose nursing as a career. Urban hospitals can work with high schools, the media, and state and national legislators to plan programs that will effectively recruit individuals into nursing. Otherwise, urban hospitals will find that their recruitment efforts of the future will be directed toward moving around a relatively fixed number of nurses between health care agencies within their geographical area. Gains for one institution will result in losses for another with no net gain for the welfare of the community as a whole.

RETENTION IN URBAN HOSPITALS

While the nursing shortage has focused efforts on the recruitment of nurses to urban hospitals to assure an adequate work force, the ultimate success of an urban hospital in providing quality nursing care services will be the retention of a nursing staff committed to making the organization the most excellent in the area. The costs of recruitment can be significant, with estimates ranging from $2000 to $8000 per recruit.[9,10] However, the effective retention of a nursing staff can free money, which then can be directed to support more programs promoting the retention of nurses, thus establishing a positive cycle of investment in the major work force in the hospital. Hospitals that fail to recognize the importance of retention of nurses will experience a monetary drain in recruitment efforts and a revolving-door phenomenon as dissatisfied nurses leave for more satisfying environments.

The keys to successful retention parallel those for successful recruitment. An urban hospital must match the incentives that competitors use while differentiating itself in one or more incentives that are significantly valued by nurses (Figure 14-2). The incentives used as distinguishing characteristics should be selected carefully, because once a program or an incentive is begun in an institution it often cannot be discontinued without creating negative feelings in those affected.

Assessment: The First Step

The retention program and its distinguishing characteristics should be cost-effective and net the greatest possible return on investment. Therefore, the urban

Match characteristics valued by nurses that are offered by competitors.

Develop and market one or more characteristics valued by nurses that differentiate oneself from competitors.

Figure 14-2 The Keys to Successful Recruitment and Retention

hospital that is serious about retention will do a thorough assessment of the needs and desires of its staff and determine a systematic and coordinated effort based on the results. The assessment should be repeated at least annually because of the changing nature of the nursing work force and the health care industry.

The assessment may be made with the use of an employee questionnaire that has been shown to be valid and reliable. Focus groups can also be an effective mechanism by which to get meaningful feedback from the staff. If focus groups are convened, the facilitator should be experienced in this type of methodology and viewed as a neutral person by the nursing staff. A committee of staff nurses and representatives from nursing management can serve as the coordinating and planning group for retention activities in the organization and oversee the assessment process and the program development resulting from it.

Characteristics of Magnet Hospitals: The Base of the Program

The study of the magnet hospitals surfaced the unique features of institutions that were able to both attract and keep nurses.[11] Current literature suggests that the information learned in studying the magnet hospitals is still true today.

The characteristics of the magnet hospitals that were identified as job satisfiers can be clustered into four major areas (Exhibit 14-1). Administrative characteristics include a clear philosophy or ''corporate'' culture, a supportive administration that recognizes staff nurse contributions, a participatory management structure, and sensitivity by management to ethical/moral issues. Organizational

Exhibit 14-1 Major Areas of Job Satisfiers in Magnet Hospitals

---

Job Satisfiers

Administrative Factors

Clear philosophy or "corporate culture"
Supportive administration
Recognizes staff nurse contributions
Participatory management
Sensitivity to moral/ethical issues

Organizational Factors

Positive relationships with peer group, co-workers and nursing administration
Collaboration with other professionals/departments
Effective use of committees
Joint practice committees
Personnel policies and programs allow nurse to better control personal and professional life
Size/complexity of organization "fits" the nurse
Salaries/benefits adequate and appropriate to expertise

Professional Practice

Workload is appropriate to number and mix of staff with sufficient support services
Access to nurse specialists for consultation
Primary nursing care delivery system
Autonomy and responsibility in position with authority
Ability to plan, implement and evaluate creative ventures
Opportunity to share practice with others via preceptor/teacher role

Professional Development

Adequate orientation program
Inservice based on staff needs/input
Continuing education programs
Support for formal education
Career development via career ladders

Source: Based on *Magnet Hospitals: Attraction and Retention of Professional Nurses* by the American Academy of Nursing Task Force on Nursing Practice in Hospitals, American Nurses' Association, 1983.

---

factors encompass positive relationships with peers and nursing administration, collaborative relationships with other professions and departments, the effective use of committees, personnel policies and programs that allow nurses better control of their personal and professional lives, a "fit" with the size and complexity of the organization, and salaries and benefits that are adequate and appropriate to the nurse's expertise. The area of professional practice includes the use of primary nursing; a workload that is appropriate to the number and mix of the staff; sufficient support services; access to nurse specialists for consultation; autonomy in practice; the ability to plan, implement, and evaluate creative ventures; and an opportunity to share practice with others via a preceptor role. The fourth area of job satisfiers is professional development. It addresses adequate orientation programs, inservice and continuing education programs based on staff needs and input, support for formal education, and career development.

The challenge for the urban hospital is to plan a creative approach to the implementation of the characteristics of the magnet hospitals that *fit* the particular staff within its organization. Not all hospitals can afford to implement every characteristic listed in the study, but creative planning can permit some aspect of each characteristic to fit within the specific limitations that an institution may face. A hospital may decide prematurely that it is impossible to implement a facet of the magnet hospital study. However, an institution can couple the results of its own assessment with the ideas from the literature to plan a unique and cost-effective way to introduce a specific nurse satisfier. For example, the ability to advance within the organization can be approached in multiple ways. This may take the form of supporting interunit transfers through effective in-house postings and advertising, offering career planning through the human resources department, or providing opportunities to learn new skills—such as by opening critical care classes to general medical-surgical nurses who are interested.

Administrative Factors

The philosophy of the hospital must be articulated clearly so that a nurse may select an environment that is congruent with his or her own values. Simply recruiting "any warm body" will not build a stable work force for an urban hospital. The organization must establish an identifiable "corporate culture" and consistently act in congruence with the norms of the culture. A nurse employed in an institution that shares his or her value system is less vulnerable to the recruitment efforts of another organization since the work environment is part of the nurse's own identity.

To be satisfied, nurses must feel a sense of worth in their jobs. Nurses must also see that their jobs are recognized and valued by nursing and hospital administrators and physicians as well as by their colleagues and patients. Therefore, hospitals must plan and implement recognition and reward programs for their nursing staff as part of a comprehensive approach to retention. Adequate compensation alone will not retain nurses. The environment in which the nurse works must convey a sense of esteem and worth for the nursing care provided to patients.

Hospital administrators often are unfamiliar with the actual work that nurses do in their organization. Despite the fact that the nurse is the only professional in contact with patients 24 hours per day and seven days per week, administrators' knowledge of what nurses do may be based more on what they have read or heard rather than what they have observed with their own staff.

Nurses are keenly aware of how much value top administration displays toward their jobs. A visible administration that frequently interacts with the nursing staff projects an attitude of openness and understanding that is highly valued by nurses. Ideally, administrators may spend a day ''shadowing'' a nurse to experience the varied and complex activities to which nurses are exposed daily. Nurses may be invited to spend a day with an administrator, as well, so that they can begin to understand how the administrator's job supports the nurse in ways that are not evident to the nurse on the clinical unit.

Personal recognition by the administrator may be a powerful incentive for many nurses. However, a recognition and reward program must be varied to meet the needs of different types of nurses and nurses who are at different stages in their careers. A hospital is likely to find that many nurses respond to concrete rewards such as five-year pins, plaques for special achievements, and dinners or receptions held in their honor. Other nurses will value more intangible rewards such as the ability to serve on special committees, accessibility to top administration or the board of trustees, or assignment of the responsibility to develop a special project of interest. Nurse managers also can help by identifying significant individual rewards. The assessment survey used to determine meaningful retention activities can include items related to recognition and rewards that may be valued by the institution's unique nursing staff. Any program that is implemented must become part of the culture of the hospital and not be used as a gimmick to pacify the nursing staff and maintain their loyalty during the current shortage.

Many organizations espouse participatory management structures but in reality practice a hybrid system that often breeds distrust. Participatory management too often means that nurses participate only in decisions for problems that upper management has been unable to resolve or in which upper management has little or no interest. The wishes of the physicians practicing in the institution may be another limitation of participatory management in nursing. Physician preferences often can take precedence over the judgment of the nursing staff. This action gives a clear message to nurses that their expertise is valuable only if it does not conflict with the decisions of the hospital administration or the medical staff.

The most successful participatory management structure is one that has clearly defined the scope of decision making for the staff and supports that scope. A self-governance model can be an excellent means of achieving maximum participation and autonomy for the nursing staff but should be used only if it is congruent with the hospital's culture, the hospital is genuinely committed to supporting it, and the staff is educated and coached in how to use the model effectively.

Organizational Factors

Nurses value supportive relationships and group cohesion. An institution that fosters a strong team spirit within the clinical unit will progress toward a work force whose ties of loyalty are more difficult to break by incentives offered by other organizations. Many individuals may be willing to accept a lower compensation rate if they feel a strong bond with their colleagues. Nurses who have worked in an environment that has been unfriendly and unsupportive are particularly drawn to an environment of warm, respectful relationships among peers.

The nurses' immediate supervisor affects the climate of the clinical unit significantly. This person has been traditionally called the head nurse, although many other titles are currently in vogue. This manager's expertise is critical in the hospital's effort to create a satisfying environment for nurses. Therefore, the institution that wants to stand out as the best place for nurses to practice must invest in hiring and developing its first-line managers into expert leaders.

Head nurses frequently are recruited for their clinical expertise. Too often, management skills are then learned by trial and error with little coaching or orientation. There is ample support in research and the literature that leadership and effective management are learned skills that must be developed through ongoing education and experience. An urban hospital that institutes a strong retention program focused on compensation, recognition, and rewards but that ignores the caliber of its first-line nurse managers will often find nurses exiting from the clinical areas because of inept or weak managers.

A hospital can pinpoint areas of ineffective management by using data from its annual assessment of nurse satisfaction and interim and exit interviews, or through monitoring turnover statistics. A poorly performing manager must be targeted for intensive remediation or removed from the position if quick improvement is not evident. The cost to the organization in employee turnover is too high to let ineffective managers remain in positions because they are due to retire in a few years or have significant seniority, excellent clinical skills, or certain credentials.

Positive, collaborative nurse-physician relationships can contribute to the professional environment that many nurses value and seek in their work lives. An urban hospital can differentiate itself from other area hospitals by implementing formal collaborative relationships between nurses and physicians through the use of joint practice committees or case management teams. In institutions where the culture does not yet support formal liaisons between nurses and physicians, collaboration may be fostered informally via the development of specialty practices at the unit level, in which the nursing staff works with a defined group of physicians to deliver care to a defined patient population. Research supports that the patient, and therefore the hospital, also can benefit from the collaborative practice between nurses and physicians. [12]

Personnel Policies and Programs. Personnel practices should be established that allow nurses to better control their personal as well as their professional lives. The culture of nursing is changing from one in which self-sacrifice is paramount to a more balanced approach between work, home, and leisure. Assertiveness-training programs teach nurses how to say "no" to requests to work beyond their personal limits without accompanying guilt. Nurses no longer look at how they can adapt to the work schedules of their organization but how the organization must adapt to them to make employment satisfying and congruent with their life styles. Therefore, flexible staffing takes on a new meaning and importance in the ongoing satisfaction of nurses within an organization.

Urban hospitals competing for nursing resources will find a distinct advantage for both recruitment and retention if they are able to accommodate the desired work schedules of nurses. Flexible staffing includes not only attention to the staffing desires of the nurse by supervisors and scheduling personnel but the actual involvement of nurses in planning their schedules with other staff members on their unit. Hospitals that can enhance the nurse's control over his or her environment in ways such as this will often find greater ownership for decisions that are made and less dissatisfaction with even potentially negative choices. To handle the many complexities that flexible staffing creates, a computerized staffing program is essential. Without it, frequent errors can occur that frustrate both staff and supervisors, and inadequate staff coverage for patient care could result.

Nurses face significant stress in their work lives. Patients are more acutely ill, technology rapidly changes, ethical dilemmas frequently occur, and life-and-death situations exist for which the nurses' skill and knowledge can be a determining factor in the success of the outcome. Stress can be a positive, motivating factor in one's work life. However, if it is not managed, stress can result in a syndrome commonly called burnout. A nurse who is experiencing burnout is less productive, a negative force on a clinical unit, and a likely candidate for resignation or termination from the institution. The hospital that successfully assists nurses to cope with stress not only retains a satisfied employee but also a more productive one.

While there is much discussion about the stress nurses experience, many hospitals do not have a systematic program to help nurses cope. This then is another opportunity for an urban hospital to differentiate itself from other health care organizations in the area.

Hospitals can use several techniques in instituting a stress-control program. For example, a cost-effective way to maximize existing resources is to incorporate a stress-control program into an existing employee assistance program. Another technique is to implement support groups for nurses that can be facilitated by a member of the hospital's social work or human resource department or by a nurse with special expertise in stress reduction and conflict resolution. It is essential that the facilitator have appropriate skills to lead such a group. In addition, this individual may be responsible for individual counseling of staff as well as monitoring the support groups.

The best approach a hospital may take is to focus on *preventing* negative stress rather than directing all resources toward coping with it once it occurs. Stress can be reduced if the factors already discussed as part of a comprehensive retention program are instituted by the hospital and sustained so that they become part of the corporate culture. Institutional ethics committees can be a significant force in the positive resolution of the ethical dilemmas in which nurses are involved. Inservices or continuing education programs on stress-management techniques can be helpful, too. However, they are effective only if the stress-management techniques are practiced and reinforced in the work environment until they become integrated into the individual's ongoing behavior pattern.

Compensation: A Major Issue in Retention. Compensation is a major issue of retention as well as recruitment. Wage increases for nurses have been compressed since the last nursing shortage, and in 1986 they were only an average of 4 percent despite the notoriety of a shortage of registered nurses (RNs) throughout the nation.[13] Once the nurse is employed in the hospital, merit increases and the salary range become potential sources of satisfaction or dissatisfaction. Because nurses are the largest single work force in the hospital, wage adjustments for them can have significant financial impact on the organization. The challenge is to plan a fiscally responsible compensation program while satisfying nurses who increasingly realize the wage discrepancies between themselves and other health care professionals. To maximize the compensation incentives instituted by the hospital, the input of employees and successful programs that are being used by competitors should be considered.

There are several options from which hospitals may choose to meet the compensation challenge. For example, an urban hospital can increase the range between the starting salary and the top salary offered to its staff. The average maximum wage for nurses is approximately $7000 higher than the average minimum wage.[14] Nurses can often meet this top salary within 7–10 years of employment. They then have no further monetary reward in a job that is increasing in responsibility, liability exposure, and stress. Hospitals must seriously consider increasing the maximum wage so that ongoing compensation can be offered to nurses as an incentive to remain within the organization.

An urban hospital may choose to increase the compensation of nurses by paying a full-time salary and/or benefits for fewer than 40 hours of work per week. In the compensation scheme, the employee works 36 hours (usually three 12-hour shifts) and is compensated for 40 hours. In order to staff weekends better, another approach may be to offer a weekend cadre in which the nurse is compensated full-time for working 24–32 hours every weekend.

These work arrangements may be very attractive to some nurses. However, an organization should carefully evaluate whether it will be able to continue to compensate its nursing work force for hours not worked. Institutions that initiate programs that they do not sustain may face considerable dissatisfaction by its nursing staff if the staff perceives that the organization is taking away something of value.

Because of the financial risk to hospitals that high nursing salaries can create, an urban hospital will want to examine other approaches to financial rewards that can act as incentives but not necessarily become a part of the ongoing wage structure of the employee. A creative use of bonuses to reward excellent nurses can be developed. Bonuses must be paid often enough to achieve their maximum motivating potential. However, bonuses are one-time rewards that can only be earned again if excellent performance is continued. In this type of system, the institution benefits because its resources are being used to reward its most productive worker and the nurse is rewarded for the exceptional contribution made to the organization.

A new method to increase the compensation of the nursing staff that is being tried in some hospitals is a profit-sharing scheme. This type of incentive program can be very beneficial to the hospital as well as the employee. The additional compensation is directly linked to the investment of the employee in the operations of the hospital, and the money for the compensation is actually "raised" by the employee. However, urban hospitals must pursue any type of profit-sharing program carefully. First, nonprofit organizations must assure that such programs do not jeopardize their not-for-profit status. Another challenge is setting up a program that is viewed as fair by employees. Many hospitals may find that this is not an appropriate alternative because the degree of "profit" they anticipate earning in the future is too ill-defined or too small to make the program credible.

There are several approaches an urban hospital may take to institute a profit-sharing program. A hospital may offer an across-the-board bonus to all staff members if the organization achieves a certain monetary goal. Another institution may arrange for the staff on a particular clinical unit to receive a monetary award if their expenses are contained within specified parameters. A third approach would be to offer additional compensation for new services that nurses plan and implement that produce revenue for the hospital.

A hospital must compete with other health care institutions in the urban area not only on the issue of salary but also on differential pay. Almost all of the nursing staff will be involved in working off-shifts and weekends. An urban hospital must successfully compete with others in the area by offering competitive differential pay for employees for these less-attractive hours. The hospital that concentrates its resources on differential pay may reap a double benefit. The nursing staff realizes an increase in the salary base and the organization may be able to recruit more individuals to work these less-desirable hours.

Professional Practice Factors

With the nursing shortage, adequate staffing that permits the nurse to deliver patient care as close as possible to his or her model of practice is a special challenge. Primary nursing is cited frequently in the literature as well as in the magnet hospital study as being the model of care preferred by most nurses. Currently, primary nursing is equated with a predominantly RN staff. Each RN is responsible for the total nursing care of a caseload of patients. However, with the nursing shortage and the increasing monetary restraints faced by hospitals, this model of primary nursing becomes increasingly difficult, if not impossible, to meet.

An urban hospital has a unique opportunity to differentiate itself from other hospitals by creating a system in which the essence of primary nursing is maintained with a mix of RN and auxiliary staff. In fact, the hospital that is able to plan a satisfactory system with its nurses is likely to be recognized as *the* place to be employed. The ability to practice as a professional nurse is one of the greatest challenges in the current health care system, and the institution that establishes a system that permits nurses to match their expectations will be a leader in both recruitment and retention.

In the development of strategies to support the essence of primary nursing, an urban hospital must carefully evaluate how it chooses to supply patient care support to the diminishing RN supply. Staff nurses must be involved in planning how auxiliary staff will be used in patient care. Automatically assigning nurse's aides or licensed practical nurses to hygiene care and other such intensive contacts with the patient can displace the RN from the very types of contacts that give the greatest satisfaction. Also, valuable assessments and teaching can occur while the RN is completing what may appear to be a low-level skill at the bedside. If staff nurses have input into how the auxiliary staff is used, their acceptance of changes in their practice will be facilitated and dissatisfaction reduced.

Urban hospitals need to assure that systems within the organization that support nurses are in place and working smoothly. Research suggests that as much as 35 percent of the nurses' time may be spent in non-nursing duties.[15] As the nursing resource continues to diminish, it will be increasingly unable to assume these duties and successfully meet the responsibility of providing nursing care for more acutely ill patients. Hospital departments will need to negotiate with the nursing division to plan how clerical, housekeeping, dietary, pharmacy, and other non-nursing tasks can be eliminated from the nurses' role and assumed by the appropriate department or level of personnel. The urban hospital that successfully achieves such a balance can earn a reputation among its own staff and those in other institutions as being the most progressive institution in the area in meeting the challenges of the nursing shortage and the economic constraints of the industry.

Another area where an organization can excel as the innovative leader in conserving its nursing resource is in the creative use of computer systems that facilitate nursing practice. For example, a hospital may seek to be a demonstration site for a new computer program that will augment the nurse's ability to meet the requirements for charting or care planning or assist the nurse to gain access to information on procedures, drugs, or a patient treatment regimen for a specific medical or nursing diagnosis. At the very least, an urban hospital must be knowledgeable about how competing hospitals are utilizing computer technology and assure it remains on the cutting edge.

As nursing becomes a more well-defined profession, the area of professional practice will provide the urban hospital new opportunities to develop innovative programs for staff nurses that are valued and that will differentiate the institution from its competitors. The urban hospital that foresees the opportunities and successfully integrates them into the work environment of the nurse will indeed have an edge in both the recruitment and retention of nurses in the geographical area.

Professional Development Factors

Retention of nurses begins with the interview and hiring process. The placement of new recruits in the clinical area that fits their knowledge, skills, and interest followed by provision of a thorough orientation are wise investments for the urban hospital. The orientation program should be planned, systematic, competence-based, and flexible. Orientees have different needs based on their education and past experience. The program that can accommodate the variable learning needs of new staff members is cost-effective and facilitates the integration of the new nurse into the life of the organization.

Orientation should address the social as well as the skill needs of the nurse recruit. One of the most effective ways to do this is through a preceptor program. This program accomplishes dual goals for the hospital. It allows competent staff the opportunity to share their practice with others—an identified job satisfier for current nursing personnel. Simultaneously, new recruits have mentors who introduce them to the norms of the organization and coach them in learning the standards of practice operant in the clinical area.

The nursing shortage may tempt a hospital to shortchange the orientation program. This strategy is short-sighted, since nurses who are insecure tend to be less productive and more frustrated with their role. They often will seek the "safety" of an orientation program in another institution rather than struggle with the daily reality of practicing in an environment that they have not had a sufficient opportunity to master.

Once a nurse successfully completes the orientation to a new organization or clinical area, opportunities for continuing education—both within the hospital and through formal degree programs—become significant. Health care technology changes faster than updates can occur. As resources become more focused on providing care and less available for training and education, hospitals will find it more difficult to provide money for formal schooling or quality educational opportunities for their staffs during paid time.

However, nurses clearly state that they expect hospitals to provide support for their education. Again, such an expectation offers the urban hospital an area in which it can distinguish itself from other institutions. The hospital can earn the reputation as the most progressive in providing the nursing staff with the factors it needs to practice in a professional manner. To maximize the benefit of the hospital's investment, the nursing staff should participate in planning the types of educational opportunities.

Meaningful continuing education opportunities can be very different for nurses depending on the stage of their career and their individual goals in the profession. A flexible plan for determining the type of education that will be supported by the organization will satisfy a greater number of nurses than one that designates a narrow range of paid educational activities. An organization may financially support certification programs, formal education programs, inservices and workshops sponsored by the hospital or other providers, and closed-circuit television programming. In addition to "things," an institution can also choose to invest in expert nurse educators and/or clinical nurse specialists who are responsible for working with nurses on a more individual level to improve the person's expertise.

Opportunities for Advancement. Because the urban hospital has many different types of health care institutions with which to compete in a relatively small geographical area, it must provide a variety of options to staff members looking for a "change" in their careers if it is going to retain the staff within the organization. A thorough review of its potential nursing positions in all departments in the hospital can identify multiple opportunities for growth for staff. These can then be marketed so that staff members are apprised of the choices available to them. The result is mutually beneficial because the staff person's need to look for new horizons is met within his or her present environment.

The judicial use of a career ladder or a similar structure can motivate excellent performance and reward employees for their clinical knowledge and expertise. A career ladder system can achieve the dual goals of providing an opportunity for nurses to advance in the clinical area and compensating nurses who exhibit exceptional performance. However, an urban hospital that is considering a career ladder approach must plan carefully, since the experience of others in the use of such systems has pointed out that the system must fit the nursing culture of the organization to be successful.

Professional development and advancement can mean different things to different types of nurses or nurses in different stages of their careers. For example, Mitchell discusses different types of nurses.[16] The "getting ahead" types need significant challenge and a career marked with timely promotions that recognize the productive energy they put into the organization. The "getting secure" types, which personify the majority of staff nurses, expect job security and an organizational commitment to lifelong employment. The "getting free" types need freedom and respond to involvement in short-term task forces that focus on projects that have quick, concrete results tied to them. The "getting balanced" types expect that the institution will work with the nurse to assure an equal balance between work and personal life.

Nurses vary not only in type but in the stage of their career. Seybolt describes the differences between five levels of employees[17]: entry level, 0–6 months; early career, 6–12 months; mid-career, 1–3 years; advanced career, 3–6 years; and later career, more than 6 years. Early career nurses need an opportunity to perform well on the job through the support of supervisors and peers and to receive adequate feedback on the contributions they are making to the organization. Mid-career nurses need autonomy to make decisions and to work more independently. Advanced career groups need incentives that maintain or rekindle their excitement in their jobs. One creative way to accomplish this is to develop nurses on units into various "expert" roles and title them as consultants in the specific area. For example, the nurse may be a discharge planning consultant, research utilization consultant, grief counselor, or patient classification consultant.[18]

Whether an institution segments its nursing staff into these classifications or another, the important point is that no single approach to advancement and career development is going to meet the needs of all of the staff. Any program must be based on the needs as expressed by nurses in assessments conducted by the institution and by the needs expressed by individual nurses to their managers.

In summary, retention must be the primary focus of the urban hospital if it is to have the nursing resource required for patient care. The characteristics of the magnet hospitals serve as a sound base for building a successful retention program. The effort should position the urban hospital as a progressive leader in creating and sustaining an environment in which a staff nurse can grow professionally, advance to new challenges, and be compensated adequately for the expertise gained from continued education and experience.

The institution must address administrative, organizational, professional practice, and professional development characteristics to compete successfully with others for the limited nursing resource available. The urban hospital that involves its own staff in the planning of the retention program will be the one that selects those characteristics that are most meaningful to its particular nursing population and creates a program that meets the widest variety of individual preferences. As the nursing work force becomes more diverse in types of personalities and career stages yet more specialized in practice, the retention factors will need to become more individual. The urban hospital that is futuristic will not stop at creating a general retention program but will plan constant refinement of the program to meet the changing expectations of its nurses.

SUMMARY

Recruitment and retention are not separate entities but parts of a continuous process. Recruitment is supported by a satisfied and stable nursing staff who "sell" their institution to the students and experienced nurses with whom they interact. Retention is fostered by the recruitment of nurses who see themselves "fitting" the culture of the hospital and who find that their career aspirations may be met by the opportunities for professional growth and advancement provided by the organization.

To successfully obtain and maintain its share of the dwindling nursing resource, an urban hospital must match the incentives provided by its competitors while differentiating itself in one or more areas as a progressive leader that visibly supports its nursing staff. The special niches created by the hospital must be marketed aggressively both to its existing staff and potential recruits. The urban hospital not only must focus its efforts in the immediate geographical area but also compete regionally and nationally.

To track its efforts, the hospital must decide in advance what are acceptable attrition rates and maintain records on the costs of RN replacements and programs aimed at retention.[19] While a 0 percent turnover is not only unrealistic but also undesirable, the institution should decide what its target rates are for turnover so that allocation of resources for recruitment can be planned. The comparison of costs of recruitment and retention can assist the organization to assure that a disproportionate amount is not directed toward recruitment. The hospital must focus continually on the fact that retention is the most cost-effective way to maintain an adequate nursing resource.

Urban hospitals cannot be satisfied with currently successful recruitment and retention activities but must work with other health care organizations and agencies on long-term ways to address the shortage of nurses. One method may be to cooperate with community efforts to introduce high school students to nursing as an attractive profession. Another approach may be to work with businesses and schools of nursing in efforts to retrain a displaced work force from another industry. Of greatest significance may be the hospital's political efforts to change the reimbursement process to allow for adequate compensation of nurses throughout their careers. Hospital nursing then becomes more attractive to experienced nurses as well as potential students.

The nursing shortage offers the urban hospital a unique opportunity to establish a competitive edge over other institutions in the area. The improved work environment that can be created by attention to the factors discussed in this chapter can result in an enthusiastic and productive work force that advances the institution toward true excellence. The benefits of a positive recruitment and retention program for nurses thus become shared by the organization as a whole.

NOTES

1. Ada Sue Hinshaw, Carolyn Smeltzer, and Jan Atwood, "Innovative Retention Strategies for Nursing Staff," *Journal of Nursing Administration* 17, no. 6 (1987): 8–16.

2. Elizabeth Duncan Burn and Mary Crabtree Tonges, "Professional Nursing Practice in Acute Care Settings," *Nursing Administration Quarterly* 8, no. 1 (1984): 65–75.

3. Karen Hart and Karen Lindquist, "Nursing Shortage: Issues and Answers," *Michigan Hospitals* 24, no. 3 (1988): 7–9.

4. Linda Aiken and Connie Mullinix, "Special Report: The Nurse Shortage: Myth or Reality?" *New England Journal of Medicine* 317, no. 10 (1987): 641–646.

5. Eldine Sanger, Jamie Richardson, and Elaine Larson, "What Satisfies Nurses Enough To Keep Them?" *Nursing Management* 16, no. 9 (1985): 43–46.

6. M. Elizabeth West, "Keeping Talented RNs in Hospital Practice," *Nursing Management* 14, no. 8 (1983): 38–41.

7. Geraldine Talarczyk and Dorothea Milbrandt, "A Collaborative Effort To Facilitate Role Transition from Student to Registered Nurse Practitioner," *Nursing Management* 19, no. 2 (1988): 30–32.

8. Crystal Richman and Gail Durant, "Education As an Active Response to the Nursing Shortage," *Michigan Hospitals* 24, no. 3 (1988): 51.

9. Hinshaw, Smeltzer, and Atwood, "Innovative Retention Strategies for Nursing Staff," 8.

10. Margaret Van Meter, "Why Hospitals Like Contented Nurses," *RN* 49, no. 9 (1986): 94.

11. American Academy of Nursing Task Force on Nursing Practice in Hospitals, *Magnet Hospitals: Attraction and Retention of Professional Nurses* (Kansas City, Mo.: American Nurses Association, 1983).

12. William Knaus et al., "An Evaluation of Outcome from Intensive Care in Major Medical Centers," *Annals of Internal Medicine* 104, no. 3 (1986): 410–418.

13. Aiken and Mullinix, "Special Report: The Nursing Shortage: Myth or Reality?" 644.

14. Ibid.

15. Lorraine Berlin, *Nursing Shortage: Building Creative Strategies To Celebrate Nursing*. Presentation to Grand Rapids District Nurses' Association, April 28, 1988.

16. Karen Mitchell, "Putting a Stop to the Nursing Brain Drain," *Nursing Economic$* 4, no. 4 (1986): 158–159.

17. John Seybolt, "Dealing with Premature Employee Turnover," *Journal of Nursing Administration* 16, no. 2 (1986): 26–32.

18. Mary Ann Haw et al., "Improving Nursing Morale in a Climate of Cost Containment," *Journal of Nursing Administration* 14, no. 11 (1984): 10–15.

19. Bessie Marquis, "Attrition: The Effectiveness of Retention Activities," *Journal of Nursing Administration* 18, no. 3 (1988): 25–29.

Chapter 15

The Implications of Unionization in Nurse Recruitment and Retention

Philip L. Ross, Gregory L. Crow, and J. Mark Montobbio

INTRODUCTION

Is a health care institution's ability to recruit and retain nurses significantly affected by the presence of a union at that institution? To examine the possible effects of unionization on nurse recruitment and retention it is essential first to consider from a historical perspective the reasons behind the unionization of nursing. With that in mind it then becomes possible to examine the legal and organization arrangements arising from unionization that affect the work environment of nurses. It goes without saying that the presence of a union does affect organizational structure, process, and outcome. However, has that impact been positive or negative, or a combination of both? This chapter explores the relationship of recruitment and retention efforts of health care institutions in an atmosphere of unionization.

THE PROMISES OF UNIONIZATION—A HISTORICAL PERSPECTIVE

Nurses unionize for a variety of reasons. Of major importance in the unionization movement within the American Nurses' Association (ANA) begun 40 years ago was the quest for more power and control over wages, working conditions, and job security. Commentator Colvin notes that nurses turned to collective bargaining as the most reasonable means of confronting hospital administration in those areas.[1] Additionally, input into policy decisions that directly and indirectly affect nursing practice and patient care were, and still are, of prime concern to all nurses.

Nearly four decades have passed since delegates to the 35th ANA convention endorsed the concept that state nursing associations could bargain collectively regarding economic and security issues.[2] What were the promises of unionization when the ANA delegates voted to endorse the collective bargaining concept? Have those promises been realized? Moreover, what are the greater implications of the promises of unionization on nurse recruitment and retention?

Promises come in four basic forms: (1) explicit, (2) implicit, (3) realized, and (4) unrealized. Certainly, there were both explicit and implicit promises brought forth when the ANA house of delegates voted to unionize.

In 1946 the ANA adopted an official economic security program. Its stated goals included (1) enactment of the standard 40-hour work week, (2) minimum salaries equal to a nurse's professional status, and (3) increased participation in the administration and planning of nursing services.[3] While these explicit promises of unionization of four decades ago were specific to economic security issues and participation in the administration and planning of nursing services, the implicit promises went much further. The implicit promises encompassed such issues as autonomy over practice and increased status associated with movement toward a more professional position within the health care bureaucracy. With this improved professional position would come the opportunity for input into policy that affects nursing and patient care.

Which of the explicit and implicit promises have been realized and which have not? Certainly, most would agree that wages for nurses have increased at least partially as a result of union activities. Commentator Alt-White, however, notes that research suggests that unions have been less successful on behalf of nurses in this area than they have been for other classes of employees. Thus, unions have increased nonprofessional wages by as much as 60 percent more than wages for nurses.[4] Moreover, wage rates, for the most part, are similar in both unionized and non-unionized hospitals.[5] Many believe that this phenomenon is due to the fact that unionized nurses pave the way for those who are not unionized and that the non-unionized nurses reap the benefits fought for by the unionized nurses. Certainly, it is not unusual for non-unionized employers to match the wages and benefits of those who are unionized in an effort to keep their non-union employees from organizing. Young and Hayne note that this is no less true for nurses.[6]

There is evidence, however, that the unions' positive impact on wages has had very little effect on overall nurse satisfaction. Commentators Pfeffer and O'Reilly note that there is not a strong relationship among turnover, wages, and collective bargaining representation.[7] They go on to report that the most significant relationship that depicts turnover is the relationship between nurses, physicians, and administrators and feel that this relationship may be more important than wages.[8] As is seen below, this is one area where unionization is not likely to have a beneficial effect.

In addition to somewhat higher wages, unionization and its resulting collective bargaining activity have also had a positive impact on some aspects of working conditions for nurses. Most collective bargaining agreements have helped to eliminate some of the historical abuses in the nursing field. Thus, unions have worked to end the practice of arbitrary shift rotation and in its place have enacted a contractual system of organized bidding for open positions on shifts viewed as more favorable. The work week has been stabilized similarly. These are some of the clear advances resulting from unionization and support the argument that unions have gone far toward realizing the historic promises of better economics and working conditions.

Where the unionization movement has clearly yet to succeed, however, is in the explicit and implicit promises of giving nurses increased participation in the administration and planning of nursing services and more autonomy over their practice resulting from a heightened professional status. Many would question whether or not these unrealized promises can ever be fulfilled using the industrial model of unionization in the present climate of health care. Certainly, nurses have not flocked to the union banner. Moloney reports that of 1,700,000 nurses holding licenses, 1,404,200 are employed in nursing.[9] Mary Foley, RN, chairperson of the ANA's Cabinet on Economic and General Welfare, states that ". . . approximately 133,000 [nurses] are represented by state nurses' associations [unions]."[10] These figures indicate that fewer than 2 percent of nurses are unionized.

PROFESSIONAL VERSUS NONPROFESSIONAL STATUS OF NURSES

The status of a career in society affects the choices of those who potentially might participate in that career. Much has been written about the choices and options now open to women. As options increase for women, they are choosing more varied and diverse careers. Women are choosing careers that are more closely identified with power, money, and prestige. In our society, those careers typically involve professional positions not associated with the trappings of unionization, such as strikes and picket lines. Nursing as an entity within health care and individual nurses have struggled with the implications of unionism on the potential of nurses to gain full professional status along with other health care providers who are considered professionals.

As previously noted, one of the implicit goals of unionization was to enhance the professional status of nurses as copartners with physicians in providing patient care. Unions promised to help achieve this status by providing nurses with a unified, and therefore more powerful, voice in establishing health care policy.

The decision to bargain collectively set up an inevitable split within the ranks of nursing. To this day, many nurses question the wisdom of the decision to engage in collective bargaining. There were nurses bitterly opposed to the concept of unionization and who therefore left the ANA. They were opposed to the use of the industrial model of collective bargaining with all of the trappings of that adversarial relationship (i.e., strikes and picket lines) and the possible negative impact that unionization would have on the struggle for full professional status. In a survey of 1643 nurses, *Nursing 88* quotes a nurse's statement: "I think the ANA and NLN [National League for Nursing] are like the unions in Pittsburgh that put the steel workers out of work, making the nursing shortage worse.''[11] The link between the blue-collar union and the steel workers and the nursing union made in the above quote is a view that many nurses and other health care professionals also share.

On the other hand, many nurses who support the concept of unionization have come to adopt the traditional view of industrial unionism that management is inherently exploitative. Commentator Colvin notes that, prior to the ANA endorsement of strike action, hospitals were seen as employers who took advantage of nurse dedication and loyalty to their profession. Many nurses viewed strikes and work stoppages as the only means of ''real'' power for them to effect change.[12] This viewpoint that seeks to separate the ''workers'' from the ''bosses'' furthers a we/they approach to nursing care among nurses who have come to view themselves less as professional ''partners'' in health care and more as exploited ''workers.'' Union activities such as strikes and picket lines may therefore in fact make nursing less attractive to men and women as it is premised on a position of weakness and semiprofessional status within the health care industry.

The decision of the ANA to unionize has also led many nurse administrators to resign from the ANA because they refuse to belong to an organization where part of their (nurse administrators') dues support the economic programs of a union, which can result in strike efforts by staff nurses.[13] Additionally, labor law prevents nurse administrators, who are supervisors, from interfering or playing a dominant role in local bargaining unit activities.[14] This further creates a gap between the nursing staff and the nursing management that enhances the well-entrenched we/they phenomenon.

Not only does unionization have an impact on the manner in which nurses view themselves, but it clearly influences how management views its staff nurses. One of the most frustrating features of nurses' working lives is the bureaucratic organizational structure found in most health care facilities. The bureaucratic model today remains the dominant form of organizational structure in the health care field.[15] In an organization that truly believes that nurses are professional employees, there should be less bureaucratic entanglement such as policy and procedure manuals and other bureaucratic measures that hamper the enactment of one's professional role. It would appear that nurses' unions have reinforced the bureaucratic structure rather than attempting to change it. Thus, for example, collective bargaining agreements entered into by the nursing unions typically result in more structure in the work place. While such contractual detail reduces the possibility of arbitrary action by the institution, it also decreases the flexibility of that institution.

Certainly, health care management's view of unionization is more aligned with nonprofessional status than professional status. Porter-O'Grady and Finnigan offer a model depicting how organizational arrangements are different for professional and nonprofessional groups (Figure 15-1).[16] Because most union activity,

ORGANIZATIONAL PERFORMANCE CHARACTERISTICS		
Characteristics	**Nonprofessional**	**Professional**
Structure	Tight Control High Degree Structure	Low Structure
Distribution of Influence	Low Total Influence Centered at Top	Even Distribution of Influence
Superior-Subordinate Relations	Directive Low Freedom	Participation High Degree of Freedom
Colleague Relations	High Coordination Few Differences	Diffuse Relations Low Correlation Many Differences
Time Orientation	Immediate, Short Term	Long Range
Goal Orientation	Technical High Task	Professional Scientific High Interactional
Management Style	Task Centered High Control	Task and Relationship Orientation

Figure 15-1 Organizational Processes and Structure in Relation to Professional and Nonprofessional Status. *Source:* Reprinted from *Shared Governance for Nursing: A Creative Approach to Professional Accountability* by T. Porter-O'Grady and S. Finnigan, p. 22, Aspen Publishers, Inc., © 1984.

especially strikes and picket lines, are closely associated with nonprofessional behavior, the mere fact that nurses are unionized puts them at risk of being viewed by administrators as nonprofessionals or at best semiprofessionals. This in turn reduces the willingness of administrators to see nurses conceptually as health care partners and grant them the autonomy that would be associated with that position. Simply, nursing unions, by adopting the industrial unions' approach, act to foster both internal and external attitudes toward unionized nurses as being nonprofessionals or semiprofessionals rather than full professionals. As a consequence, the movement of nursing toward full professional status is restricted, which in turn leads to renewed dissatisfaction and an exodus from the occupation in general.

Having arguably failed in the effort to advance nursing toward full professional status, the question remains whether the efforts of nursing unions have nevertheless assisted nurses in gaining entry into the circles where health care policy is decided. Many staff nurses would answer this question with a resounding no. The connection between policy making and autonomy is clear for most staff nurses:

those in power (administrators and physicians) not only decide what health care policy will be but decide who will have input into that policy formulation. Huey and Hartley's report on what keeps nurses on the job notes that one of the ten most important reasons a nurse plans to leave nursing is that the nurse is not allowed to exercise nursing judgment for patient care.[17] In other words, autonomy is not a benefit nurses currently enjoy. Autonomy over one's practice is a hallmark of professional status. Reports indicate that respect, autonomy, and flex-time would make nursing more attractive to those already practicing.[18]

Unionization not only restricts the ability of nurses to have some say in the hospital policies that affect them by coloring the manner in which nurses and administrators view the position of nursing—as not being fully professional—but additional legal considerations exist that further hamper health care institutions' ability to work closely with its nurses. These legal considerations arise from the National Labor Relations Act (NLRA), which sets forth the rules for labor-management conduct. Most of these rules were developed in an industrial setting, and the application of these industrial rules to health care facilities is not always a smooth one.

Quality of work life has received much attention in the last ten years as a means of creating an improved work environment and of encouraging increased productivity from employees. Schuler and Youngblood define quality of work life programs as programs that enable employees to have ". . . some say in job design in particular and the work environment in general."[19] One tool commonly used in the health care field to facilitate two-way communication between management and nurses on issues concerning patient care and nursing standards is the nurse advisory committee (NAC). NACs, however, present a special problem when those discussions expand to matters involving nurses' working conditions or grievances.

Section 8(a)(2) of the NLRA makes it unlawful for an employer "to dominate or interfere with the formation or administration of any labor organization or contribute financial or other support to it. . . ."[20] The NLRA in turn defines a "labor organization" as "any organization of any kind, or any agency or employee representation committee or plan, in which employees participate and which exists for the purpose, in whole or in part, of dealing with employers concerning grievances, labor disputes, wages, rates of pay, hours of employment, or conditions of work."[21] The National Labor Relations Board (NLRB) and the courts have interpreted this definition broadly and have held that a group of employees may constitute a "labor organization" despite having no elected officials, dues, or other formal structure.[22] The term "dealing with" has also been broadly defined to encompass an employee committee that represents employee interests in discussing grievances, wages, hours, and working conditions.[23]

In applying these broad standards, NACs have been found in certain cases to be statutory labor organizations where they exist at least in part to discuss such nursing issues as staffing, scheduling, salary increases, benefits, and on-call rules.[24] The fact that an NAC may also discuss with management professional matters not involving wages, hours, or working conditions does not change its status as a labor organization.[25]

Where an NAC comprises a labor organization it becomes unlawful for a health care facility to encourage its formation, control its activities, or give it various forms of financial or administrative assistance or support.[26] An unfair labor practice can occur even when the institution's domination or assistance was done for the purpose of providing a forum for the discussion of principally professional matters, rather than in an attempt to undermine a potential or existing union.[27] As such, health care institutions must tread carefully in working with groups of nurses over issues of health care and working conditions in order to avoid both recognizing a nursing group as a labor organization in a nonunionized setting and undermining an existing union in a unionized setting.

In all, the impact of unionization on recruitment and retention of nurses relative to professional standing and ability to affect professional issues is clear. Enrollment in the schools of nursing is down nationwide, and nurses are leaving the hospital setting and the occupation in record numbers. Professional status and the resulting control over nursing by nurses have not been answered by union status.

COMMUNICATION

The presence of the union in the health care environment affects not only the frame of reference by which nurses and administrators view each other but also the manner in which the nursing staff and management are able to communicate with each other. Communication is an area of critical importance in efforts to retain and recruit. It is only through effective communication that the changing needs and interests of nurses and management can be made known to one another.

Commentators Young and Hayne note that a union represents a barrier to communication within an organization.[28] This occurs in several ways. Two prime components of effective communication are that (1) direct feedback should be encouraged and (2) direct channels of communication are best.[29] These components are extremely difficult if not impossible to achieve in a unionized setting, as many legal limitations exist on the ability of nurses and administrators to "bypass" the union and communicate directly with each other.

These legal limitations on direct communication are no better illustrated than in the area of communication between management and staff nurses regarding nurses' complaints and grievances. A health care facility's ability to communicate directly with its nurses about their complaints concerning working conditions generally becomes restricted with the very advent of union organizing activity. Unless a health care institution has a preexisting policy of soliciting employee grievances by requesting that nurses come forward with their complaints, as soon as union organizational efforts begin it becomes unlawful for the employer to solicit grievances and directly or implicitly promise to remedy them. Such conduct is both an unfair labor practice under the NLRA and can be the basis for a union's overturning the results of an NLRB election.[30] Thus, for example, "an attitude survey" conducted by a hospital to determine the types of complaints that led employees to an interest in unionization has been held illegal.[31]

Once a union is recognized as the nurses' collective bargaining representative, a health care facility's right to bypass the union and deal directly with nurses over their grievances is similarly circumscribed. Although the NLRA expressly provides that individual employees have a right to present grievances directly to their employer without the intervention of the union,[32] several significant rules exist that effectively restrict that right. First, the union representative must be permitted to be present at the adjustment of any grievance.[33] An adjustment of a grievance can occur at the lowest level, where employees first express their concerns to their direct supervisors.[34] Technically, union representatives should therefore be invited to be present at any discussion between an employee and any manager or line supervisor that might result in a resolution of any employee complaint. Unions can, by contract, waive the right to be present at any adjustment of grievances, and most collective bargaining agreements typically provide that an employee may first discuss any grievance with his or her supervisor or department head without the union's having to be present. Even that right, however, is restricted, as an employer is generally prohibited at all stages from adjusting any employee grievance in a way that is inconsistent with the terms of a collective bargaining agreement.[35]

Thus, instead of direct communication, information between administrators and the nursing staff must pass through a third party—the union—who will in turn likely interpret, evaluate, and filter the message before sending it on. In practical terms, given the basic adversarial nature of industrial labor relations, communications between management and nursing unions will typically be viewed by each side with suspicion and mistrust. Often, the parties spend more time in developing responses for purposes of effective posturing than in listening to and dealing with what the other is saying. At no time is this more true than during what has become the almost ritualistic practice of periodic contract negotiation or renegotiation. During negotiations, the process of communication becomes especially elaborate; complicated; and fraught with noise, filtering, emotion, values, and preconceived beliefs. Add to this the legal ramifications of what can or cannot be said in order to avoid claims of "bad faith" bargaining, and the result is that the ability to communicate *effectively* is virtually destroyed at one of the few times when productive change to the mutual benefit of the health care facility and the nurses can be made lawfully.

Thus, while unionism promised to give nurses a louder and clearer "voice" with management, in reality, a union more often acts as a barrier to effective communication with management when the message must be transferred through so many channels (Figure 15-2). The implication of this lack of communication for recruitment and retention is again clear. The inability of nurses effectively to

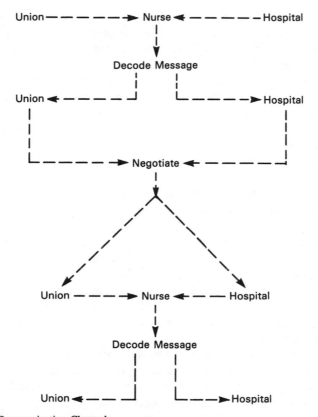

Figure 15-2 Communication Channels

make their needs and interests known increases the level of frustration. This frustration leads to burnout, and burnout leads to turnover, which increases the need for recruitment, a resource that no longer exists—and the cycle is established.

UNIONIZATION AND THE ABILITY TO EFFECTUATE CHANGE

The final factor affecting nurse retention and recruitment focuses on the health care facility's ability to respond promptly and effectively to the changing needs and interests of nurses. Here again, the existence of the union often acts to restrict rather than to facilitate change. Once a collective bargaining agreement has been entered into, the terms of that contract will define not only the existing wages, hours, and working conditions of nurses, but also a health care facility's ability to respond to changing conditions and nursing needs.

It is unlawful for an employer to unilaterally change or to modify any of the terms of a union contract during the life of that contract. It is both a violation of Section 8(a)(5) of the NLRA (a refusal to bargain)[36] and a breach of contract enforceable either through contractual arbitration or civil lawsuit for an employer to deviate from the established terms of a collective bargaining agreement.[37] Most frequently, a health care facility's deviation from the terms of its union contract will result in a contractual grievance and arbitration. Recent reported arbitration decisions involving hospitals and nursing unions include disputes over many of the most pressing issues involved in nurse retention and recruitment today, including alleged employer violations of such issues as staffing, scheduling, wages and benefits, use of on-call or temporary nurses, and of course, discipline and discharge matters.[38] A health care facility's violation of its union contract as a result of instituting a unilateral change in that contract can result in significant potential monetary liability in the form of back pay or lost benefits.

Thus, where a collective bargaining agreement exists, changes in wages, hours, and working conditions can be made only with a union's *prior* approval. This, in turn, can occur in two ways. First, provision for future employer changes in existing working conditions can be drafted into the contract itself. This is most typically done through the negotiation of a "management rights" clause. Management may lawfully bargain for the retention of traditional management powers.[39] The negotiation of a management rights clause is a recognition by both parties that management retains the right to make basic operating decisions. Most management rights clauses, however, also expressly provide that, in exercising the rights retained, the employer agrees not to vary from, or otherwise conflict with, any other term of the collective bargaining agreement.

The other manner in which an employer can make changes in existing working conditions during the life of a collective bargaining agreement is by requesting the union's permission to make those changes. Nothing, however, requires a union to acquiesce to an employer's proposed modification during the term of an agreement.

Several significant forces are also at work that in turn limit a labor organization's ability to agree either to contract language providing the health care facility with contractual flexibility or specific proposed employer changes during the life of a collective bargaining agreement. The most significant of these forces is the union's own rhetoric. Traditional labor dogma provides that one of the most important benefits of unionization is the protection that a collective bargaining agreement affords. By strictly defining the wages, hours, and working conditions of employees and thereby reducing employer flexibility in those areas, the collective bargaining agreement is said to protect employees from arbitrary or discriminatory conduct by employers. Moreover, midterm changes in existing contract language may be seen by employees as a take-away or loss of previously hard-earned benefits. Thus, a union may find it politically difficult if not impossible to acquiesce in many proposed employer modifications to the terms of an existing collective bargaining agreement.

In addition to those political ramifications, a union also has a legal obligation to act as the representative of all bargaining unit employees and to work for their interests as a whole.[40] A union has a duty to represent fairly all employees in the collective bargaining unit.[41] Therefore, under certain circumstances a union may not lawfully be able to agree to an employer's proposed modification that might benefit a small number of represented nurses, if that modification is detrimental to the interests of nurses as a whole.

If a health care facility is unable to obtain a union's acquiescence in a midterm modification, then the facility will have to wait until the expiration of the agreement (which can be as long as three years later) in order to address that issue during negotiation for a new agreement. The adversarial nature of collective bargaining in turn frequently reduces the likelihood of a quick negotiation of substantive contractual changes. Under existing law, once a collective bargaining agreement expires, an employer still is not able to make unilateral changes in its terms until it has at least negotiated to "impasse" with the union.[42] Once impasse has been reached, while the health care facility can finally institute its proposed changes, not only will significant time likely have lapsed, which may in turn have reduced the effectiveness of the proposed contractual change, but impasse also generally leads to the specter of strike activity by the union.

Loss of income during strikes, picket lines, and the organizational conflict associated with labor disputes are significant disadvantages to unionization. A nurse writing a letter to the *American Journal of Nursing* noted that when a strike the nurses had participated in was over, they were angry at both the union and the hospital. The nurse felt that the "physicians harassed them" and that the "hospital administration did not care." Additionally, it was noted that the union just moved on to the next contract negotiation and left the nurses to "pick up the pieces" on their own. The strike this nurse was speaking of had happened "several" years ago, and it was obvious that the wounds had not yet healed.[43]

SUMMARY AND CONCLUSION

As suggested above, the impact of unionization on nurse recruitment and retention is varied. While unions can rightfully point to increased wages and contractual limitations on arbitrary conduct by health care institutions, those benefits are not sufficient to stem the flight of nurses out of the profession.

On the contrary, because the nursing unions have chosen to adopt the approach of industrial unions, unionization has had a negative effect on the very areas seen as most critical in the effort to recruit and retain nurses—namely, advancement of the professional status of nurses and the ability of nurses to have some governance in their own working environments. By approaching collective bargaining in an industrial mode, nursing unions foster the view, both among their member nurses and importantly among health care administrators, that nurses are nonprofessional or semiprofessional "workers" rather than health care "partners." This viewpoint not only colors the way in which the parties perceive each other but the manner in which they communicate, which often becomes clouded by traditional management/union rhetoric.

Existing labor laws, which were developed for an industrialized setting, also severely restrict the ability of a health care institution to respond directly to changing nursing needs and interests. Thus, health care institutions are legally limited in their ability to deal directly with nursing groups, either in fear of recognizing them as a labor organization, or of unlawfully bypassing an existing union. Where employers do try to effectuate change through a union, the ability to make that change promptly and effectively is adversely affected both by further legal restrictions and a frequent failure by the parties to work cooperatively rather than adversarily.

In sum, unionization clearly has not been able to fulfill the most important promises made 40 years ago. Indeed, unless nursing unions can somehow remove themselves from the industrial union approach, the likelihood is that nursing unions will continue to act more as a detriment than a benefit to effective nurse recruitment and retention.

NOTES

1. Constance C. Colvin, "Conflict and Resolution: Strikes in Nursing," *Nursing Administration Quarterly* 12, no. 1 (Fall 1987): 45–51.

2. Laura C. Young and Arlene H. Hayne, *Nursing Administration: From Concepts to Practice* (Philadelphia: W.B. Saunders Co., 1988).

3. A.C. Alt-White, "A Comparison of Salaries of Nurses and Other Professionals in Hospitals," *Nursing Administration Quarterly* 12, no. 1 (Fall 1987): 13–18.

4. Ibid.

5. Young and Hayne, *Nursing Administration: From Concepts to Practice*.

6. Ibid.

7. Jeffrey Pfeffer and Charles A. O'Reilly, "Hospital Demography and Turnover Among Nurses," *Individual Relations* 26, no. 2 (Spring 1987): 158–173.

8. Ibid.

9. Margaret M. Moloney, *Professionalization of Nursing: Current Issues and Trends* (Philadelphia: J.B. Lippincott Co., 1986), 201.

10. Mary Foley, "Letter to *American Journal of Nursing*," *American Journal of Nursing* 87 (April 1987): 39.

11. Editors of *Nursing 88*, "Nursing Shortage Poll Report," *Nursing 88* (February 1988): 39.

12. Colvin, "Conflict and Resolution," 45–51.

13. Eleanor J. Sullivan and Phillip J. Decker, *Effective Management in Nursing* (Menlo Park, Calif.: Addison-Wesley Publishing Co., Inc., 1985), 452.

14. Moloney, *Professionalization of Nursing,* 201.

15. Timothy Porter-O'Grady and Sharon Finnigan, *Shared Governance* (Rockville, Md.: Aspen Publishers, Inc., 1984), 23.

16. Ibid.

17. Florence L. Huey and Susan Hartley, "What Keeps Nurses in Nursing?" *American Journal of Nursing* 88 (February 1988): 187.

18. Ibid., 187–188.

19. Randall S. Schuler and Stuart A. Youngblood, *Effective Personnel Management*, 2nd ed. (St. Paul: West Publishing Co., 1986), 255.

20. 28 U.S.C. § 158(a)(2).

21. 28 U.S.C. § 152 (5).

22. See, e.g., *Colombia Transit Corporation*, 237 NLRB 1196 (1978).

23. *NLRB* v. *Cabot Carbon Company and Cabot Shopes, Inc.*, 360 U.S. 203 (1959).

24. *South Nassau Community Hospital*, 247 NLRB 527 (1980).

25. Ibid.

26. *South Nassau Community Hospital*, 247 NLRB 527 (1980); *Saint Vincent's Hospital*, 244 NLRB 84 (1979); *Alta Bates Hospital*, 226 NLRB 485 (1976).

27. *South Nassau Community Hospital*, 247 NLRB 527 (1980). In *Alta Bates Hospital*, 226 NLRB 485 (1976), the NLRB specifically rejected as a defense the argument that the hospital created its advisory committee upon its belief that if its employees had easy access to an advisory committee with their unanswered problems or requests that they would be happier with their work environment and, since satisfied employees tend to do better work, they would take better care of the hospital's patients.

28. Young and Hayne, *Nursing Administration: From Concepts to Practice*, 376.

29. Sullivan and Decker, *Effective Management in Nursing*, 87.

30. *Montgomery Ward Inc.*, 225 NLRB 112 (1977).

31. *Saint Joseph's Hospital*, 247 NLRB 869 (1980).

32. 29 U.S.C. § 159(a).

33. Ibid.

34. Ibid.

35. 29 U.S.C. § 158(a)(5).

36. 29 U.S.C. § 185.

37. See, e.g., *Miller-Dwan Medical Center*, 83 LA 1059 (1984) (staffing dispute); *Kapiolani/ Children's Medical Center*, 81 LA 214 (1983) (staffing dispute—use of on-call nurses); *Albany General Hospital*, 77 LA 1121 (1981) (scheduling dispute); *Marshalltown Area Community Hospital*, 76 LA 978 (1981) (job bidding dispute).

38. *NLRB* v. *American National Insurance Co.*, 343 U.S. 395 (1952).

39. *Steele* v. *Louisville and Nashville Railroad*, 323 U.S. 192 (1944); *Ford Motor Co.* v. *Hoffman*, 345 U.S. 330 (1953); *Vara* v. *Sipes*, 386 U.S. 171 (1967).

40. *International Brotherhood of Electrical Workers (IBEW)* v. *Foust*, 442 U.S. 42, 47 (1979).

41. *NLRB* v. *Katz*, 369 U.S. 736 (1962).

42. *Taft Broadway Ins. Co.*, 163 NLRB 475 (1967).

43. Name withheld, "Letter to Editor," *American Journal of Nursing* 87 (April 1987): 443.

Chapter 16

Nursing's Changing Roles

Pamela S. Erb

Changing the unacceptable has been recognized as a responsibility of nursing practice since the 19th century. During the first days of military hospitals, patient care was provided by uneducated women of the poorest reputation working in an environment that contributed more to patient morbidity and mortality than did primary war injuries. The challenging nursing values of Florence Nightingale conflicted with the existing poor sanitary conditions tolerated, if not accepted, at the time. Chinn and Jacobs have stated, "When individual or professional values are in conflict with and challenge societal values, there is potential for creating change in society."[1]

The individual and professional values of today's nurse are in conflict and continue to undergo change. In many situations change has been quite subtle; however, subtlety is lost as the nation at large begins to address the byproduct of conflicting values—the nursing shortage.

While the nursing shortage speaks to many conflicting values inherent to the profession, such as salary compression, short staffing, and lack of recognition, it is seen by many to offer an opportunity for accelerated transformation, allowing the profession to move forward at a much faster pace or at least at a pace that is more in step with the dramatic changes of the health care industry. Forces within our environment, external to the profession, are further influencing our values and transforming the role of the registered nurse (RN). These forces include financial instability, data generation, and principles of patient case management. The predominant focuses of transformation are in control of professional practice, autonomy in practice, and patient care management.

TRANSFORMATION

Control of Professional Practice

Increased control of professional practice from the days of total physician domination is now accelerated, primarily as the result of continued professional

214

educational growth and nursing research. Nursing training programs were nonexistent prior to the 1870s, and physicians resisted formalized training even if it meant that patients were attended primarily by the rodents roaming the filthy halls of the almshouses. The sentiment of physicians expressed at the turn of the 20th century was that training would produce within nurses a "resistance to do as they were told."

Aid to the hospitals and almshouses of the times did not come from organized nursing but rather from women of the upper class who were sufficiently influential with men in high places of authority and power to effect a transformation to organized training programs. Florence Nightingale was one of those influential women, and she is recognized as the founder of modern Western nursing. Today, nurses continue to take an active role in the transformation of professional practice. Nurses now hold positions of authority and power, and influence health care policy at the institutional level and at local, state, and federal levels. There are now approximately two million nurses, and the political influence of such numbers is rapidly gaining recognition and clout.

Today's nurse is more frequently educated beyond traditional hospital-based training programs, which indicates a direct response by nursing to meet the increasing complexities of our health care settings. In a recent report by the American Association of Colleges of Nursing (AACN) nursing supply statistics relate that enrollment in master's and doctoral programs in nursing is up 19 percent and enrollment of RNs obtaining the baccalaureate degree is up 11 percent in the past two years.[2] The AACN concludes that these figures identify the trend of nurses seeking advanced education to increase their knowledge and skill commensurate with the demands of today's health care systems. Demands and complexities within today's dynamic health care systems include intensive technology, growth of the frail elderly population, complex health care organizations, increasing ambulatory health care models, differentiated practice settings such as computer and accounting firms utilizing nursing expertise, and the endless dilemma of how to finance all of this.

Virginia Henderson has said,

> When nurses' sensitivity to human needs (their intuition) is joined with the ability to find and use expert opinion with the ability to find reported research and apply it to their practice, and when they themselves use the scientific method of investigation, there is no limit to the influence they might have on health care worldwide.[3]

Thus it has become more commonly recognized that the power to control professional nursing practice by nursing professionals is directly supported by expanding nursing knowledge through nursing research. This is evidenced by the growing volumes of nursing literature. Advanced education and nursing research continue to build the knowledge guiding nursing practice. These efforts will continue to transform roles and to expand levels of practice. Likewise these forces will further stimulate the evolving diverse models of nursing practice controlled by professional nursing.

Patricia Donahue further validates the significance of nursing research, as she has stated,

> The value of nursing research, which has already been demonstrated, will become even more important as nursing continues its march toward professional status and excellence in performance. Research has proven to be a mechanism of generating new knowledge for nursing that will ultimately ensure quality of nursing care. A growing acceptance of nursing research has occurred as this area has become recognized as an effective method of cost containment. The most efficient and most effective modes of nursing can be identified through nursing research.[4]

Independent Practice: Autonomy in Practice

Controversy continues to rage within the profession as to who is best prepared to do what. The process of defining the different performance levels of RNs with varying levels of preparation is a complex task. While this controversy is primarily confined to the issues of entry into practice and the undefined levels of competence of bedside nurses, it must come to resolution. Concurrence on two levels of nursing practice, technical and professional, with clear job delineation and standards of practice is necessary to accelerate other elements of professional practice that are undergoing transformation. Resolving these issues will provide the unity required to articulate autonomous nursing practice further and to advance nursing practice generally.

Whereas organized medicine still does not give full credence to formalized nursing education at the baccalaureate and advanced levels, the growing demands for coordinated case management in a fragmented health care delivery system require these skills. The indigent population has provided the greatest impetus for the development of advanced nurse practice models. These settings allow the greatest flexibility of independent or autonomous practice. In teaching hospitals, public health clinics, and sparsely populated or socioeconomically deprived areas throughout the country where patient demand exceeds physician availability or accessibility, nurses are demonstrating their effectiveness and efficiency in managing certain patient populations with optimal outcomes. The areas of maternal-child care and nonemergent ambulatory care are rapidly providing protocols consistent with nurse practice acts. They demonstrate cost-effective health care delivery by ARNPs and clinical nurse specialists that can ill be refuted by physicians or others who may wish to thwart entrepreneurial nursing care delivery models.

Of major importance in stimulating further entrepreneurial models is the attainment of third-party reimbursement for nursing services. Through the use of nursing's political influence legislative changes can occur, and are occurring, allowing direct payment for nursing services rendered. The further challenge was stated by Griffith: "Clearly passing legislation enabling third party legislation for nursing services is easier than implementing it. This is particularly true for nurse practitioners and clinical specialists, but less true perhaps for nurse midwives and nurse anesthetists."[5]

Independent practice or autonomy in nursing does not equate to freedom from restraint or nonadherence to professional practice standards. Rather, at the bedside within the acute care setting it implies the creation of a work milieu that is conducive to maximization of professional knowledge and skills in an environment where mundane and repetitive tasks do not detract from the professionalism of the nursing role.

The need for hospitalization has changed in emphasis from a terminology of caring for the sick to the broader concept that hospitals exist primarily to provide 24-hour nursing care for patients who cannot be cared for in any other setting. With the growing acceptance of this concept, the service provided by support and ancillary departments is being revisualized to reduce demanding functions to their proper skill levels. Such functions include transporting specimens and dirty linen and making repeated telephone calls to obtain physician orders.

Support and ancillary departments must assess who their customers are and must recognize that patient care managers, the RNs, require their full support. It is the patient's perception that the nurse is responsible for all activity that affects his or her stay. If the meal is cold, the pharmacy does not send a medication, or the room is dirty, the patient expects that the nurse will provide the appropriate satisfiers as well as provide quality care.

Expectations of the nurse in current typical work environments have been largely unrealistic, contributing to the burnout syndrome so often spoken of when nurses leave the profession. Whereas the misconception of nursing practice may be task-oriented, the very essence of the nursing process is the collection of data with implementation of appropriate nursing actions in response to those data. According to Griffith-Kenney and Christensen, professional nursing has evolved from an intuitive base of subjective impressions gathered from the medical diagnosis and patient observation to a base including the behavioral, social, nursing, and medical sciences, which provide concrete indicators of health as cited within theories, norms, and standards.[6] Voluminous amounts of information are thus produced.

To support quality care and the nursing process of assessing, planning, implementing, and evaluating patient care, the traditional tools of data collection and information analysis have been the thermometer, stethoscope, and other paraphernalia related to body orifices, organs, and cavities as well as the patient's voluminous paper chart. Advancing computer technology and information management in the real-time mode have been slow to develop products that would allow clinicians to immediately access and input information to multiple data bases, thereby augmenting the decision process, eliminating paperwork, and improving accuracy.

Combined with the nursing shortage, the financial health and well-being of today's hospital under regulated and contractual payment systems have provided an impetus to improve effectiveness and efficiency at all levels while maintaining quality outcomes. Developing computer technology will provide shared or integrated data bases that will identify the costs of patient care, collect patient care information at the point of its generation, and display trends toward quality outcomes.

The professional nurse is impatient to gain access to this technology and clearly realizes that information-management tools will support decision making as well as enhance productivity. Providing computer technology to the nurse that has been available to other hospital business, particularly finance, will improve the image of nursing and enhance self-esteem. Functional changes in work systems will occur to transform clerical tasks to structures that assist decision making and the efficient management of patient care. Computer technology is capable of replacing the stethoscope as nursing's primary work tool.

As this technology evolves within the work setting, providing additional opportunities to restructure the environment and work flow of professional nursing, and maintaining a consistent philosophy of computerized patient care information management is vital. It is indisputable that all of nursing's wants and expectations are presently unattainable. It is also indisputable that, with dedicated resources, the functionality of systems can support the nursing process. A philosophy may be constructed such as that adopted by the department of patient care services and the department of systems and procedures of The Tampa General Hospital for support and selection of a new patient care information system.

Patient Care Information System Philosophy of The Tampa General Hospital

Today's healthcare environment demands creative, innovative solutions which provide a competitive advantage, increase physician loyalty, nurture productive hospital medical staff relationships, and increase consumer awareness and satisfaction.

The patient is a unique individual, the most important person in the healthcare system and the focal point of all patient services. Healthcare is the dynamic process of action, reaction, interaction and transaction (King, 1981) whereby patients and providers share information, identify goals and explore the means of attaining the goal of optimal health. Healthcare providers utilize specialized skills, understanding and knowledge to interact with others to attain the goal of optimal achievable health.

To support this philosophy, we believe that the patient directly or indirectly generates data which is essential in providing quality medical and nursing care. Assessment is the primary component which drives the nursing process for planning, implementing and evaluating the attainment of mutually accepted goals, and supports the work effort of the healthcare team. Primary providers of care input, and access this data base, with respect to their functions and need-to-know, as close to where the patient/provider interaction occurs.

Patient care data entered into a system should form a central data base that links clinical personnel with the information required to manage patient care and to produce financial/statistical information for managers, and can be accessed by all areas of the healthcare facilities. The system should be patient centered and provide an on-line, real-time, paperless record of patient activity, and information should be captured as close to the source as possible. Patient confidentiality is of utmost importance and security of the system must be effective.

The system should be user friendly, supporting professional use at all levels. Data should be gathered by instrumentation, with minimal data entry. The system should be integrated with physicians' offices, clinics, public health facilities and future external sites. The system should support the medical education and research efforts of The Tampa General Hospital and the University of South Florida.[7]

Management of Patient Care

Although changes in roles continue to occur, a basic value of nursing is held dear; that value is the RN, the professional patient manager, must maintain responsibility for the management of patient care. In the face of the nursing shortage, management of patient care is not synonymous with a predominant RN staff providing primary patient care; rather, the focus is planning, coordinating and evaluating care based on patient outcomes.

The practice of nursing in the 1960s and 1970s related to team nursing with an emphasis on increasing leadership skills. The primary care models of the past decade have emphasized autonomy and accountability. Developing models for professional nurse practice of the next decade will integrate these values while articulating patient care in terms of managed patient care systems, frequently referred to as medical case management models. A generic definition of case management is "a systematic approach to identifying high-cost patients, assessing potential opportunities to coordinate their care, developing treatment plans that improve quality and control costs, and managing patients' total care to ensure optimum outcomes."[8]

While not a new concept, case management today is grounded in third-party reimbursement and long-term managed care. We see the evolution of case management from long-term or rehabilitative support to the medically necessary hospitalization. Clearly the push by insurance companies and governmental bodies is to impose standards on hospitals in an effort to decrease costs. Within the hospital, however, we can alter this scenario with case management and managed patient care systems. The opportunity exists for health care facilities to become hospitals without walls, with the management of patient care pivotal to the institution and not the third-party payer. The premises for success are

- early intervention
- hospitalization only as long as medically effective
- appropriate care interventions
- appropriate resource management
- identified patient outcomes
- autonomy in professional nursing practice
- delineated standards of care

The development of patient care managers within the current health care environment fraught with financial turmoil and transition has created the necessity to broaden nursing's knowledge to include an awareness and comprehension of predominant financial issues. From the hospital's perspective these issues include

- any adjustment to diagnosis-related group (DRG) rates
- restructuring the delivery of services because of the critical shortage of RNs
- inflation
- indigent care
- demand for discounted care (managed care)
- acquired immune deficiency syndrome (AIDS)
- human resource needs—recruitment and retention costs
- staggering costs associated with advancing technology and medical management protocols
- the physical plant—replacement and renovation

Clearly, providing an expanded educational base for professional nurses as patient care managers not only is responsive to the industry changes and demands but it prepares the professional nurse to influence directly the future of the industry. The components of this educational base, as defined by Kersey,[9] are inclusive of, but not limited to, the following:

1. alternative delivery systems
2. reimbursement
   a. capitation agreements and process
   b. federal regulations
   c. state regulations
   d. DRG-based reimbursements
      (1) overview of process
      (2) case mix index
      (3) blended payment rates
      (4) cost outliers
      (5) day outliers
      (6) cost-based payments
   e. hospital cost-based reimbursement
3. auditing process
4. utilization management
   a. PRO—denials/appeals
   b. recertification
   c. physician attestation
5. billing process
   a. overview
   b. financial codes
   c. charge entry
   d. UB-82 forms
   e. charge master
   f. room and bed master
   g. patient types
6. variance analysis
7. reports for financial management
8. operations
   a. inventory management
   b. forms management
   c. standardization

Managed patient care systems are practice models that support and promote optimal patient outcomes utilizing cost-effective practice patterns. Managed patient care systems are patient-centered and enable the optimal participation of patient and family throughout the entire episode of illness. Other health care professionals may also manage patient care in collaborative relationships, but it is the professional nurse who is best prepared to manage patient care within a model of professional nursing practice. The principles of team nursing resurfacing most strongly are those of Kron,[10] who believed that whatever her or his position—staff nurse, team leader, or head nurse—the professional nurse has the opportunity and the obligation to apply the principles of management in planning, directing, controlling, and evaluating the care of patients.

These principles of management combined with the principles of independent decision making as to patient need versus task completion are infinitely responsive to the current and projected shortage. They create a framework for professional nurse management of patient care in keeping with the values of the profession.

Managed patient care systems provide the opportunity to restructure the work setting by responding to the conflicting values contributing to the nursing shortage and promoting a professional practice climate with the following goals:

- to create an environment in which professional practice can occur and can be enhanced
- to maximize professional practice while increasing productivity
- to utilize health care resources effectively and efficiently
- to build a health care team in an environment that fosters clinical excellence, commitment, and continuing professional development
- to develop professional practice models that will image, influence, and have an impact on the profession

Briefly stated, managed patient care systems address conflicts in the current environment. This transformation offers an opportunity to address the issues of mundane work for professionals, improved professional interaction, and conserving human resources while striving for balances between cost, acuity, and improved clinical outcomes.

Managed patient care systems, to be most clearly articulated and developed, should be based upon a conceptual framework and theory such as King's dynamic interacting systems and the theory of goal attainment,[11] which interact with political, financial, and environmental systems. Resource utilization may then be tested against nursing theory to be efficient and effective based on clinical nursing research.

More clearly in managed patient care systems than in past patient care delivery models, the professional nurse as a primary provider has the greatest influence in the balance of cost and quality. As the health care industry has been transformed radically and the macroeconomics driving the industry exerts new and untold dimensions of pressure on the work environment, it is not unreasonable to project or contemplate this evolutionary role of the RN—professional patient care manager. Surrounded by increasing technologies, increasing costs, and an awareness of the breakdown of a growing system with the end result of fragmented care, substandard care or the absence of care, the professional patient care manager becomes pivotol. The professional nurse is responsible for the integration of the medical plan into a *managed* plan of patient care that considers the unique requirements of resource allocation and discharge planning.

Patient case management models may be as simplistic or as complex as the system within which one works. Examples within the tertiary setting may include organ transplantation programs and nurse midwife programs for low-risk patients. The most familiar models can be found at the nursing unit level, where geographic and human resource constraints drive the development of care delivery systems.

Recognizing that the physician is the primary team leader of managed care with the key role of directing the medical plan, real patient care cannot occur without nursing interventions. The professional nurse as patient care manager becomes the main contributor to maximization of cost-effective and efficient patient management. Nursing knowledge and skill are integrated with the medical plan to achieve nursing and patient case management protocols—to actualize the nursing process toward optimal patient outcomes.

Perhaps as best described by Gulitz,

> Nursing can manage groups of patients, counsel, teach, coordinate resources and services, evaluate care, and work with individuals of any age, sex or economic status. We understand the social, psychological, political, and economic impact of health care on our patients whether they are healthy or sick in any setting. Who else can do that?[12]

SUMMARY

Whatever the model, Thelma Schorr, editor of the *American Journal of Nursing*, may have offered the greatest challenge:

> If we fail, however, to get in on every level of decision making where cost cuts are considered, we will have wasted our concerted energies and violated our professional trust. Certainly there is inefficiency that must be corrected. Certainly there is misplacement of human and technological resources that must be realized. But nurses know best what is essential to patient care in a nursing setting. And nurses had better fight to preserve those essentials.[13]

By utilizing the tools of case management, a systematic approach to analyze, coordinate, and evaluate patient care and treatment plan development, points of measurement are established and outcomes trended that provide professional models of nursing practice that can best measure patient acuity, cost, and outcomes. In light of the nursing shortage, the profession of nursing cannot survive without new and innovative models of practice that complement the values of control of professional practice, autonomy in nursing practice, and control of the management of patient care. Hospitals cannot survive without quality care at a reasonable price. *The registered nurse as professional patient manager has the greatest influence over the delicate balance between cost and quality.*

NOTES

1. P. Chinn and M. Jacobs, *Theory and Nursing: A Systematic Approach*. (St. Louis: C.V. Mosby Co., 1983).

2. American Association of Colleges of Nursing, Report, February 1988.

3. V.A. Henderson, *On the Role of Research in Nursing*. Paper presented at Clinical Excellence in Nursing: International Networking, Sigma Theta Tau International Research Symposium, Edinburgh, Scotland, 1987.

4. M. Patricia Donahue, *Nursing: The Finest Art in Illustrated History* (St. Louis: C.V. Mosby Co., 1985), 452.

5. Hurdis M. Griffith, "Direct Third Party Reimbursement for Nursing Services: A Review of Legislation and Implementation," *Nursing Administration Quarterly* 12, no. 1 (Fall 1987): 23.

6. Janet W. Griffith-Kenney and Paula J. Christensen, *Nursing Process, Application of Theories, Frameworks, and Models*, 2nd ed. (St. Louis: C.V. Mosby Co., 1986), 58.

7. Department of Patient Services and Department of Systems and Procedures, *Patient Care Information System Philosophy of the Tampa General Hospital*, Tampa, Fla., 1988.

8. C. Delaney and D. Aquilina, "Case Management: Meeting the Challenge of High-Cost Illness," *Employee Benefit Journal* 12 (March 1987): 2–8.

9. James H. Kersey, *Proposal for Basic Financial Management for Registered Nurses*, Tampa General Hospital, Tampa, Fla., May 1988.

10. Thora Kron, *The Management of Patient Care: Putting Leadership Skills To Work* (Philadelphia: W.B. Saunders Co., 1971).

11. Imogene M. King, *A Theory for Nursing, Systems, Concepts Process* (New York: John Wiley & Sons, Inc., 1981).

12. Betty Gulitz, "We Cannot Teach for Today: An Educator's View," *The Florida Nurse* 36, no. 4 (April 1988): 5.

13. T.M. Schorr, "Cost Not Care Containment," *American Journal of Nursing* (July 1977): 1129.

Chapter 17

The Role of Supplemental Nursing Services

Ellen Thomas Eggland

The American Hospital Association recently reported that, in a random survey of 2000 hospitals, 75 percent of hospitals relied on overtime and 41 percent employed temporary or agency nurses to ease their nursing shortage.[1] And a vice-president for nursing in California states that local hospitals use 30 to 40 percent of outside supplemental staffing.[2] Reports like these are becoming more common throughout the country as the nursing shortage affects more areas and supplemental services have grown to meet resulting needs.

But the emergence of supplemental nursing services has been met with a number of different viewpoints. Like burnout and career options, supplemental nursing is categorized sometimes as being a cause, sometimes an effect, or most often just a related issue in the nursing shortage. Many in the industry believe that the emergence and growth of the supplemental nursing industry represent a response to the nursing shortage in two ways: first, supplemental nursing keeps more nurses active in nursing because of flexibility and control in scheduling; second, it meets facility (hospital and nursing home) and home health care staffing needs for supplemental help. Furthermore, some facility administrators feel that supplemental nursing services contribute indirectly to the facility's goal of nurse retention by providing off-shift relief to their own nursing personnel in areas experiencing a critical shortage.[3] For "when the staff feels there's too few nurses around to get the job done, an atmosphere of complaining, dissension, slack motivation, lateness, absenteeism, apathy, and then high turnover may develop—which can result in many unfilled and unfillable positions."[4]

SUPPLEMENTAL SERVICES

Let us first look at the identifying factors of the supplemental services, what makes them different, and what services they can provide.

Registries

Registries are the earliest form of temporary nursing help, in the context of outside personnel assisting facility staff nurses with nursing care (although usually in the form of private duty). Today, some registries also provide referrals of independent contract personnel for supplemental staffing (i.e., staff relief). Licensed as employment agencies, these groups of independent contractors have traditionally been directly employed by an individual patient for private duty in the facility or in the home.

By the nature of the federal regulations defining private contractors, these nurses should be licensed, not directed and not supervised. They must set their fees with the patient, who is responsible for the independent contractor's workers' compensation coverage if the nurse does not have his or her own. If the independent contractor is judged to be an employee and not an independent contractor for the above or other reasons (IRS private letter ruling no. 8753042, October 7, 1987, and *Brock v. Superior Care, Inc.*, 108 L.C. 135, 029, February 16, 1988), the patient or the hospital as the employer is responsible for insurance required by that state (usually workers' compensation and state and federal unemployment) and for withholding taxes (federal, FICA, and sometimes state, city, and county taxes). The employer should further be assured of liability and malpractice insurance. In addition to payroll responsibilities, the employer must file 941s quarterly and W2s annually. Even patients or hospitals using independent contractors need to file form 1099 annually for each contractor.

Administration of the registry is by a single owner (who may or may not be a nurse) or a group of private nurses. Member fees to the registry are made on a percentage of hours worked and/or a flat fee for referral. Some registries employ nonlicensed care givers who by definition cannot be independent contractors and who subsequently raise an important issue of the supervision they need by nature of their training and established standards of practice.

Because of the increased use of supervised services and because of a trend in state laws and certifications, registries are not as prevalent as they were decades ago.

Temporary (Supplemental) Agencies

What has been known as "pools" in earlier stages of growth have actually evolved into full-scale nursing service organizations. Because of agency competition, voluntary certification, state-imposed licensing (in some states), consumer demands, and professional standards, these private corporations seem to have peaked in proliferation and are currently being sifted out by quality control utilization.

These supplemental services are independently owned or are part of a national or regional organization in which they are structured as a branch (company-owned) office, a "licensed" office, or a proprietor franchise.

Services include almost any level of nursing care around the clock for private duty in facilities, supplemental staffing in facilities, and discharge planning assistance and home care. Supplemental agencies provide adequate insurance for their employees. Supervision of agency employees is provided by their own nursing/administrative staff. A round-the-clock communication by nursing supervisors to facilities and by nursing supervisors to employees assures prompt response to staffing needs and/or problem solving.

Because they are a full-service nursing agency, you should expect that

- Employees are screened and hired according to standard employment practices, including personal interview.
- Assignments are made according to the nurse's past experience and individual training and capabilities.
- Documentation, including complete employee files and client files, is maintained according to established policies and procedures on standard forms.
- Physicians' orders are obtained and kept current, and collaboration with all team members is orchestrated by the nursing supervisor who is the case manager.
- On-site, routine (RN) supervisory visits are made for the purpose of assessment, supervision, problem solving, teaching, and coordination of health resources for home care. The necessary frequency of visits is initially established, then later reevaluated, but on-going frequency should never be less than every few weeks.

High-technology care is fast becoming the trend in the larger supplemental nurse organizations. Especially in these situations (e.g., ventilator, I.V. therapy, etc.), very detailed discharge planning and nurse inservice training is done in the facility during private duty and/or prior to discharge planning.

On the other hand, private-duty care as basic as home health aide or companion/sitter can be initiated during hospital or nursing home stays, then continued at home. Here again a patient's condition can change rapidly, so regular RN supervision for both the patient and the employee is important.

Hospital Pools

Traditionally, most hospitals have had a few designated "floaters" who worked part-time or full-time and were assigned to units according to where they were most needed at the start of a shift. As hospital administrators saw the numbers of staff nursing vacancies increase and watched the increased use of supplemental services as it affected the nursing budget, the development of in-house (''internal agency'') hospital pools was introduced.

Hospital pools employ part-time or full-time nurses; instead of the guaranteed work and pay of the former ''floaters,'' pool (per diem) employees are paid only for the hours worked.

The administration of the hospital nursing pool is designated within the nursing department. Most pools provide nurses to their hospital for supplemental staffing, but some do private-duty assignments as well. Pools consist of RNs and LPNs and provide care for shifts of 4, 6, 8, or 12 hours. Some hospitals find that, with the development of their own hospital pools, they have decreased the utilization of outside supplemental services, although they have increased nursing scheduling time. An advantage to the facility is that these supplemental nurses complete a full staff orientation program because of the hospital's exclusive use of the supplemental nurse. A disadvantage is the cost involved in the loss of that nurse if his or her services are not needed for a period of time and the nurse seeks employment elsewhere.

Travel Nurses

National travel nurse companies are the newest trend in meeting the nursing shortage. Through these companies supplemental nurses may accept assignments lasting usually from 4 to 13 weeks, or they may make commitments of 3 to 12 months. Round-trip tickets to the facility's city is provided to the nurse, and free or subsidized housing is arranged.

Travel nurses are utilized solely for staffing needs, very often in specialized areas for unpopular shifts (e.g., critical care night shift). A disadvantage of this program to the hospital is the cost of travel and housing, but an advantage is a specified contract with the hope of recruiting that nurse into the position he or she has temporarily relocated to fill.

What about Standards?

To date, there are few rules and regulations regarding supplemental and registry nurses. The federal government has rules for private contractors that primarily affect registries but also affect anyone who uses private contractors even on a lesser scale. It has become more and more evident that private contractors in the nursing and therapist fields DO NOT often qualify as private contractors. There is no effective monitoring, however, to see that these IRS and lawsuit precedent guidelines are currently being followed by everyone.

Many states have instituted comprehensive licensure laws, but they are in the area of home health care. These laws have an impact on an agency's supplemental staffing quality, however, because of the guidelines in hiring, screening, orienting, inservicing, assigning, and evaluating all employees. They also address the requirements of the administrator and nursing director and supervisor, which are always determining factors in the quality of any service.

Certifications such as those sponsored by the National League for Nursing (NLN) and the National HomeCaring Council have long been available to supplemental agencies if they provide home care and if they choose to undergo certification.

Newest on the scene, and promising to make a tremendous impact on the attention to certification, however, is the newly renamed Joint Commission on Accreditation of Healthcare Organizations and their new certification for home health agencies and related services. As implied by its former name, the Joint Commission on Accreditation of Hospitals, the Joint Commission until now has focused on hospital certification only. Now, however, it is turning its attention to all services and agencies dealing with the hospital and health care. It is not only seeking certification for its members but is requiring it of those to whom members refer for services. Among those service providers are durable medical equipment suppliers, group therapists, and home health agencies—which often provide supplemental staffing and private duty services as well. The effects of the certification for home care affect the organization and the quality of the entire agency.

Another standard setting certification is Medicare. Agencies that have chosen to be certified for Medicare-reimbursed care have met very detailed requirements, policies, and procedures, which again affect the entire supplemental organization.

In reference to supplemental staffing in hospitals, Joint Commission certification has traditionally had specific requirements for hospital nursing services in their use of outside agencies, especially regarding licensure check, orientation, and evaluation of supplemental personnel.

WHY NURSES CHOOSE A SUPPLEMENTAL SERVICE

In Chapter 2 various reasons why nurses "dropped out" were presented. Because of supplemental services, some of those nurses likely to drop out did not leave nursing, and some who did returned to active nursing on a part-time or full-time basis. Over a decade of interviewing supplemental nurse applicants and employees supports this.[5] But a different view is that to offer employment services outside the hospital setting sets up an arena in which hospitals and supplemental services are competing for the recruitment and retention of nurses.[6]

What Are the Advantages?

Undoubtedly the main reason nurses are attracted to supplemental services is the flexibility of scheduling available in most agencies. Also with this, the nurse has control of her schedule with days off according to her choosing.

As a supplemental nurse employee, the nurse gives her or his availability for the days, shifts, and types of assignments she or he would like to work for the upcoming 1 to 4 weeks. If the nurse wants to travel with a spouse on a business trip or take 3 months off for summertime with school-aged children, she or he merely states an unavailability to work. The nurse gives the agency at least a 2-week advance notice so that a replacement can be found, and there is no guilt or concern for the time off.

Students, whether studying for an LPN, RN, BSN, or PhD degree, find that flexible work hours fit in with class schedules and can be readjusted when final examination time approaches. Nursing instructors, too, often work on their "time off" to keep their skills current, to keep abreast of new methods and treatments, and to be better oriented to the unit where their students do their clinical practice.

Baccalaureate graduates find that the experience in clinical areas gives them a better background for choosing a specialty for postgraduate study leading toward a master's degree.[7]

A nurse moving to a new city because of a spouse's job change likes to work as a supplemental nurse in various settings to preface a choice for permanent employment.

More often, retirees are eager to continue fulfilling roles, especially in private duty, and yet work only enough to still qualify for their social security benefits.

Supplemental nurses enjoy a variety of assignments on different units and in different facilities. Working in this way, they can try a variety of settings without the expected one- to two-year commitment to a single unit or facility, they avoid unit politics, and they are often welcomed by staff members who treat them amiably in the hope that they will want to return for future unit needs.

Salaries are attractive and competitive to recruit quality nurses who do not require the benefits that hospitals offer.

A last advantage for some is that a few agencies provide "instant pay," and many offer unique bonus programs for recruitment of new nurses to the supplemental agency.

What Are the Disadvantages?

The disadvantages of working for a supplemental service are primarily fourfold. First, a supplemental nurse may not always get the number of hours she or he would like to work each week. Although the agency tries to meet requests for days, shifts, and assignments, if they are not requested by a hospital or client, the nurse does not work and payment is not received (because it is pay for hours worked). Second, the duration of an assignment is often not known and continuity may suffer; also, if a nurse requests a vacation, the same assignment is not guaranteed upon return (if the client requests to continue the replacement nurse instead). Third, benefits have increased in working with supplemental services, but some benefits such as life insurance and extensive health insurance may not be comparable with those of large-facility programs. Fourth, most supplemental agencies do not have a mechanism for longevity, seniority pay, or career ladder benefits. All categories are usually paid one salary according to job classification (RN, LPN, aide, homemaker, or companion/sitter).

Orientation

The type and extent of orientation are important determinants of how well the supplemental nurse performs.[8] In one agency, for example, Healthcare Personnel$_{sm}$, the following procedure is recommended.

After the initial application, interview, and reference-checking procedure, applicants are scheduled to attend an orientation to the agency, its policies, and procedures. The orientation includes

1. policies and procedures of Healthcare Personnel$_{sm}$
2. job descriptions
3. orientation to other members of the health care team and how they relate to one another in care of the patient
4. ethics and confidentiality
5. assignments, scheduling, and uniform code
6. responsibilities to staff, clients, and facilities
7. emergency measures, safety precautions, and infection control
8. charting and other documentation, sign-in and out procedures, etc.
9. health certificates
10. facility information and basic orientation (according to information provided by each area facility)

A Healthcare Personnel$_{sm}$ orientation manual and packet are given to each new employee for further reference during employment.

General information concerning a facility is given to employees before they accept an assignment at that hospital. Orientation to facilities can be in the form of group or individual orientations. Methods include a choice or combination of in-house facility manual review, a slide/tape program, facility orientation manual, and/or an orientation checklist. Facilities may choose whatever on-site orientation they prefer. Orientation may be prescheduled before the day of assignment, and/or orientation to the nursing division is done by a head nurse or charge nurse 20 minutes before the shift. This orientation should include introduction to the physical layout, hospital procedure book and forms, shift personnel and routine, and a complete patient report. Furthermore, emergency procedures, codes, and access to emergency equipment should be pointed out. Upon satisfactory completion of the orientation, the agency orientation checklist should be signed, dated, and returned to the agency office to be retained in the employee file. In addition, a copy of the form may be retained by the facility, if they so choose. The fundamental premise and success of an efficient, concise, orientation program is the philosophy that nursing is a profession with universal standards of practice; the nurse is oriented to somewhat different methods and forms that are to some extent generic.

An experienced hospital staff nurse co-worker is an asset to an agency nurse during the entire shift. He or she can answer any questions pertaining to a routine or procedure unique to that floor or unit.[9]

The Joint Commission requires orientation to supplemental nursing personnel and states that it may be

> conducted by the hospital or in another manner approved by the hospital or nurse administrator. . . . The nursing department/service is to determine the scope of orientation necessary for nursing personnel who are not hospital employees. However, orientation for nursing personnel who are not hospital employees is to include pertinent information relative to the safety and infection control requirements described in the *Accreditation Manual for Hospitals*.[10]

Nursing homes do not have any federal regulation regarding orientation of supplemental personnel, but Medicare and Medicaid certification carries with it a need to have responsibilities, objectives, and terms of agreement delineated in writing. Orientation programs are usually provided because those same rules state that the nursing home assumes professional and administrative responsibility for services rendered.

Beyond orientation programs, supplemental agencies should have continuing education programs that are planned and presented in response to requests of the agency staff, the identified needs of the staff (from evaluation or from the request of the facility in which they work), the types of patients the agency or facility services, and established and progressive goals of the agency. Also, information regarding community and facility continuing education programs should be made available to supplemental employees via the agency's employee newsletter and employee bulletin board. In facilities, supplemental nurses should be able to attend programs on their own time. Occasionally, facilities may invite a nurse to attend a program during shift time if it directly benefits the facility.

In addition to orientation programs, agencies should have an office library for their staff so that pertinent professional books, current nursing periodicals, and other resource materials are available to and utilized by employees.

Evaluation

Supplemental nurse evaluations assist in assuring continuous quality service to the facility toward the ultimate goal of quality patient care. Also, an evaluation procedure is an effective means of bringing even the smallest problem to the agency's attention, so that all problems may be remedied or averted.

Job descriptions should be utilized during the procedure of employee performance evaluations. Employees should be routinely evaluated within three months of the start of employment during their probationary period, and annually thereafter. Input to evaluations of agency employees can be given by staff supervisors, head nurses, or charge nurses in the hospitals in which the agency employee is working. Although the agency supervisor or director of nursing makes periodic evaluations of agency personnel, it has proven beneficial to have facility staff with whom agency personnel work also contribute to the evaluation of their skills and performance. The facility personnel's working exposure to agency personnel allows them the opportunity to evaluate during a greater period of time and thus assess a greater number of skills of supplemental nurses. The agency supervisor or director of nursing should be available to make on-site evaluations, facilitate solutions to problem situations, and assist the agency nurse to acquire skill review when necessary. Additional evaluations by the agency, beyond the initial and routine, are obtained as necessary should a problem arise or a weakness be noted. Like evaluation, problem solving is the responsibility of the agency but is performed with communication at each appropriate level of facility nursing management. Employees should be counseled by agency nursing supervisors or the director of nursing services. All evaluations and counseling reports should be kept on file in each employee's folder in the agency office. Copies or summaries of any incident reports should also be kept in the employee's file.[11]

SUPPLEMENTAL HELP AS AN AID TO FACILITY RECRUITMENT AND RETENTION

Twenty years ago, it was not uncommon to encounter a hospital that did not hire part-time nurses; they required full-time help. There were hospitals, too, that required shift rotation, especially if a nurse was primarily assigned to the day shift. Differentials helped to attract nurses to unpopular shifts, but they still were not incentive enough to acquire a full staff. Hospital administration had to change its staffing philosophy to include part-timers.

With the advent of supplemental service agencies, the hospitals had to change their staffing philosophies again. Many directors of nursing look upon agencies as an undesirable necessity. But temporary nursing services have filled a lot of staffing holes in advance; within planned staffing schedules; and at the last minute for hospital staff illness, patient census fluctuation, or abrupt change in patient acuity level.

Internal nursing services (or per diem hospital pools) followed; then travel nurses were introduced.

As the shortage of nurses became more critical, the options for supplemental help grew, and the need for a change of attitude was apparent. No longer could the hospital be the autocratic ruler of a captured labor market of nurses. Instead, administrations are now looking toward steps to improve the practice environment and organizational strategies to improve the motivation of nurses.[12] This attitude has to extend to the acceptance of the supplemental nurse as well—beyond the occasional hope that the supplemental nurse could be recruited to join the hospital staff.

Appropriate Use and Avoidance of Overuse

Supplemental nurses have always been meant to supplement staff, not replace hiring of permanent, full-time nurses. However, a few large agencies are marketing a program to contract services for an entire nursing unit. However, we will deal here with the supplemental issue only.

The single most important factor in the appropriate use of supplemental nurses is planning. Without planning, acquisition of a supplemental nurse a few hours before a shift is difficult, to begin with. Besides, at the last minute, agencies may not be able to get in touch with the nurses who have the particular skills and experience for that position, or who had worked on that unit before, for continuity. With charge nurses and supervisors counting staff to patient ratio one or two shifts in advance, unpredictable staffing can be felt by all. This can only result in discontent and concern by permanent and supplemental staff alike, being manifest in increased staff tardiness and absenteeism,[13] which further contributes to the problem of recruitment and retention of nurses.

By planning a two- to four-week schedule of supplemental nurses along with the permanent staff, the same supplemental nurse could be scheduled for continuity and would be more willing to work some weekends and/or unpopular shifts because he or she would feel a responsibility to the unit as part of their team. Such planned staffing allows the permanent staff to have a better schedule of days off, and requests for special days off are more easily accommodated in the schedule.[14]

Scheduling is an important part of planning, especially to avoid overuse of temporary staff. When more than one supervisor or designated secretary is calling agencies scheduling supplemental nurses, orders are duplicated or the need is overestimated, because a comprehensive study of the staffing distribution is not made. One designated scheduler and one other alternate are suggested for easier scheduling. In scheduling, when the hospital informs the agency of all duties and responsibilities involved in the assignment, the agency informs the employee before the employee accepts the shift, which results in a better skill and performance match. Upon the employee's acceptance of the shift, the agency should call the hospital with the employee's name as designated for that particular assignment.

The review of staffing patterns and preplanning for staffing is a key concept in use and not overuse. It is also the basis for identifying the true supplemental need, cost-effectiveness, and budget capabilities. It is best based then on the method for staffing that the facility uses (full-time equivalents, patient care hours, acuity levels, etc.). Coordinating supplemental nurses' scheduling into permanent nurses' scheduling gives a free flow for focusing on adequate staffing for quality patient care. This method also sets a precedent to avoid overuse or inappropriate use of supplemental nurses merely as last-minute replacements, for errors in scheduling, and last-minute absenteeism of permanent staff. Last-minute need for supplemental nurses does occur, but be sure that first-line management determines that it is a need and not just a reflex when a nurse is ill or on vacation.

Budgeting decisions need to be made in light of the comparison of rates paid to the facility's own staff for overtime versus rates paid to the agency for supplemental staff. For prolonged use, rates should be compared with the cost of recruitment, orientation, and benefits for a full-time person if needed only temporarily.

Appropriate Role of the Supplemental Nurse

The appropriate role of supplemental nurses is simple. Accept them and use them as if they were facility staff. Expectations for any nurse—staff or supplemental—are conveyed in many ways, perceived by most, and usually met with that same certainty. Quality patient-centered nursing should be an expectation of any and all nurses regardless of the setting or the employer. With good orientation and delineation of patient and task responsibilities, supplemental nurses can be important contributors to the facility's goal-centered patient care nursing.

If a particular unit is task-oriented, all assignments should be made accordingly, with the supplemental nurse assigned to the tasks least needing experiential knowledge of the unit if he or she is new to the area (i.e., assignment to patient care versus treatment rounds). If a particular unit is using total-care assignments, assign the supplemental nurse his or her own patients—but not consistently the difficult or isolation cases whom the in-house staff complains about. On the other hand, if the staff nurses have "taken turns" on a more difficult assignment, use the supplemental nurse as a welcome break for the staff. It will be a "new challenge" for the supplemental nurse, and an opportunity for teamwork with a new or fresh insight to patient need, and possibly a new approach for nursing intervention. No matter what the type of unit assignment (even primary nursing), it is ineffective to assign a supplemental nurse as a "floater," helping out wherever and whoever she or he can. This adds to the supplemental nurse's frustration from poor utilization and only emphasizes to the staff a feeling of disorganization and lack of professional collaboration and teamwork.

Refer back to "similar expectations": consistent supervisor communication with supplemental and staff nurses alike creates benefits to the facility in two ways. First, the supplemental nurse performs better within the same expected boundaries as the staff nurse; second, the staff nurse does not become disgruntled because the supplemental nurse has an easier job or role expectation or is allowed infringements on the facility's standard expectations, policies, and rules for permanent staff.

Be sure the supplemental nurse knows who is the first line of supervisory communication; i.e., does the nurse report to the charge nurse, or is she or he directly responsible to the head nurse? As mentioned earlier, problem solving and counseling can be initiated by facility staff members who report to the agency administration any nurse requiring immediate follow-up, with in-office discussion and resolution of the situation. Facility input toward the agency's evaluating and problem solving with supplemental nurses not only assists the facility in quality control, it makes the supplemental nurses feel important through awareness of their contributions and their needs.

Peer/Staff Relations and Communication

Administration's downward communication toward their own staff is an important preface to good peer/staff relations and communication between supplemental staff nurses and in-house staff. The components of this communication should be (1) why a decision for using supplemental service was made; (2) the decision was made for the benefit of the staff in their goal for quality patient care; (3) how best to utilize supplemental staff; and (4) a method for reporting and handling problems and staff input is established.

The facility supervisor sets the tone for the introduction, utilization, and often the effectiveness of supplemental nurses. If the administration and supervisors feel that supplemental nurses are a "necessary evil to be endured in dire circumstances," then that is the attitude the floor staff will have. If a head nurse implies that a temporary is a poor-quality outsider who contributes little, is paid more than most, and requires more staff time for guidance, then that is the attitude the floor staff will have also. How can any person, no matter what the background or experience or quality of care, be an effective team player with that image to overcome? Instead, prepare the staff in a positive way. A head nurse at shift report can inform the staff collectively that, because of a concern for them and their workload, a supplemental nurse will be assigned the next day and that the nurse will have the same expectations, workload, and feedback/supervision that they as staff have. To help the supplemental nurse work at optimal efficiency for everyone's benefit, encourage the staff to respond positively, and in a helpful way, to any questions or concerns the temporary may have.

Encourage the staff to help the supplemental nurse feel part of the team—even if assigned for only one day—so that they all can work together for quality care of the patients on the unit, which should be every staff person's goal.

A negative factor in cohesion can be a discussion of salaries. Salaries should not become a topic of conversation, but if they do the facility would benefit if the head nurse points out to the staff that when the monetary values of fringe benefits are considered, the staff's salaries are roughly equivalent to supplemental nurses' salaries, even though the supplemental base salaries could be higher.[15]

During the course of use, if hospital staff members respond negatively to supplemental nurses, facility administration should find out why, to remedy the situation as well as the unproductive stress it creates. If it is due to insufficient orientation, review the orientation given and provide more information and/or team a supplemental nurse with a very capable, experienced staff nurse. If it is a problem of group dynamics because of staff social ostracism or supplemental nurse isolationism, or simple bilateral avoidance, open the lines of communication: set the stage for acceptance as social and professional equals. Plan coffee breaks or lunches to encourage communication and conversation. Provide the supplemental nurse with every opportunity to contribute to the unit workload in a routine manner and, if the nurse is consistently assigned to the unit, assign him or her to a special project if he or she has particular expertise in that area. Slowly opening avenues to exhibit the supplemental nurse's experience and capabilities not only benefits the supplemental nurse by professional recognition and expectation, it points to a common ground for acceptance by the hospital staff. As an example, this author experienced first-hand a physician who refused to have a supplemental nurse care for his patient in critical care until she was introduced as having been a former head nurse in critical care at a large hospital in an adjacent city. Furthermore, when this nurse had been assigned consistently to this unit for two months, the hospital frequently requested that she be assigned as the evening charge nurse while they had a vacancy. She functioned well and very competently, receiving excellent reports from the doctor and the hospital, and good performance evaluations from the agency. As in this case, an introduction that includes a supplemental nurse's past experience allows the staff initially to feel more comfortable with the supplemental nurse's competence and later to feel more comfortable in utilizing the nurse's full potential.

In terms of recognition, when supplemental nurses have been particularly helpful, cooperative, or efficient, let them know. Positive reinforcement begets further positive performance—staff and supplemental alike.

The Facility Perspective

Determining criteria for choosing agencies to be used sets a standard for the quality of services you will receive. When you contract with an agency versus a registry, you are buying the services of temporary nurses backed by a management team. Old adages of "You get what you pay for" and "An organization is only as good as its leaders" ring true in many situations, including the supplemental nursing field. For your own benefit, look at an agency's administration, background, training, and support systems; their philosophies, policies, and procedures; and job descriptions. Who have they serviced in the area? What is their volume of service and potential volume? How long have they been serving the local area? Check others who have used them; the best services are referred by satisfied clients. What are their recruitment and retention practices? Learn how they hire, screen, orient, and evaluate. How do they make assignments for continuity and skill needs? Do they use skill inventories? What security measures do they use for licensure assurance, identification (photo) badges, incident reports, and insurance? How reliable are they and how quickly and thoroughly do they respond to problems or needs? Can they fill your particular staffing needs?

Advantages of Temporary Staff

Predictable and adequately staffed units definitely contribute greatly to the recruitment and retention of a nursing staff. When patient census or acuity level fluctuates, supplemental staff can be used or not used, with no carryover of people or benefits when they are not needed.

Illness such as rampant flu can understaff a unit as quickly as seasonal and unplanned vacancies during vacation season.

When new positions or units open, supplemental agencies can provide the necessary human resources to adequately accommodate planned, timely, and beneficial growth.

Unpopular shifts, weekends or nights, may always remain the nemesis of the schedule. Supplemental nurses can help fill those voids. To this advantage, add caution. It is important to learn from the agency their policy toward how often and under what conditions their supplemental nurses can work these shifts. An important restraint here is a policy of limiting shift hours or consecutive double shifts worked by supplemental staff nurses. An advantage of covering difficult shifts with a nurse's prolonged compressed schedule is quickly offset if fatigue hinders or threatens the quality of patient care. Care may also be hindered if, after a supplemental nurse is assigned, a unit is still short-staffed and/or a strong staff person is not also assigned.

Disadvantages of Temporary Staff

Some administrators try to avoid the use of supplemental nurses or other levels of caregivers because of the lack of continuity they have experienced with some agencies. They say that the staff nurses then seem to spend their time constantly orienting, directing, and guiding supplemental staff nurses, which takes away from their own activities and responsibilities.[16]

Other disadvantages are that the facility staff is discontent if salaries are compared; and the facility does not "know" the supplemental nurse because the employee file, including references and evaluations, is in the employer's (supplemental agency) office. Some nursing supervisors also feel that supplemental nurses are not as committed to the facility's patient care as staff nurses are, because chances are the supplemental staff nurse may or may not return. Other nursing administrators feel that the commitment and performance toward quality care is determined by the personal integrity and professional competence of the individual nurse, not his or her employment choice.[17]

The quality of supplemental nurses is sometimes criticized. Be assured that a nonregulated (or even a regulated) supplemental agency can be a haven for nurses who have been "let go" from facilities for quality of care or personal impairment reasons. Choosing an agency is comparable to making a major investment. All avenues and all aspects should be investigated as such with emphasis on the local agency office and its administration.

Some Legal Concerns

Among the most important aspects to be investigated is the supplemental agency's or registry's relationship with its personnel as it complies with all governing regulations. Are the personnel employees with employer responsibilities taken care of by the agency or are they private contractors? If they are private contractors, be aware of the federal requirements of private contractors in regard to scheduling; supervision; the direction or control of the manner in which services are performed (control, coordination, and evaluation); and reimbursement. Note that there cannot be "supervisors" for contract nurses even though some registries advertise supervision. Why is this important? Because:

> Now that private duty nurses are usually obtained from a nurses registry and the hospital may insist that its approval be obtained for anyone who is allowed to care for patients in it or that a nurse be under the supervision of the hospital's nursing supervisor, private duty nurses may be regarded as hospital employees.[18]

The patient or facility then must be sure to complete all associated responsibilities, as discussed earlier. If the patient has not obtained workers' compensation insurance, for example, the facility will be, and in some suits has been cited as, liable.

Next, be aware of the need for—and source of—a realm of insurance coverage and tax responsibilities: malpractice insurance, liability insurance, workers' compensation insurance, bonding insurance, unemployment insurance, and withholding taxes. Are the independent contract nurse and patient supplying these for each other? Is the supplemental agency supplying all of these for its employees? Will the hospital or nursing home be responsible should an incident occur? Early determination before an incident protects the patient and protects the facility.

Employment contracts also need to be respected. To defray some of their own recruitment and orientation costs, some supplemental agencies have applicants at the time of employment sign an agreement not to seek or accept employment from a facility to which they have been assigned for a specific number of days after their written resignation from the agency. The employee may continue to work at the facility but is still considered an agency employee during those interim days. When a facility does not want to "wait" for an employee, a few large companies have a policy of outright "selling" the contract to the client for a specific sum. Either way, the contractual agreement between the supplemental agency and supplemental nurse requires the respect of a legal contract. To assure this, some agencies, at the start of service, have the client/facility sign a similar contract so that they are bound to wait those specific number of days for hiring also.

It is often the hospital or nursing home's hope that supplemental nurses who work at their facility will want to join their permanent staff. Too often the facility administration or staff seeks too enthusiastically to encourage this conversion, which can leave a cumulative deficit of agency supplemental nurses from which to draw when there is a need. On the other hand, supplemental agencies should inform their nurses that, while working in the facility, they should not seek to recruit facility nurses to work for supplemental agencies.

An important area of legal concern, too, is the effect of understaffing on liability and the quality of patient care. The Joint Commission Nursing Service Standard III addresses the requirement of sufficient nursing personnel, and precedent-setting suits have established the requirement of orientation to a new unit.[19] A yet-untested area, though, may be a suit environment in which there is a facility staffing shortage that is not addressed when at the same time supplemental nurses are available.

> Sooner or later some hospital on the receiving end of a blockbuster lawsuit, is going to be charged with failing to draw on the nursing personnel resources of a supplemental staffing company in its area. The allegation will be related to lack of adequate coverage at a time when the supplemental staffing company had a number of available RNs or LPNs. We believe a hospital's argument relative to standards of quality care will pale in the face of controverted evidence of available nurses at the local supplemental staffing office.[20]

A FINAL NOTE

The nursing shortage has already made a profound effect on hospitals, nursing homes, and patient care settings in general. It appears that the effects will be with us for quite a while. The recruitment and retention of nurses is a prime, viable and challenging goal, be it a long-term, tedious, and progressive one. A short-term goal, in the meantime, can be the appropriate use and not misuse or abuse of supplemental nurses.

The shortage is here to stay; supplemental nurses are here to stay; and change is forever with us. Harmony of purpose, goals, and standards can assure quality nursing and patient care, which is what health care is all about.

NOTES

1. Associated Press Release, *Naples Daily News*, May 13, 1988.

2. Priscilla Scherer, "Hospitals That Attract (and Keep) Nurses," *American Journal of Nursing* (January 1988): 40.

3. Isabel Boland, Executive Director, Booth Memorial Hospital, Cleveland, Ohio, telephone interview May 4, 1988.

4. Margaret Van Meter, "A 'Magic' Solution for All Our Staffing Ills," *RN* (January 1982): 49.

5. Pat Hrehocik, a supplemental service office manager since 1976, Cleveland, Ohio, telephone interview April 25, 1988.

6. P.A. Prescott, "Use of Nurses for Supplemental Services: Implications for Hospitals," *Nursing Administration Quarterly* (Fall 1986): 84.

7. Pamela Jacobson, RN, BSN, a travel nurse. Raleigh-Durham, N.C., correspondence dated April 16, 1988.

8. Marjorie H. Casey, RN, BSN, Nurse Educator, Naples Community Hospital, Naples, Florida, personal interview February 20, 1988.

9. Orientation information from Healthcare Personnel, Inc., "Presentation for Hospitals Using Supplemental Staffing and Private Duty" and *HEALTHCARE PERSONNEL$_{sm}$ Facility Manual,"* by Ellen Eggland, RN, MN, © 1984.

10. C. Patterson et al., *A Guide to JCAH Nursing Services Standards* (Chicago: Joint Commission on the Accreditation of Hospitals, 1986), 113–114.

11. Evaluation information from Healthcare Personnel, Inc. See n. 9.

12. Linda Aiken, "Solutions to Nursing Shortage Bear Repeating," *The American Nurse* (March 1988): 4.

13. K. Shanks and K. Potempa, "A System for Using Supplemental Staff," *Journal of Nursing Administration* (October 1981): 44.

14. Ibid., 42.

15. Prescott, "Use of Nurses for Supplemental Services," 85.

16. Pamela Cox, Administrator of Lakeside Plantation, Naples, Florida, telephone interview April 12, 1988.

17. Boland. See n. 3.

18. Helen Creighton, *Law Every Nurse Should Know* (Philadelphia, W.B. Saunders Co., 1986), 111.

19. Ibid., 68–69.

20. William Regan, "Supplemental Staffing: Nursing Personnel Pools," *Regan Report on Nursing Law* (December 1981): 1.

FURTHER READING

Alt, Joyce, et al. "We Bit the Bullet," *RN* (January 1982): 52.

American Nurses' Association. *Guidelines for Use of Supplemental Nursing Services* (Kansas City, Mo.: American Nurses' Association, 1979).

Baird, J.E. "Changes in Nurse Attitudes: Management Strategies for Today's Environment," *Journal of Nursing Administration* 17, no. 9 (September 1987): 38–43.

Buccheri, Robin. "Nursing Supervision: A New Look at an Old Role," *Nursing Administration Quarterly* 11, no. 1 (Fall 1986): 11–25.

Gulack, Robert. "Why Nurses Leave Nursing," *RN* (December 1983): 32–37.

Hamilton, J.M. "4 Tips To Take the Fear Out of Floating," *Nursing* 17, no. 2 (February 1987): 60–61.

Internal Revenue Service. *Technical Advice Memorandum*, February 10, 1987.

Lewin, Barbara, and Brown, Lillian. "Monitoring Supplemental Staffing Agencies," *Nursing Management* 12, no. 9 (September 1981): 56–63.

Longo, R.A., et al. "Why Nurses Stay: A Positive Approach to the Nursing Shortage," *Nursing Management* 18, no. 7 (July 1987): 78–79.

Prescott, P., and Langford, T. "Supplemental Agency Nurses and Hospital Staff Nurses: What Are the Differences?" *Nursing and Health Care* (April 1981): 200–206.

Rabinow, J. "Inadequate Staffing? Don't Take Chances with Risky Solutions," *Nursing Life* 5, no. 4 (July/August 1985): 28–30.

Regan, William. "When the 'Agency's Nurse' Becomes 'Hospital Employee'," *Regan Report on Nursing Law* 26, no. 4 (September 1985): 2.

Robertson, M., et al. "Temporary Staffing: A Positive Approach," *Nursing Management* 18, no. 7 (July 1987): 80–82.

Tillman, Eugene. "Contract Workers Providing Home Care Could Be 'Employees' under IRS Rules," *Home Health Line*, Port Republic, Md., April 18, 1988, 142.

Chapter 18

Alternative Care Providers: Are They the Answer?

Patricia K. Findling, R. Edward Howell, and Cecelia K. Golightly

BACKGROUND DISCUSSION

The preceding chapters in this book describe the techniques, methods, and approaches for recruiting and retaining professional nursing personnel. This chapter discusses a staffing approach under study at a major teaching hospital in the Southeast that is geared toward the expansion of existing nursing staff capacity in any given health care facility by the use of what is termed here the *alternative care provider*. The alternative care provider is defined as a non-registered nurse whose primary function is bedside patient care.

Why are expanders of the registered nurse (RN) capacity being considered? It is estimated by federal projection that by 1990 the demand for baccalaureate-prepared nurses will exceed the supply by 340 percent.[1] It is projected that the current nursing shortage will grow and will be greater and longer than previous shortages. This is due to the decreasing numbers of enrollments and graduations from baccalaureate nursing programs. By the year 2000, the projected shortage will be even greater. Chapter 1 describes in more detail the issue of the nursing supply.

It is clear from all of the projections that insufficient numbers of RNs will be available to meet the demands of the various components of the health care system, even if retention and recruitment strategies are effective. Thus, the enhancement of the "capacity" of the RN to function in specific situations has been evolved as a potential solution by hospitals and other health care providers to address this major labor shortage issue.

For many in the nursing profession, expansion of the use of the alternative care provider seems like a step backward in time. In fact, many U.S. hospitals began moving toward increasing the ratio of RNs to non-RNs during the 1980s. The goal of an all-RN hospital has been associated with the well-managed magnet hospitals that have been described in the literature; magnet hospitals have a reputation for being good places in which to work and to practice nursing.[2,3] When a high value

is placed on increasing proportions of the RN staff within the hospital organization, there is a natural reluctance to consider the alternative care provider as a
possible solution to the problem of any given institution's nursing shortage. One
author suggests, "Like sex and death, nursing assistants may be essential, but that
does not make them suitable topics for polite conversation."[4]

Recognition of the inherent concern of the nursing profession—that the gains in
the development of the professional practice of nursing that have been made over
the past two decades must be preserved, if not enhanced, as solutions to labor
shortages are developed and implemented—is essential. By definition, some may
believe that the professional practice of nursing and use of the alternative care provider are mutually exclusive. It is hoped that the work described in this chapter will
allay some of these concerns and bring the alternative care provider into focus as a
support for the professional practice of nursing when properly structured into a patient care delivery system. We also touch on recent proposals put forward that
recommend the development of a non-nurse technologist as a solution to the
nursing shortage.

TRADITIONAL CARE PROVIDERS

Alternative care providers originated during World War II as a response to an
acute shortage of RNs. During that period, "health care workers were trained in a
variety of technical skills on a wide range of levels that included aides, practical
nurses, and diverse technicians."[5] This pattern of filling the staffing gap in patient
care areas with alternative care providers has repeated itself each time shortages of
RNs have developed. In 1981, a national survey of RNs reported that the gap
created by the nursing shortage was once again being filled by non-RNs, in this
case licensed practical nurses (LPNs).[6] In the study referenced earlier regarding
the magnet hospitals, which provide an exceptional environment for the professional practice of nursing, the percentage of nursing staff that was non-RN ranged
from a low of 2.76 percent to a high of 33.14 percent with an overall mean of
20.54 percent.[7] Thus one might conclude that, even in hospitals that have mastered the problem of creating an environment that is conducive to attracting and
retaining the professional RN, significant numbers of alternative care providers
are utilized as an essential element of staffing. The use of the alternative care provider—the nursing assistant, LPN, or licensed vocational nurse (LVN)—will
likely continue.

The LPN typically has a 9- to 15-month program of training and is licensed
under each state's nurse practice act. Nursing assistants, in general, have been
trained in-house, although some formal educational programs in community and
technical schools have provided training. In many cases nursing assistants' roles
have been filled by nursing students themselves. Operating room (OR) technicians
are another category of nursing care providers who are specially trained to function
in the OR.

For each category of alternative care provider there are skill levels that are defined in a given institution for both nursing assistants and LPNs. These skill levels relate directly to the training and experience of the individual, which provide the individual with the capacity to perform various technical tasks in relation to patient care. More than half of all nursing functions are performed by all levels of nursing personnel, from the nursing assistant to the RN. In general, these are considered the fundamental tasks of nursing. LPNs and RNs carry out the more complex activities related to nursing care. One study indicated that 28 percent of the more complex nursing activities were carried out by both RNs and LPNs.[8] From this study only 12 percent of the tasks of nursing fell within the skill level exclusively of the RN. The study described later in this chapter found this percentage to be approximately 14 percent. Thus the alternative care provider, whose training ranges from one-year programs of education to in-house training, functions in a significant way to carry out the tasks of nursing. Later we discuss skill levels and how these skill levels dovetail with the training of the individual and the quality of the nursing care provided.

NEW PROVIDERS OF CARE

The American Medical Association (AMA) in December 1987 approved a report entitled "Nursing Education and the Supply of Nursing Personnel in the United States," which contained a recommendation for a proposal to establish formal educational programs to prepare bedside caregivers with the title of registered care technologist (RCT). The RCT would "execute medical protocols at the bedside with special emphasis on technical skills."[9] This proposal suggested three levels of RCTs: assistant, basic, and advanced. The assistant RCT would receive two months of training; the basic RCT would receive approximately 9 months of preparation; the advanced RCT would receive an additional 9 months. The basic RCT would function in low-technical areas to provide patient care, such as on general medical-surgical units. The advanced RCT would work in intensive care areas, special care areas, or emergency rooms. As defined by the AMA's proposal, the advanced RCT would also function in any kind of patient care setting—the hospital, the patient's home, or long-term care facilities. The basic prerequisites for entering into the program would be similar to those for the LPN and, as of the time of this publication, the proposal presumes that the RCT would be licensed under the state medical practice acts. It is also proposed that the RCT would somehow be integrated into the nursing organization of hospitals, skilled nursing facilities, etc. How this would occur is not as yet specified.

With the current shortage of nursing personnel throughout the U.S., it is no surprise that one of the groups most affected by the shortage, that is, the medical profession, has put forward a proposal to assist with solving the problem. It appears that one advantage of the proposed RCT may be simply that the title of this new bedside caregiver may be "flexible enough to attract a broader range of recruits"[10] than the nursing profession, which is dominated by female applicants and is not expected to attract sufficient numbers of individuals from both sexes to meet the growing demands. Aside from this advantage, which should not be underestimated, new problems may be created by this proposed solution. The addition of yet another caregiver into the spectrum of already licensed, trained health care workers presents another opportunity for fragmentation of patient care within hospitals and skilled nursing facilities. If this technical group is not well integrated within these organizational and professional structures, more problems will surely arise in the continuity of the delivery of care. Furthermore, given the current absence of career advancement opportunities within already existing health care technical providers, this would certainly create yet another group with limited potential for career growth.

At the time of this publication, the future of the RCT is unclear. It is hoped that, if this concept moves forward, the need to address the integration of this technically trained person into nursing professional practice will be given the necessary consideration.

MODELS OF CARE

In order to understand the role of the alternative care provider in contemporary patient care, a brief review of the evolution of models of patient care is provided. Within nursing there are five common, well-accepted models of patient care. These are case, functional, team, primary, and, most recently, case management. An evolution of different models of nursing care has occurred, beginning with the public health nurse caseload. Caseload is the approach where one nurse has the sole responsibility for planning and administering care for patients. Functional nursing was developed according to industrial engineering principles where efficiency was felt to be gained by dividing various functions of nursing among the nursing staff, with each nursing patient caregiver having responsibility for certain functions; for example, one would administer medication, another would serve meals, and another would change linens. The nursing profession has moved significantly away from functional nursing, as it caused the patient to be treated by numerous individuals in any given 24-hour period without any significant integration of planning for that individual patient's care.

Team nursing developed during World War II, simultaneously with the rise of the alternative care provider. In team nursing, a group of workers is assigned to an individual team leader, typically an RN, who is responsible for a designated group of patients. A team leader plans for the care of all of the patients assigned to the team and delegates that care to the individual members of the team. The benefit of this approach is that this does utilize to an advantage the more advanced knowledge base of the RN in organizing care and does provide for some accountability for the personal nursing care plans for an individual patient. The disadvantage of team nursing is that it is task-oriented. This approach lacks continuity and 24-hour accountability for patients. In addition, as with functional nursing, the RN who expects to enjoy the satisfaction of caring for patients personally oftentimes becomes much more involved in the supervisory functions as a team leader and becomes removed from direct patient care.

Primary nursing evolved as a professional model in the late 1960s because of the increasing dissatisfaction among professional nursing staffs with the fragmentation of care that functional and team nursing models created. In primary nursing, a primary nurse is responsible for a group of patients. The primary nurse's responsibility will extend over a 24-hour period and the primary nurse will delegate to associate nurses responsibilities for executing care plans throughout the other shifts when she or he is not present. The primary nurse retains control over planning and evaluating the effectiveness of the nursing care of his or her primary patients.

Primary nursing is considered a pivotal point in the development of the professional practice of nursing. This is so because with primary nursing comes 24-hour accountability, authority, and autonomy in the care of a particular group of patients. This results in the development of a set of expectations for work by nursing professionals that has been found to be very satisfying. Today's shortage of nurses is perceived as a threat to the gains that have been made in the development of the professional practice of nursing. In some settings, primary nursing has become "synonymous with an all RN staff, which is highly impractical during the (labor) shortage of the century."[11] Clearly an all-RN staff is not feasible in most hospitals, given today's labor shortage. Thus, the challenge becomes how to retain the professional practice gains and yet meet the service and care needs of today's hospitalized patients.

Case management is "second generation" primary nursing according to Zander,[12] who has developed and implemented this nursing model at the New England Medical Center. Case management promotes collaborative practice between nurses and physicians because it requires the integration of the nursing plan of care with the medical plan of care. This is achieved by nurses and physicians who develop a critical pathway for specific diseases/diagnoses. It includes identifying specific anticipated patient outcomes at given points in time during an expected length of stay. The critical pathway is influenced by the individual physician's practice patterns and accepted standards of nursing care. Zander reports the following preliminary results of a study implementing the case management model: improved patient outcomes, shorter lengths of stay, improved patient and family satisfaction, increased autonomy and job satisfaction for nurses who are case managers, and increased physician satisfaction with nurse interaction and patient outcomes.

PROFESSIONAL PRACTICE IN NURSING

Nursing professional practice has developed throughout the 20th century, and a significant turning point occurred with the introduction of advanced, trained nursing professionals, such as the nurse practitioner. The introduction of primary nursing has also been significant in bringing the necessary autonomy to the nursing profession that other health care professional groups enjoy.

The current and repeated shortages of RNs threaten the concept and sense of professional practice. Staffing shortages create different impacts on the professional RN, the most immediate of which is increased workload. With more acutely ill hospitalized patients and fewer co-workers, nursing practice begins to be compromised, creating a sense of dissatisfaction. Ultimately, left unchecked, burnout occurs and the RN exits either the work setting or the profession itself.

Other factors come into play in the loss of a sense of profession. When the professional nurse must substitute for the lower-level worker during periods of staff shortages, role integrity can be lost and professional responsibility potentially diminished.[13] Because significant advances have occurred in the development of the nurse as a professional practitioner, this development having a direct bearing on the quality of patient care, any plan that expands the explicit use of the alternative care providers needs to provide for the assurance that the professional practice of nursing will be not only sustained but enhanced.

THE NON-RN PRACTICE PARTNER

At a major academic medical center in the Southeast, a pilot study is currently underway that tests the concept of expanding the capacity of the RN through the use of currently trained alternative care providers. The study project has been developed within the existing state practice act and licensure codes for nursing. In this study, the alternative care provider is called the primary practice partner. In its most basic form, the primary practice partner is an extension of the RN. The partner works under the direction of the RN. When the partner is an LPN, he or she functions under his or her license. This method of expanding the capacity of the RN is intended to reinforce the professional role of the nurse by using a primary nursing model of care and yet address the very real problem of shortage of sufficient numbers of RNs to carry out patient care functions. In a sense this approach may help to strengthen the ''boundary'' for professional nursing practice. Starr refers to the strong boundaries created for physicians in the professional practice of medicine.[14] Once an individual becomes an MD, the scope of practice is clear and understood, whereas in nursing, various levels of skill have been defined, each one able to perform an incremental increase in patient care functions. The boundaries for practice at each level are narrow and not well understood, particularly by those outside the profession. Additional training and education are required to advance to the next increment, i.e., nursing assistant to LPN to RN. We have already referenced the fact that 88 percent of all inpatient nursing functions can be performed by either the RN or LPN. If alternative care providers are not carefully structured in their role and relationship to the RN, the professional practice boundary for nursing may be compromised and the nursing professional practice level diminished.

Primary nursing enhanced professional boundaries by better defining the responsibility and scope of authority of the RN in the care of the hospitalized patient. Primary nursing, which utilizes a care partner in the process, reaffirms, if not strengthens, the professional RN's accountability and responsibility for a patient's care. The care partner is an extension of the nurse, just as the physician's assistant (PA) is an extension of the physician. The PA does not diminish the professional role of the MD; rather, he or she enhances the capacity of the physician to see and care for larger numbers of patients.

ALTERNATIVE CARE PROVIDERS

The Primary Partnership study was initiated in the fall of 1987 at an academic medical center in the Southeast. The purpose of the study was to determine the feasibility of enhancing nursing capacity through the use of non-RNs, and thus permitting the hospital to maintain and expand inpatient bed capacity, particularly the intensive care unit capacity. The study was jointly undertaken by the hospital nursing service administration with support from the school of nursing and a consulting firm specializing in nursing management.[15]

The study focused on determining the type of work being done on three nursing units, including a medical intensive care unit, a general medical-surgical unit, and a pediatric medicine unit. The type of work being done on the unit was categorized and analyzed according to quantity and the skill level required for each category of work. The categories of work included were

1. performance of medical treatments (patient-specific)
2. daily care (not patient-specific)
3. nursing management
4. communication-documentation-coordination

Subcategories were developed for each of the four major categories.

Once the categories were established, the overall work of the unit was assessed according to the skill level required to accomplish the work of the specific unit. When this was completed, the work on each unit was assessed by subcategory for the skill level required for that subcategory of work. This percentage of skill was then converted to an actual full-time equivalent staffing estimate.

The results were then aggregated for each category by unit so that an estimate could be derived of the percentage of work performed on the unit by skill level. The skill level was identified as skill level 1, 2, or 3; skill level 4; and skill level 5. This analysis resulted in a distribution of actual work for the category by skill level. The percentage range for the skill levels by category of work was as shown in Figure 18-1.

| | Patient Care Unit | | | |
Skill Level	Intensive Care	Pediatric Medicine	Medical/ Surgical	Over All
1, 2, 3	45.48%	56.57%	52.9%	53.34%
4	45.71%	32.87%	25.55%	34.21%
5	8.8%	10.56%	21.55%	13.47%

Figure 18-1 Percent Distribution of Work by Skill Level

Skill level 5 work was considered by the investigators to be primarily cognitive work such as "forecasting how a patient will respond to a medication or intervention"[16] and the work that the RN was best prepared to undertake as opposed to other care providers.

The work distribution analysis was then reviewed in relation to existing staffing patterns for the three units. It was determined that the greatest opportunity for enhancing the capacity of the nursing service was in the intensive care units, where staffing patterns approached an all-RN staffing model. At this stage of the project the role of the alternative care provider and his or her relationship to the RN was conceptualized. The concept of a practice partnership, previously discussed in this chapter, was developed. This concept envisions an RN and an LPN working together in a joint practice mode, with the RN focusing attention on what is termed "knowledge" work (skill levels 4 and 5) and the LPN focusing attention on "technical work" (skill levels 1, 2, and 3). A pilot project is now under way that tests the efficacy of this joint practice model. The pilot is expected to show the following benefits.

- RNs will function at higher levels when responsibilities are redefined.
- A higher job satisfaction level is expected to occur among both RN and LPN staff.
- No decrease in the quality of patient care is expected.
- Nursing capacity is expected to increase through the partnership model by 10–15 percent.
- Increased capacity will result in the institution's ability to open additional intensive care beds and to staff additional services within the existing supply.

SUMMARY AND CONCLUSIONS

This chapter has reviewed the role and usage of alternative care providers in patient care. Given the likely future use of alternative care providers in delivering nursing care because of continuing shortages of RN professionals, the authors suggest how the professional practice of nursing can be preserved, if not enhanced, through the use of the alternative care provider in a modified primary nursing model of patient care. Nursing care distribution studies are described that reveal the skill level required for work actually accomplished on patient units. Further studies are under way that will test the concept of a joint RN-LPN practice model intended to increase the satisfaction of the RN with his or her work and to increase the capacity of nursing to care for patients.

There is no test site for the RCT proposal at the time of this writing. Studies, such as the joint practice model described here, are under way in hospitals nationwide. Although the future is still in the making, it is clear that ways to expand the capacity of the RN will continue to be explored.

NOTES

1. American Nurses Association, *The Nursing Shortage* (a briefing paper) (Kansas City, Mo.: American Nurses Association, 1987).

2. M. Kramer and C. Schmalenberg, "Magnet Hospitals: Part I. Institutions of Excellence," *Journal of Nursing Administration* 18, no. 1 (January 1988): 14.

3. M. McClure, et al., *Magnet Hospitals: Attraction and Retention of Professional Nurses* (Kansas City, Mo.: American Nurses Association, 1982).

4. M. Hardie, "Nurse's Little Helper?" *Nursing Times*, March 11, 1987, 24.

5. J.P. Young et al., *Factors Affecting Nurse Staffing in Acute Care Hospitals: A Review and Critique of the Literature*. DHEW Publication No. HRA 81-10 (HRP 0501801) (Washington, D.C.: U.S. Government Printing Office, January 1981), 3–8.

6. F.B. Friedman, "As the 'RN Gap' Becomes a Chasm LPNs Move in," *RN* (December 1981): 51.

7. Kramer and Schmalenberg, "Magnet Hospitals," 16.

8. L. Wood, "Proposal: A Career Plan for Nursing," *American Journal of Nursing* 73, no. 5 (1973): 832.

9. American Medical Association, *Implementation of Report cc (I-87)* (Chicago: American Medical Association, January 1988), 3.

10. Ibid., 2.

11. Marie Manthey, "Primary Practice Partners (a Nurse Extender System)," *Nursing Management* 19, no. 3 (March 1988): 58.

12. K. Zander, "Second Generation Primary Nursing—A New Agenda," *Journal of Nursing Administration* 15, no. 3 (March 1985): 18–24.

13. Carol S. Weisman, "Recruit from Within: Hospital Nurse Retention in the 1980's," *Journal of Nursing Administration* 12, no. 5 (May 1982): 24–31.

14. P. Starr, *The Transformation of American Medicine* (New York: Basic Books, Inc., 1982), p. 225.

15. The Primary Partnership Study was undertaken in October 1987 at the Medical College of Georgia Hospital and Clinics, Augusta, Georgia, the academic medical center for the University of Georgia system, in conjunction with Creative Nursing Management, Inc., Minneapolis, Minnesota.

16. Thomas M. Jenkins, "Primary Partnership Study, Preliminary Report," (unpublished), December 1987, p. 4.

Chapter 19

Foreign Nurse Recruitment and Authorization for Employment in the United States

PART I. FOREIGN NURSE RECRUITMENT

Barbara L. Shockey

Why go outside the United States to recruit nurses? There are not enough registered nurses (RNs) in the labor pool to meet the increasing demands for RNs in the United States. "Hospitals are now being used for the acutely ill while alternative settings are being used for other kinds of health services. These new settings need highly qualified registered nurses as do specialty units in hospitals," says Margretta Styles, president of the American Nurses Association.[1] The available supply of RNs has indeed been shrinking even as the need increases. This deficit will become even more prominent in 1990 and beyond, when the declining enrollment in nursing schools makes itself felt. RN program enrollment went from a high of 250,000 in 1983 to a low of 198,000 in 1986. With a shrinking supply and an increased need for RNs, it is just good business practice to recruit from another source, i.e., foreign-educated nurses.

If your organization is interested in this option, the first step is to find out what are your state's laws governing the practice of nursing by foreign-educated nurses. Each of the 50 states sets its own laws governing the practice of RNs, and the laws vary widely. An example of a state with liberal laws for RN licensure is Arkansas. For RNs educated in many English-speaking countries, Arkansas will grant licensure by endorsement rather than licensure by examination. California is an example of a state that grants an interim permit to a foreign-educated nurse once he or she has met the educational requirements and has been accepted to take the next scheduled RN licensing examination. This National Council Licensing Examination for Registered Nurses (NCLEX-RN) is given every February and July in all 50 states. The interim permit that California issues allows the nurse to work before the examination as well as while awaiting the results of the NCLEX-RN examination. Hawaii is an example of a state with conservative licensure laws. If you are a foreign-educated nurse and wish to work in Hawaii as an RN, you must first pass the NCLEX-RN examination before you will be granted a license that allows you to practice. Once you are knowledgeable about your own state's licensure laws governing RNs, you are ready for the next step in a foreign nurse recruitment plan.

There are several countries to consider for foreign nurse recruitment. Canada, England, Ireland, Scotland, the Philippines, Australia, and New Zealand are the most popular countries. Once you decide what country or countries you wish to recruit from, your organization will need to decide on the most cost-effective method of doing this.

A number of factors will influence the method you choose. First of all, how many nurses do you plan to recruit and what time frame is acceptable to your organization? What commitment of manpower and financial resources is your organization willing to invest in a foreign nurse recruitment plan?

The first recruitment method is one by which the organization plans and implements a foreign nurse recruitment effort totally on its own. This includes an advertising campaign in the country of choice, actual travel to the country of choice, and interview and selection of qualified nurses for actual follow-up. In this situation, the organization's own staff does all of the work. This method works best for an organization that is committed to recruiting a significant number (at least 25) of foreign-educated nurses per year. This method also requires considerable staff time to coordinate all of the necessary follow-up paper work.

The second recruitment method is one by which the organization contracts with a foreign nurse recruitment firm. The firm does all of the advertising, travel, and interviewing and selects qualified applicants to market to the organization. The recruitment firm does this for a set fee per nurse.

The third recruitment method is actually a combination of the first two. The organization's recruiters actually travel to foreign countries to participate in nursing job fairs that are organized and advertised by a recruitment firm. Once candidates are interviewed and selected, the follow-up is done by the organization's recruiters.

The usual fee to a recruitment firm in England is 10 percent of the first year's salary or $2,500.00. This does not include a relocation package for the nurse or preparation and filing for the H-1 (temporary worker) visa. An all-inclusive fee for recruiting the nurse, securing an H-1 visa, and a relocation package from an English firm would run approximately $5,000.00 per nurse.

One way to justify this kind of recruitment cost is to look at the cost of supplemental staff on 13-week contracts used to fill core staff positions that you have been unable to fill.

13 - week contract	
40	work hours/week
520	
34	hourly cost for supplemental staff from a traveling nurse agency
$17,680	13-week cost

$15.00	your own staff nurse salary/hr
$ 2.75	11–7 shift differential
$ 3.75	25% allowance for 1st year's benefits
$21.50	

```
$21.50  cost/hr your own staff
   520  hr/13 weeks
$11,180.00
```

```
$17,680.00  cost of 13-week contract nurse
$11,180.00  cost of staff nurse on your payroll
$ 6,500.00
```

You recruit foreign-educated nurses for a minimum of a one-year contract. In one 13-week period, you more than offset the recruitment cost of a foreign-educated nurse versus the cost of a traveling nurse. What do you pay your own staff who cover your staffing vacancies by working double shifts? Compare the cost of numerous double shifts with the cost of foreign nurse recruitment. It is quite common not to look at temporary staffing costs when preparing a nurse recruitment budget, and this is a poor business practice.

If your organization is located in one of the many states that grant an interim permit, time frames for licensure and visas will be very important. Thirty-four states require foreign-educated nurses to pass the examination given by the Commission on Graduates of Foreign Nursing Schools (CGFNS) and give evidence that they have completed an approved course of study before they can take the NCLEX-RN examination. The CGFNS examination covers nursing knowledge and English comprehension. It is administered twice yearly, in April and October, in United States embassies and consulates in 25 countries around the world. The examination fee is $95.00. The deadline for receipt of completed applications is three months prior to the actual examination date. For example, the deadline for completed applications for the October 5, 1988, examination is July 1, 1988. For further information contact:

> Commission on Graduates of Foreign Nursing Schools
> 3624 Market Street
> Philadelphia, PA 19104-2679
>
> Telephone (215) 349-8767

When you recruit foreign-educated nurses, the ideal candidate is one who already has taken and passed the NCLEX-RN examination. The time frame from when you make a job offer to a nurse with a current active license to practice in your state until his or her actual hire date will depend partially on acquisition of a visa to work in the United States.[2] Other time factors relate to the nurse's closing out his or her affairs (often abroad) and traveling to this country.

In many states, a nurse who has a CGFNS pass is automatically an acceptable candidate for the NCLEX-RN examination, and will quickly be granted an interim permit and again be able to travel and go to work for your organization in approximately three months. California does not accept the CGFNS pass as evidence that the nurse is an acceptable candidate for the NCLEX-RN examination. The candidate must submit a completed application, including a transcript from his or her school of nursing, which the California Board of Registered Nursing then evaluates to determine whether the nurse meets the educational standards. If the Board of Registered Nursing finds that the recruit meets its standards, it will schedule the candidate for the next NCLEX-RN examination and issue an interim permit. The NCLEX-RN examination is given twice yearly also, in February and July. The deadline for completed applications varies from one to two weeks, depending on the state in which the candidate is applying to take the examination. In California, the deadline for completed applications is November 15 for the February examination and April 30 for the July examination. For both the CGFNS and the NCLEX-RN examinations, two factors can cause problems with completion of applications by the deadlines: schools of nursing that do not see the issuance of transcripts as a high priority and international air mail, which can be very slow at times.

If the nurse is going to work on an interim permit,[3] it is best to plan his or her arrival at least two months before the NCLEX-RN examination. This time to practice nursing in the American system is of great value in helping the nurse pass the NCLEX-RN examination.

In the time from when your organization first makes a formal job offer to a nurse to when the nurse actually arrives to start work, it is imperative that you stay in touch with the nurse or you will lose the candidate to another organization, as foreign recruitment is very competitive at present. This time can be as short as 3 months, if the nurse has already passed the CGFNS examination and has applied for and been granted an interim permit, or as long as 12 to 15 months, if he or she has not even applied for the CGFNS examination. Letters and an occasional telephone call are very helpful to both the candidate and the organization in collecting all of the necessary information and documentation needed for licensure and a visa.

When you recruit foreign-educated nurses, you are primarily dealing with young single women. Because of the time lag of 6 to 12 months between job offer and hire date, you need to plan a loss rate averaging 50 percent. Much can change in one's life in a 12-month period when one is young and single. You will also recruit some older candidates who are married and may even have children. These can be excellent candidates as long as their spouses understand that they cannot work as long as the nurse is on an H-1 visa.[4]

When you gave the nurse a formal job offer in writing, the nurse signed a contract with your organization to work for you for a minimum of one year in return for the job offer and relocation package. The organization typically will need to provide one-way air fare and a minimum of two months' free housing for the nurse. The housing must be close to good public transportation or close enough to the hospital that it is an easy/safe walk from the apartment/home to the hospital. Someone should meet the nurse at the airport and help him or her get settled in temporary housing.

It is advisable if you can arrange a buddy system with someone on your staff who is perhaps from the same country as the newly recruited nurse and has an interest in helping a newcomer get settled. Be prepared to help the recruit complete the new hire paper work, as this will be new to him or her, especially forms such as W-4s and I-9s. The nurse will need to apply for a social security card, get photo identification from your state's department of motor vehicles, open a checking account, and the like. You will need to have addresses and telephone numbers for these services available for him or her. Information from your local chamber of commerce is also helpful. It usually includes information on housing, and a local map. You need to go over your dress code with the nurse, and you may have to help shop for some uniforms. I also recommend to the nurses I recruit to come with a major credit card as they have no credit record in the United States, and it takes a minimum of six months to establish credit. Often, nurses arrive with no linens, cookware, or furniture, so be prepared to introduce them to thrift shops and garage sales. Again, a buddy can help with all of these things. If you help make the transition to the American way of life easier and less a hassle, the nurse will make the transition to American nursing more smoothly. If the nurse feels good about his or her job and about living in the United States, he or she will be much more likely to continue to work at your facility beyond the minimum of the one-year commitment in your formal contract.

Of the first group of 25 nurses whom I recruited to California from England, Ireland, and Scotland in 1981–1982, 20 stayed the minimum of one year. Of those 20, 10 were still on staff 5 years later. Only one nurse in this group did not successfully complete her probation period, and four others chose not to fulfill their minimum one-year contract.

There are two main reasons for this excellent retention rate. First of all, many hospital staff members went out of their way to be helpful and friendly to these nurses. Second, the hospital has an excellent orientation to help these nurses convert to safe practitioners of American nursing. We provided them with a six-week orientation with special emphasis on pharmacology, forms and documentation, and equipment and procedures. It is not that these nurses do not know how to nurse; they are just not familiar with the American health care delivery system. We found these nurses to be an excellent and very welcome addition to our nursing staff.

We continue to recruit foreign-educated nurses, as we are not able to fill all of our staff vacancies with new graduates and experienced RNs who choose to relocate.

PART II. EMPLOYMENT AUTHORIZATION FOR FOREIGN-BORN NURSES WORKING IN THE UNITED STATES

David P. Berry

The Immigration Reform and Control Act of 1986[5] requires employers to ascertain that all employees are lawfully eligible to work in the United States. Hospitals and other medical organizations must therefore assure that the Immigration and Naturalization Service (INS) authorizes employment of foreign nurses.

In general, the Immigration and Nationality Act facilitates the employment of foreign-born RNs. This article discusses the applicable visas, analyzes eligibility criteria, and discusses procedures for acquisition of visas.

IMMIGRANTS VERSUS NONIMMIGRANTS

The employer who wishes to hire a foreign-born RN must decide whether to offer the prospective employee temporary or permanent employment. Our immigration laws divide entrants to the United States into two broad categories. Immigrants (persons with a "green card") are those people permitted to live and work in the United States indefinitely. An immigrant has authorization to work anywhere in the United States that she or he pleases and usually can freely enter and depart this country. While an RN may be eligible to enter the United States as an immigrant, this process is limited by quotas, which often result in substantial delays.

In contrast, nonimmigrants generally are those aliens coming to the United States only temporarily, and who have a foreign residence to which they intend to return. The issuance of nonimmigrant visas is not limited by quotas, and therefore nonimmigrants are not subject to numerical backlogs. While a nonimmigrant visa is often received much faster than an immigrant visa, the visa is issued only for a limited duration. Only one nonimmigrant visa is generally available to RNs seeking temporary employment in this country. This visa is referred to as an H-1 nonimmigrant visa and usually allows nurses to remain in the United States for a period of up to five years.[6]

Because of the relative speed by which employers may secure H-1 status on behalf of an RN, most RNs begin employment using an H-1 visa. Many of these nurses are able to remain permanently in the United States with the same employer. Provided that the employer's initial intent to offer temporary employment is bona fide, immigration regulations permit the employer to possess the dual intent ultimately to secure employment through the same job.[7]

H-1 VISAS—ELIGIBILITY CRITERIA

Generally speaking, the H-1 visa is available to medical personnel holding entry-level degrees whose field is one for which a baccalaureate degree or its equivalent is the usual minimum entry-level requirement. Licensed RNs are among those professionals who qualify for H-1 visas. Licensed vocational nurses and various medical technicians typically do not qualify for H-1 status unless a baccalaureate degree is the usual entry requirement to employment and the individual possesses such a degree.

In order to be eligible to secure H-1 status on behalf of an RN, the employer must intend to have the alien fill the position for only a temporary period of time. While the need for an RN may be ongoing, the specific desire for that RN must be temporary in nature. Correspondingly, the RN must intend to remain in the United States temporarily, and must maintain a foreign residence in order to be eligible to receive an H-1 visa.

The H-1 visa status does not depend upon demonstrating a shortage of American professional employees. Even if an American employee desires the job, an employer may utilize the H-1 visa to hire a professional employee from outside the United States. No advertising or special permission from the Department of Labor is required before an H-1 visa may be issued.

Regulations propounded by the INS establish special eligibility criteria for H-1 RNs.[8] Under these regulations, the nurses must have obtained a full and unrestricted license to practice professional nursing in the country where she or he obtained nursing education, or evidence that the education was obtained in the United States or Canada in order to qualify for an H-1 visa. The nurse must also have either passed the examination given by the CGFNS or have obtained a full and unrestricted license to practice professional nursing in the state of intended employment. In addition, the employer must certify that the beneficiary is fully qualified and eligible under the laws governing the place of intended employment to engage in the practice of professional nursing immediately upon admission to the United States, and that under those laws the employer is authorized to employ the beneficiary to perform services as an RN.

The process of securing an H-1 visa for an RN requires the employer to file a petition for H-1 classification. An employer may initially petition to accord H-1 status to an RN for up to three years. Thereafter, H-1 status may be extended for an additional two years.

Regardless of whether or not the alien nurse is in the United States, the employer must first petition the INS to accord the H-1 eligibility to him or her. Once the INS approves the employer's H-1 petition, the overseas nurse then takes the notice of approval to the American Consulate to secure the H-1 visa. If the nurse is in the United States and eligible to change nonimmigrant status, H-1 status can be accorded to the nurse in this country concurrent with the petition's approval.

Employment is not authorized until the H-1 petition has been approved and the nurse is granted H-1 status.

An approved H-1 petition authorizes employment only with the petitioning employer. Thereby, if a nurse wishes to change employers, both a new petition and a new extension application must be filed and approved before the nurse may begin work for the latter employer.

While the regulation itself is less than clear, INS practice is to deny H-1 visa status to an alien RN who has an interim permit to practice nursing in the United States but has not passed the CGFNS examination. Thus, in practice, a nurse either must have a full and unrestricted license in the employer's state or have passed CGFNS and have an interim permit.

When an RN is married and/or has children, the family members may also enter the United States under the terms and conditions of the principal H-1 visa holder. Such individuals are granted derivative H visa status (H-4) but are precluded from employment authorization. This lack of authorization may cause hardship to a family that depends on two incomes to support itself. This disadvantage is one of the reasons H-1 employees may be anxious to convert their status to that of permanent residents, whereby the spouse and children become derivatively eligible for "green cards" and all family members are entitled to work.

PROCEDURES FOR ACQUIRING AN H-1 VISA[9]

Employers are often guided through the maze of immigration visas with the assistance of attorneys specialized in this field. In such cases, once a decision to offer a job is made, attorneys can accomplish all necessary screening for visa eligibility and evaluate any potential problems. Typically, competent counsel will prepare all documents for the employer's review and signature, and reduce the burden on nurse recruiters. Changes in procedure with the INS arise so frequently that the petitioner who only occasionally seeks an H-1 visa with the INS may be unable to keep apace. Nonetheless, all employers benefit from understanding the basic procedural guidelines; those medical institutions preparing and filing their own cases must master these procedures thoroughly.

Every H-1 visa petition consists of the INS petition (Form I-129B), a letter from the employer to support the petition, and documents that support the letter and petition. Petitions and accompanying documents must be filed in duplicate with a filing fee of $35.00. When the RN is lawfully in the United States under another nonimmigrant status, such as tourist, a petition may also be accompanied by an application to change nonimmigrant status (Form I-506). An additional fee of $15.00 is required for the change of status application.

The petition itself must be supported by a letter from the employer that describes the need for temporary professional employment. Generally, this letter will describe the alien's professional-level credentials and relate the credentials to the nursing position. The letter should also indicate the period of desired employment (remembering that the offer must be temporary) and the salary.

Supporting documents must include certified copies or originals of the nursing diploma, foreign license, domestic license, and if relevant, CGFNS passage. Regulations permit licensed attorneys to certify that they have compared a photocopy with its original, and that the photocopy is a true and correct copy. Original documents should not be submitted to the INS, as they are rarely returned. In the event that an attorney is unavailable to certify the photocopies, either the petitioner or beneficiary is well advised to proceed to the nearest INS office with the original and two photocopies, whereupon the INS will certify the photocopies as being true and correct.

The INS recently instituted a direct-mail filing procedure for all H-1 visa petitions. The United States is divided by regulations into four geographic areas, each area containing one remote adjudication center. H-1 visa petitions must be filed by mail with the remote adjudication center having jurisdiction over the place of employment. Those medical institutions filing their first visa petition without legal assistance are best advised to call the local INS office for the address of the remote adjudication center, technically called a "Regional Service Center."

There are four remote adjudication centers. As a result, it is impossible to advise employers uniformly as to the processing time for an H-1 visa. The INS has devoted considerable resources to reducing processing backlogs for H-1 visa petitions, and most of the remote adjudication centers typically complete an adjudication within four to six weeks of receipt. Some remote adjudication centers reliably process H-1 petitions in less than one month.

Once an H-1 petition is approved by the INS, the alien is free to make application to enter the United States with an H-1 visa. If the petitioner has designated that the approved petition be sent to a particular American consulate, there is often a considerable delay before the American consulate receives the INS notice of approval. It is generally advisable for the employer/petitioner to forward the *original* copy of the approval notice, Form I-171C, directly to the alien outside the United States. Most American consulates around the world will issue H-1 visas within one day of being presented with an application from the alien and the original H-1 approval notice. Thereby, the alien is quickly eligible to enter the United States and commence lawful employment after the H-1 petition is approved.

In some instances, the RN is lawfully in the United States and concurrently files an application to change nonimmigrant status along with the employer's H-1 petition. In such a case, the nurse may start employment upon receipt of the notice of approval and change of status from the INS. It must be emphasized that the filing of the petition does *not* automatically yield authorization to start employment, and employment may not lawfully begin until after approval notice and change of status are received.

PERMANENT EMPLOYMENT AUTHORIZATION

While the H-1 visa status is an excellent vehicle with which to secure up to five years (and sometimes six years[10]) of employment authorization for foreign-born nurses, it proves inadequate thereafter. Additionally, as discussed above, the H-1 visa status does not authorize employment for spouses and accompanying children. In cases where employment is likely to exceed five years, it is appropriate for the employer to contemplate petitioning for permanent residence for the RN.

The Department of Labor has greatly facilitated the process by which RNs may become permanent residents based on their professional skills. Before most professionals can immigrate, they must secure individualized labor certifications establishing a shortage of other minimally qualified workers. In contrast, RNs are eligible for a blanket certification known as "Schedule A," whereby the process of immigrating is greatly simplified.

Under Department of Labor regulations referred to as Schedule A, Group I,[11] RNs offered permanent employment who have passed the CGFNS examination or who hold a full and unrestricted license to practice professional nursing in the state of intended employment are eligible for precertification. This precertification authorizes such nurses to proceed directly to the INS with a petition for permanent residence.

Even though Schedule A greatly alleviates the uncertainties associated with job-related immigration, it does not solve all problems. Petitions for permanent residence under Schedule A unfortunately are subject to the numerical limitations provided by our quota system for immigrants. The Immigration and Nationality Act sets a worldwide annual limitation of 270,000 immigrants who may immigrate under the preference system. In addition, an annual limit of 20,000 visas is established for each country, and 5,000 for each dependent territory. While most countries do not approach their annual limitations, a few countries are severely backlogged.[12] Of the total number of visas in the preference system, 20 percent, or 54,000 visas, are reserved for skilled and unskilled workers, including RNs.

Because of the constant changes in quota backlogs, it is impossible to give an accurate estimate of the delay in processing Schedule A, Group I cases. In some instances, the procedure for securing permanent residence through Schedule A, Group I may be almost as fast as the one described above for H-1 visas. More often, immigration takes many months or even years. Petitioners contemplating filing such cases may wish to call the State Department recorded message for visa availability[13] in order to estimate present quota backlogs.

It frequently occurs that the nurse initially offered temporary employment is ultimately offered permanent employment. A nurse granted permanent residence is free to work in the location of his or her choosing.

PROCEDURE FOR SECURING PERMANENT RESIDENCE[14]

An RN becomes a permanent resident through a two-step procedure. The first step involves the employer's petition for third or sixth preference status. The second step involves an application by the nurse for permanent residence.

The employer's petition for permanent residence is usually filed by mail with the remote adjudication center having jurisdiction over the employer's residence.[15] The petition comprises INS Form I-140 and Department of Labor Forms ETA 750 A and B. The latter forms, and all supporting documents, must be filed in duplicate, with a filing fee of $35.00. Supporting documents include a letter from the employer documenting the desire for permanent full-time employment as well as evidence of the nursing degree and licensure. Interim permits will not make a nurse eligible for permanent residence unless the nurse has also passed CGFNS.

The application for permanent residence may be filed when the quota number is "current." The nurse who has obeyed our immigration laws may apply to adjust his or her status to that of a permanent resident while remaining in the United States. Family members lawfully in the United States are eligible to apply concurrently for permanent residence. The process usually is completed within three to six months of filing, and employment authorization may be granted for the interim period.

The application for permanent residence, Form I-485, is filed with the local INS office having jurisdiction over the alien's residence. Form I-485 must be accompanied by Form G-325A, fingerprints, photographs, and a medical report that includes a human immunodeficiency virus (HIV) test. The applicant is interviewed by the INS. When the case is approved, the nurse receives a notice granting permanent residence. The actual green card is forwarded to the alien months later.

CONCLUSION

H-1 visas and Schedule A labor certifications are excellent vehicles with which to secure the lawful employment of foreign-born nurses. Many hospitals and medical institutions have successfully hired highly qualified foreign nurses. Hospitals and medical institutions that have yet to engage the services of foreign-born RNs should not be deterred from doing so, as the INS readily facilitates the petition/application process. The initiation of a direct-mail filing for INS petitions promotes a more uniform and reliable system that is compatible with the business needs of medical institutions experiencing shortages of qualified RNs.

NOTES

1. *Wall Street Journal*, November 11, 1987; see also *Wall Street Journal*, May 16, 1988 at 7C, col. 3.

2. Acquisition of work-authorized visas for RNs is discussed in Part II.

3. The availability of employment authorization to nurses holding only interim permits appears to be limited by the INS to nurses who have already passed CGFNS. See Part II.

4. See Part II for a full discussion of spousal and employment authorization.

5. Pub. L. 99-603; 8 U.S.C. §1324a.

6. A sixth year of temporary employment authorization for H-1 visa holders may be granted in "extraordinary circumstances." 8 CFR §214.2(h)(11). A May 31, 1988, cable from the Assistant Commissioner of Adjudications for INS suggests that the sixth year extension will be readily granted to RNs through December 31, 1988, without an individualized showing of "extraordinary circumstances."

7. See 8 CFR §214.2(h)(12); 52 Fed. Reg. 5748 (Feb. 26, 1987).

8. See generally 8 CFR §214.2(h)(2)(vi).

9. Specific aspects of the described procedures are in constant flux. However, most of the analysis related to both H-1 visas and Schedule A, *infra.*, is generic in nature. Employers will find this procedural discussion a reliable guide to the rudiments of approaching H-1 visas and Schedule A petitions, but should always be cognizant of the possibility for procedural changes.

10. See n. 6.

11. 20 CFR §656.10.

12. The 20,000 per country limitation is particularly vexing to nurses born in the Philippines. It is presently taking at least four years for Philippine-born RNs to secure permanent residence through Schedule A, Group I because of that country's oversubscription of quota numbers.

13. The telephone number of the Department of State is (202)647-0508. This recording is updated each month.

14. See n. 9.

15. When quota numbers are "current," the employer's petition and nurse's application for permanent residence may be jointly filed with the local INS office having jurisdiction over the alien's place of residence.

Index

Note: Page numbers in *italics* indicate figures, tables, or exhibits.

About the Editors

Terence F. Moore, MBA, MHA, is president and chief executive officer of Mid-Michigan Health Care Systems, Inc., Midland, Michigan, which operates Midland Hospital Center, Clare Community Hospital, Gladwin Area Hospital, two nursing homes, and seven other subsidiaries. He holds a Master's Degree in hospital administration from Washington University School of Medicine, St. Louis, Missouri, and BS and MBA degrees from Central Michigan University where he has done additional graduate work in economics.

Mr. Moore is a fellow of the American College of Healthcare Executives. He is a member of the boards of the Michigan Hospital Association, treasurer of the board of the Michigan Molecular Institute, and past chairman of the board of the 23-member East Central Michigan Hospital Council. In 1986 he received the Regents Award for the state of Michigan from the American College of Healthcare Executives.

He has published more than 35 articles and is the co-author of *Organizational Burnout in Health Care Facilities: Strategies for Prevention and Change* (Aspen Publishers, 1985). He is also co-editor of *The Effective Health Care Executive: A Guide to a Winning Management Style* (Aspen Publishers, 1986) and *The Health Care Executive Search: A Guide to Recruiting and Job Seeking* (Aspen Publishers, 1989).

Earl A. Simendinger, PhD, is Professor and Chairman of the Department in Health Education and Health Sciences at Central Michigan University. Formerly he held a joint Adjunct Associate Professorship in the Schools of Medicine and Engineering at Case Western Reserve University.

He has been a practicing hospital administrator for 19 years. Former positions include the President of St. Luke's Hospital, San Francisco, California, and Vice President at University Hospitals of Cleveland, Ohio.

Dr. Simendinger holds a Doctoral Degree in Organizational Behavior from Case Western Reserve University, a Master's Degree in Health Care Administration from Washington University, St. Louis, Missouri, a Master's Degree in

277

Industrial Engineering from Cleveland State University, and a Bachelor's Degree in Business Administration from Ashland College.

He is a Fellow of the American College of Healthcare Executives and a member of the Editorial Review Boards of both the *Journal of the American Medical Association* and *The Journal of Clinical Engineering*.

He has published over 30 articles in seventeen different health care and management journals and has co-authored *Organizational Burnout in Health Care Facilities: Strategies for Prevention and Change* (Aspen Publishers, 1985) and co-edited *The Effective Health Care Executive: A Guide to a Winning Management Style* (Aspen Publishers, 1986) and *The Health Care Executive Search: A Guide to Recruiting and Job Seeking* (Aspen Publishers, 1989).

About the Contributors

David P. Berry, Esq., is a partner in the law firm of Berry and Appleman, San Francisco, California. The firm practices exclusively in the field of immigration and nationality law. He has served as chairperson of the American Immigration Lawyers Association of Northern California as well as the Bar Association of San Francisco Immigration Committee. Mr. Berry represents hospitals and medical institutions involved in the hiring of foreign born registered nurses as well as their medical personnel.

Fay L. Bower, RN, DNSc, FAAN, is vice president for academic affairs and dean of the school of nursing, University of San Francisco, San Francisco, California. She is active in nursing as president of the California League of Nursing, a board member of the National League for Nursing, and president of the Beta Gamma Chapter of Sigma Theta Tan International.

Kathryn L. Bray, RN, MBA, is the Regional RN Recruitment Coordinator for Kaiser Permanente, Northern California Region. The region includes more than 6,000 registered nurses. She has held numerous positions in nursing management and as a senior consultant for a software firm producing nurse information systems.

Gregory L. Crow, RN, MS, is a member of the faculty at the University of San Francisco School of Nursing teaching undergraduate management, leadership, and graduate nursing administration. Mr. Crow also acts as a consultant in program service development in clinical ladder systems, management and leadership development, and cardiac services. He was formerly the assistant administrator of patient care services at Merritt Peralta Medical Center, Oakland, California.

Catherine DeVet, RN, EdD, currently is the manager of Ernst & Whinney's office in Grand Rapids, Michigan. Formerly, she was the director of medical/surgical nursing, Blodgett Hospital, Grand Rapids, Michigan. She received her

EdD degree from Western Michigan University and has served in numerous educational and administrative roles prior to her current position. She is the author of *Monitoring Sourcebook*: *Volume II: Nursing Practice*, and co-author of Volumes I and III. She is a national speaker and consultant.

Ellen Thomas Eggland, RN, MN, is vice president of Healthcare Personnel$_{sm}$, Inc., in Naples, Florida. She received her bachelor's degree from Georgetown University and her master's degree from Emory University. She has extensive experience as a nursing administrator and is a book reviewer for Springhouse Corporation and frequent author in *Nursing*.

Pamela S. Erb, RN, MPA, CNAA, is vice president of patient services at The Tampa General Hospital, Tampa, Florida. She has 19 years of hospital management experience. She received her MPA from Nova University and is a fellow of the Johnson and Johnson Wharton School Program for Nurse Executives. She is certified by the American Nurses' Association.

Patricia K. Findling, MHA, is associate hospital director at the Medical College of Georgia Hospital and Clinics. Prior to her appointment at MCG, she served as vice president for clinical/support services at The Tampa General Hospital, Tampa, Florida. She received her master's degree from the Ohio State University Program in Hospital and Health Services Administration.

Carolyn E. Fraser, RN, currently is the vice president at Midland Hospital Center, Midland, Michigan. She graduated from Holy Family Hospital School of Nursing, Manitowoc, Wisconsin, and has taken additional course work at Central Michigan University, Mt. Pleasant, Michigan. She received her certification in nursing administration from the American Nurses' Association in 1986. Ms. Fraser is a member of the Michigan Organization of Nurse Executives and the American Organization of Nurse Executives.

Cecelia K. Golightly, RN, MPH, is director of nursing, responsible for inpatient operations at the Medical College of Georgia Hospital and Clinics. She is a widely published author with nineteen years experience in nursing administration. Ms. Golightly graduated from Presbyterian Hospital School of Nursing in Charlotte, North Carolina, and received her master's degree in public health from the University of Minnesota, Minneapolis, Minnesota.

Laurin Paul Hafner is a doctoral candidate in social psychology at the University of Connecticut. He has received many awards and honors. He has co-authored several papers and presented them at the American Educational Research Association and the American Psychological Association.

Abby M. Heydman, RN, PhD, is the dean of the Samuel Merritt and St. Mary's Intercollegiate Nursing Program in Oakland, California, and past president of the California Association of Colleges of Nursing. Dr. Heydman received a BSN from

Duchesne College, Omaha, Nebraska; an MN from the University of Washington, Seattle; and a PhD from the University of California, Berkeley. Dr. Heydman has held numerous clinical nursing positions and served on the faculties of Creighton University, Omaha, Nebraska, and the University of California, San Francisco.

Bernard S. Hodes is founder and president of Bernard Hodes Advertising, which has offices throughout the United States, Canada, and the United Kingdom. It is one of the leading advertising agencies specializing in recruitment and employee communications. Mr. Hodes is also the author of *The Principles and Practice of Recruitment Advertising*.

R. Edward Howell, MHA, is currently executive director of the Medical College of Georgia Hospital and Clinics. Mr. Howell previously served as associate hospital director, University of Minnesota Hospital and Clinics. He received his master's degree from the Ohio State University Program in Hospital and Health Services Administration.

Janet Y. Jackson, RN, MSN, is the vice president for nursing at Munson Medical Center, Traverse City, Michigan. She is a graduate of Wayne State University and has held several faculty positions. She is the past president of the Michigan Organization of Nurse Executives.

Marlene Kramer, RN, PhD, FAAN, holds the first Orvis Chair in Nursing Research at the University of Nevada, Reno. She has had a distinguished career and has published numerous research papers, articles, and books. She is also a well known lecturer. She received her MSN from Case Western University and her doctorate from Stanford University. She is best known for her work in reality shock and biculturalism.

Jean C. Lyon, RN, MS, MSN, is currently a doctoral student in nursing administration at the University of California, nursing and health sciences. Ms. Lyon holds master's degrees in both nursing and health science. She is employed as the director of education at Valley Memorial Hospital, Livermore, California. She has worked in health care for the past fifteen years, and for the past eight years in education and staff development positions.

Pamela A. MacFalda, RN, MS, is the nursing administrator of Rogers City Hospital, Rogers City, Michigan. She is president elect of the North Central District of Nursing Administrators.

Kathleen A. McManus, RN, is vice president, Nursing Care Services, Traverse City Osteopathic Hospital, Traverse City, Michigan. She has held numerous nursing management positions prior to assuming her present position.

Nancy Madsen, RN, MS, is the associate administrator for patient care services at Samuel Merritt Hospital, Merritt Peralta Medical Center, Oakland, California. Ms. Madsen received her BSN and MS in nursing at the University of Utah School of Nursing. Ms. Madsen has held numerous staff nursing positions and had a faculty appointment at the University of Utah, School of Nursing. She has held administrative positions in the Department of Nursing at Stanford University Hospital and the Oregon Health Sciences University Hospital.

Doris M. Modly, RN, PhD, is the assistant professor of Psychiatric Mental Health Nursing at the Francis Payne Bolton School of Nursing, Case Western Reserve University, in Cleveland, Ohio. Dr. Modly has held numerous positions in both nursing education and nurse management, including the position as director of professional nursing affairs at the Cleveland Clinic Foundation.

J. Mark Montobbio, Esq., is a partner in the labor relations group of the San Francisco law firm of Severson, Werson, Berke, and Melchior. He has practiced labor law representing management throughout Northern California and Nevada for many years. His experience includes litigation of labor and employment law disputes and the negotiation of union contracts for a variety of medical centers, hospitals, and other health care facilities.

Joanne Olsen, RN, MSN, is currently employed as the senior vice president and chief operating officer, Valley Memorial Hospital in Livermore, California. She holds a master's degree in nursing, and with more than 14 years' experience in health care, Ms. Olsen has devoted the past 10 years to nursing and hospital administration.

Philip L. Ross, Esq., is a partner in the labor relations group of the San Francisco law firm of Severson, Werson, Berke, and Melchior. He has extensive experience in labor relations and is the author of articles on employment discrimination and labor law. Mr. Ross specializes in representing employers, including many health care facilities, in the defense of wrongful termination lawsuits in state and federal court and in the arbitration of union contract disputes.

Claudia Schmalenberg, RN, MS, received her master's degree in nursing from the University of California, San Francisco. She has had a distinguished career in both nursing administration and nursing research. She served as the vice president for nursing of Mt. Sinai Hospital in Hartford, Connecticut. She has authored numerous articles and several books and now serves as a lecturer and consultant in nursing service administration.

Barbara L. Shockey, RN, BS, is the associate director of Medical Recruiting Consultants in Palo Alto, California. She has more than 30 years of nursing experience and has been a nurse recruiter for many years. Her present company has 15 years of experience in the field of international nurse placements.

Joseph M. Smith is president of Gladwin Area Hospital, Gladwin, Michigan, and Gladwin Pines Nursing Home, a 120-bed skilled nursing facility. He is a graduate of Indiana University and is pursuing an MBA at Central Michigan University. He serves on numerous boards and on the associate faculty at Ferris State University in the School of Health Science Administration.

Terry Stukalin, RN, MA, is president and senior consultant of The Terry Stukalin Health Care Management Services, Inc., in Houston, Texas. The firm provides consultation and executive search services to hospital management in areas of health care on a nationwide basis.

John F. Turck III, is the senior partner of the National Center for Recruitment and Retention Resources, a management consulting firm based in Ann Arbor, Michigan, and Chicago. He has been involved in contemporary nurse recruitment and retention issues and programs since the 1970s and was formerly the associate director of planning and marketing for the University of Michigan Medical Center in Ann Arbor.

Kathleen M. Weiss, MSN, RN, received a bachelor of science degree in nursing from the University of Maryland. She received a master's degree in nursing from Kent State University. She has held a variety of nursing positions as clinician, educator, and administrator. In her current position at the Cleveland Clinic Foundation, she is an active member of the Advisory Council for Recruitment and Retention and is co-chairman of the Teambuilding Steering Committee for the Division of Nursing.

Donna D. Young, RN, MAM, is the director of nursing of the Healthcare Medical Center of Tustin, Tustin, California. She has held numerous positions in nursing since 1959. She has been very involved in activities to enhance the development of the professional nurse and the professional nurse image.